SECOND EDITION

Nurturing Readiness in Early Childhood Education

A Whole-Child Curriculum for Ages 2–5

Ellen S. Cromwell

Allyn and Bacon

Boston ■ London ■ Toronto ■ Sydney ■ Tokyo ■ Singapore

Series editor: *Frances Helland*
Series editorial assistant: *Bridget Keane*
Marketing managers: *Ellen Dolberg/Brad Parkins*
Manufacturing buyer: *Suzanne Lareau*

Library of Congress Cataloging-in-Publication Data

Cromwell, Ellen
     Nurturing readiness in early childhood education : a whole-child
curriculum for ages 2-5 / Ellen S. Cromwell. -- 2nd ed.
          p.   cm.
     Rev. ed. of: Quality child care: a comprehensive guide for
administrators and teachers. c1994.
     Includes bibliographical references and index.
     ISBN 0-205-28863-4
     1. Day care centers--United States.   2. Child care--United States.
3. Early childhood education--United States. 4. Child development--
United States.   I. Cromwell, Ellen, (date).   Quality child care.
HQ778.63.C76   1999
362.71'2'068--dc21   98-56042
                                                                                    CIP

Printed in the United States of America

10 9 8 7 6 5 4 3 2   03 02 01 00

Permissions: p. 1, p. 239, and p. 256: From *Everychild's Everyday* by Cindy Herbert and Susan Russell. Copyright © 1980 Learning About Learning. Used by permission of Doubleday, a division of Random House, Inc.

This book is dedicated to my husband, William C. Cromwell, who has made an indelible imprint on students at the School of International Service, American University, Washington, DC, and who has supported my work by challenging me as he has challenged his students to reach beyond self-imposed limitations.

CONTENTS

PREFACE

The purpose of *Nurturing Readiness in Early Childhood Education* is to provide a tested and effective educational and developmental program for children ages 2 through 5 years. It is designed for use by college students, teachers, professionals and practitioners in the field, and parents, particularly those who are teaching children in a home/school environment.

In the five years since the publication of my earlier book, *Quality Child Care: A Comprehensive Guide for Administrators and Teachers*, the child care industry has grown remarkably. While child care choices and facilities have proliferated, there has been little advancement in the quality of child care programs offered. Only recently has important new research in the field of child development begun to influence and shape early childhood programs.

Quality Child Care was the product of extensive research and reflection in theories of child development from both a historical and contemporary perspective. I attempted to synthesize and apply the insights and knowledge of leading twentieth-century educators to today's child. Evolving from time-tested principles of child development, the program developed in that book effectively connected and integrated theory, philosophy, and practice *around* the child. The premise was that children must be given the opportunity to fully experience the stages and needs of childhood while expanding and giving expression to their many strengths and talents. This is best accomplished by designing a program that provides a variety of experiences in an unhurried, supportive environment—one that cultivates self-identity as well as group awareness and belonging. An open, child-centered environment encourages children to seek and find many opportunities for self-satisfaction and learning. Like *The Little Engine That Could*, a combination of self-belief, initiative, and encouragement enables children to climb mountains.

Nurturing Readiness in Early Childhood Education develops and refines the whole-child approach to teaching and learning identified as the *PLAN* model in *Quality Child Care*. The model's primary components, *play, learning, the arts,* and *nurturing,* provide the cornerstones for designing a child-centered environment appropriate to all levels of development. In a PLAN environment, children are treated with respect and given love. They are encouraged to develop their interests as they engage in constructive play or project work. They are given the time and space required for cooperative play, independent play, and creative thinking. In a PLAN environment, children are gradually introduced to a world that is large enough to inspire imagination, yet small enough to investigate in the palm of a hand. Within a nurturing and challenging setting, children are cared for and educated until they are ready to assume responsibility for their own lives. In the process, they will do the following:

- See value in work and play.
- Plan, begin, and complete projects comfortably as they interact with friends and practice emerging skills.

- Learn to play responsibly as they solve problems and make choices.
- Identify with and respect their environment.
- Practice self-care, good habits, and good manners.
- Construct meaning from a range of experiences that facilitate learning and encourage attitudinal development.
- Experience an idea-centered curriculum that promotes inquiry and reflection.
- Have the courage to take risks by believing in themselves.
- Develop healthy values and practice good judgment.
- Appreciate the perspective and needs of others.
- Express love and kindness toward all living things.
- Become productive and caring members of a community.

Acknowledgments

My appreciation and gratitude go to the following:

- To Jeanne Roller, Ed.D., St. Ambrose University, and to Kim Townley, Ph.D., Director, Early Childhood Laboratory, University of Kentucky, for their helpful comments on the manuscript.
- To Frances Helland, former series editor at Allyn and Bacon, for her contribution and commitment to this book, to her assistant, Bridget Keane, and to Suzanne Pescatore, TKM Productions, for her attentiveness to the manuscript in its final stage of production and her unfailing helpfulness.
- To Peter C. Cromwell, attorney and spokesperson for quality child care, who has carefully and critically edited this book while applying his own expertise and sensitivity to the complexities and challenges of the field.
- To Dr. F. Gunther Eyck, Professor at the School of International Service, American University, outstanding teacher and dear family friend, who is a model for the principles that all children should follow: integrity, commitment, and love.
- To my friends and colleagues at Georgetown Hill Child Care Center—especially to John B. Cromwell, Elsie Reid, and Arnold Schweizer for their outstanding leadership and faithful service to the center since its inception in 1980.
- To Senator Jennie Forehand, Senator Laurence Levitan, and to Miles Shulman for their steadfast advocacy for quality child care and children's programs at county and state levels in Maryland.
- To Ken Cobb for the charming cover photo, and Tannaz Etebarian for several delightful photos of children at play.
- To Doubleday for giving me permission to use several verses from *Everychild's Everyday*, tenderly and beautifully written by Cindy Herbert and Susan Russell, in its Learning About Learning Educational Series, 1980; thank you for allowing me to share this lovely writing in my book.
- And finally, to you, the reader, in whose hands children will place their trust.

About the Author

Ellen Cromwell is the director/founder of Georgetown Hill Child Care Center, Inc., a not-for-profit school located in Montgomery County, Maryland, now celebrating its twentieth anniversary. The center was recognized as a model for quality child care by the state of Maryland when, in 1991, an eight-room building was constructed through collaborative resources and assistance from the state, the Department of Business and Economic Development, and the Montgomery County Public School System. The center's educational program for children ages two through five is approved and accredited by the Maryland State Department of Education. In addition to directing the center, Cromwell's greatest satisfaction has been teaching at the kindergarten level and following the many footprints of students through early adolescence and on into maturity.

Cromwell received a Bachelor of Arts in History and in Art Education from the University of Maryland, College Park, in 1976 and a Masters in Education from American University, Washington, DC, in 1981. Her professional contributions include:

Author: Quality Child Care: A Comprehensive Guide for Administrators and Teachers, Allyn and Bacon, Needham Heights, MA, 1994; *Early Reading Through Experience,* Acropolis Books Ltd., Washington, DC, 1981.

Trainer: Approval for training workshops in child development in the state of Maryland.

Presenter: Featured speaker at legislative briefing on behalf of a child care bill presented before members of Congress in the U.S. House of Representatives, 1998.

Presenter of her Whole-Child Model and Related Topics at National Conferences, including Southern Early Childhood Conference, 1999, 1994; Association of Early Childhood Education International, 1999, 1998, 1996, 1995; International Play Conference, 1997; National School Age Consortium, 1995; Frederick College, 1998; National Association for the Education of Young Children, Maryland Chapter, 1997; and Maryland Child Care Conference, 1994.

An Introduction to Child Care

Some Models of the Past and Present

I like to think
In my room alone,
I like to dream
In a tree,
I like to invent on
The kitchen table,
In the backyard,
I like to run free,
I like to ponder,

On the living room couch,
In the big chair with you,
I read,
I like to watch things
Outside my window
Each place in my home
Is a special place
That fits the life
I lead.

—From *Everychild's Everyday*
by Cindy Herbert and Susan Russell

The Beginnings of Child Care

Day Nurseries

Traditionally, childrearing has been seen as the responsibility of parents. Good childrearing practices have been identified with common values that have been passed on from generation to generation. Throughout much of our history, however, parents have not always been able to provide proper care for their children. Since the national government, for the most part, has been reluctant to support child care, efforts to care for children in poverty were begun and promoted not by national policies but by individuals.

At the turn of the century, early reformers were successful in raising consciousness about children in poverty. Rescuing neglected children from urban squalor became a mission of mercy for early reformers like Jane Addams. Settlement houses, such as Hull House, founded in Chicago in 1889, sprang up in industrial areas to help immigrants assimilate into a new world and to provide children with basic care and training that was meant to lift them out of poverty and make them productive citizens.[1] The provision of comprehensive care to children of needy families through day nurseries began the modern child care industry. Throughout the century, and particularly during the World Wars when women were expected to work, day nurseries were considered integral support systems for families and society.

Contemporary child care should be seen as a full-service system providing families and centers with a network of support and resources to draw upon. All children need access to high-quality child care programs. Families need support and training in caring for their young, in selecting appropriate out-of-home environments, and in finding the resources that enable them to raise their children with a sense of pride and dignity.

The German Kindergarten

Friedrich Froebel (1782–1852) organized the first kindergarten in Germany in 1837. Characterized as "children's gardens," these kindergartens were intended to awaken the child's inner spirit through creative activities. Froebel believed that all children were born with a capacity for beauty and knowledge that could be fostered in an environment of harmony and tranquility. This was best accomplished through playlike experiences that encouraged cooperation and natural expression.[2]

Froebel's activities for children's play were designed to arouse interest and investigation. Children engaged in games and constructive activities that were carefully designed to hold interest. He defined ten "gifts" (objects)—the first three consisted of a ball, a cube, and a cylinder. These gifts were designed to awaken perceptions of unity, relations, connections, and diversity in the young child.[3] The precise nature and use of the gifts reflected Froebel's penchant for logical thinking. He designed the gifts with materials such as craftwork or clay in order to foster curiosity and a desire to learn. The curriculum was augmented by pleasureful group activities that also were carefully prescribed by Froebel, such as group singing, games, and nature study.

A curriculum for young children should reflect their developmental levels and interests. Learning by doing is fundamental to understanding. A program must provide alternating periods for active and quiet play so that children can exercise and rest their bodies and their minds. Children need to become familiar with the gifts of nature. Nature contains a vast reservoir of materials for teaching and learning through hands-on, sensory experiences. In a natural, outdoor environment, children are their happiest and most resourceful. They learn about shapes and textures and living things as they experiment with nature. They discover rainbows, spider webs, and the happenings of early spring.

Child care programs must therefore reflect these trends. Early learning should be considered a natural outgrowth of awareness and active participation. Children in child care centers should have ample time and space to construct with blocks and to play cooperatively. A growing child should be exposed to hands-on experiences that encourage self-awareness and the acquisition of both general and specific knowledge. The child should have the opportunity for group interactions and cooperative learning through teacher-initiated projects and activities. He should participate in the planning and organization of his room, his activities, and his own learning. Children develop habit formation when they learn to respect and care for their environment. Their educational experience should prepare them for developing the tools for lifelong learning. Therefore, value training and training in basic readiness skills also are essential components of a five-year curriculum.

Frank Newman (1991), President of the Education Commission of the States from 1991 to 1992, wrote:

> Every school in America—preschool and kindergarten, elementary, secondary, and post-secondary—should be a place where students learn to investigate, discover, and create. And schools should teach the youngest and the oldest students to think critically, solve problems, analyze, synthesize, reflect, and work collaboratively in ways appropriate to their age. Exploring, wondering, examining, creating, questioning, and investigating are natural dispositions in children—all children—and they should be encouraged and regarded as the building blocks for learning—lifelong learning.[4]

Montessori Education

Maria Montessori (1870–1952) opened the first "Children's House" in a poor district of Rome, Italy, in 1907. In theory and in practice, her approach was to revolutionize early education for years to come. The school taught children manners, good work habits, hygiene, and basic skills, all before they were five years of age.[5] The environment was carefully prepared for hands-on experiential learning through sensory exploration (i.e., touching, smelling, listening, tasting, seeing) that required specific tasks and materials for children to master in a sequential order. Montessori's no-fail, "learn-by-doing" approach provided children with a positive self-concept.

In Montessori schools, all materials are self-taught so children can see and correct their mistakes as they manipulate objects and perfect skills. In this way, children are allowed to direct and take responsibility for their own learning.[6] The tactility and aesthetic appeal of Montessori materials holds the attention of the young child. Children work at their own pace in mixed age groups. After initial instructions on the proper use of materials, little adult intervention is needed. Many of the tasks are oriented toward practical life skills—polishing shoes, washing tables, learning to button and snap. In traditional Montessori schools, children's play/work is purposeful; they do not typically engage in free and imaginary play. In less orthodox Montessori schools, children are given opportunities for creative, noninstructional play.

Noncompetitive, independent learning is *fundamental* to early development. Children develop confidence when they are not being compared to others or criticized by adults. When children know what is expected and feel in charge of their own learning experience, they need less adult coaching. Children also need to learn organizational skills at an early age. To encourage organization, materials should be selected carefully and arranged so as not to overwhelm the child/learner. The sorting and placement of play items on shelves encourages self-mastery and concept building. An organized environment does not inhibit creativity, it provides a sense of *harmony* that is conducive to exploration and discovery. When materials and equipment are seen by the child as an extension of her- or himself, it is the child who takes responsibility for their care. A criticism of the Montessori system, is that a child, restricted in the selection and use of materials, is not given sufficient opportunity to be inventive, or to self-initiate his own learning.

The English Infant/Primary School

In 1910 the McMillan sisters opened a nursery school in the Deptford slums near London laying the foundation for the English system of educating young children. The sisters chose the word *nursery* to represent the love, and nurturing that children would receive and the word *school* to acknowledge that children would learn as well.[7] Like most day nurseries, the school was primarily a caregiving environment for impoverished, neglected children. Once the physical needs of the children were met, educational concerns were addressed. The nursery had a garden that became a learning environment for children. Children learned to identify colors and shapes from flowers, and they learned to count by sorting vegetables. Within a short time, homemade wooden letters and geometric toys became part of a child's interior environment.[8] Through natural, hands-on experiences, children learned basic skills. Children's learning was facilitated by a loving and able staff and a comfortable and inspiring environment.

In contemporary English schools, a friendly, informal atmosphere immediately impresses a visitor. Children play and work in an unhurried, comfortable, and childlike environment. As in Montessori schools, children are not grouped by age. By mixing children in age groups, cooperation and cross-bonding are facilitated.

Teachers are well trained in education and respected as important contributors to children's school and home life. Visiting children at home is an important part of their responsibility. Because early childhood teachers are integral to the education process, they take pride in their work and have little incentive to make career changes. Children, therefore, have the benefit of continuity and stability. In an English infant/primary school:

- Creative activities abound; children enjoy art work, dramatic play, vocational and instrumental music, and original writing.
- Student projects promote socialization, cooperation, and motivation.
- There is an emphasis on trust, self-discipline, and respect.
- The head mistress is an educator and a role model who is revered and respected by teachers and families.
- Every nook and cranny in a classroom is used to promote independence, interaction, and the efficient management of space.
- Teachers have a warm, gentle style that promotes interaction and a friendly atmosphere.
- There is an absence of tracking and testing.
- The schools are community based and bonded to the families they serve.[9]

A child's day must be seen as too precious to waste or to mishandle. A happy child is an *involved* child who identifies positively with the surroundings. He is a child who smiles a lot and who looks forward to coming to his child care center. Feeling secure, he can break hands with mom and say good-bye without undue trauma. Quickly occupied, the child does not need to be coaxed or bribed to behave appropriately. The English system is ideal for all child care environments because of its emphasis on nurturing and active, child-initiated learning. A child always should want to return to his friends at school—he should never feel like he has to! Every child should experience a real garden outside and inside the classroom with lots of flowers to smell, vegetables to eat, worms to watch, and objects to paint.

Bank Street: A Model for Contemporary Child Care

Throughout the century, the Bank Street College of Education in New York City has championed open education. Its child-centered approach represents a child's world. The center, located in an old, restored building in mid-town New York, offers a homelike environment. Like the English infant school, children are free to play expressively and creatively in an unhurried, comfortable environment. They move from room to room choosing activities that attract or interest them. Hands-on materials, such as blocks, paint, and clay, provide opportunities for self-initiated exploration and discovery. [10]

In this kind of environment, the primary catalyst for learning is the child. The tools for learning have meaning and interest for the child. Learning is experiential.

What a child can see, feel, hear, or touch, he can identify with. In the process, an awareness of the interplay between environmental and human factors develops. For example, a child may perceive that a cloudy day endangers a planned outing to a park or that a chilly day requires buttoning up before venturing outdoors.

To the visitor, the homelike environment of Bank Street projects a sense of authenticity. Children and staff interact through friendly and supportive communication. The furnishings are comfortable yet unpretentious. Charming and child-like paintings adorn the walls and affirm the uniqueness of childhood. Nearby is Central Park—to run, to swing, and to play the games that Froebel's teachers once played with children in a distant time and at a distant place.

Direct experiences that generate children's own learning potential are essential at early childhood levels. Communities are filled with unlimited opportunities for learning that can be directly experienced and interpreted in ways that are understandable to a child. A surrounding neighborhood can be a primary resource for teaching and learning. Children love outdoor activities. They love going places and seeing things. Trips to a supermarket, to a construction site, or to a bakery help children connect their center with their community.

Classroom projects should, in part, develop from firsthand experiences. What a child experiences firsthand has more relevancy than what he experiences through teacher-initiated activities. Rather than isolating learning within the boundaries of a classroom, teachers should bring children into their community. Children need to derive meaning through *personal* experience that brings them in touch with their senses, their feelings, their perceptions, and their world. On a community outing, they can learn to read signs, to identify objects, and to develop concepts. They can also make observations and develop ideas.

Oftentimes, adults assume the ordinary is boring, failing to understand that for a child, the ordinary is almost always extraordinary. Often it is easier for adults to substitute vicarious experiences for the real thing. To a child, however, art is a real building, math is counting the steps at a zoo or jumping rope, language is how people talk, science is the sound of a cricket or the sight of leaves being whipped up by the wind. For the child, learning is derived, in large part, from *authentic* experiences—those *spontaneous* moments that occur and capture the interest and imagination of the spectator.

Reggio Emilia Schools for Young Children: A Model for Early Learning

The city of Reggio Emilia, located in the prosperous Po valley region of Emilia Romagna, Italy, is the birthplace of an early education program that is commanding international attention as a model environment for young children. A remarkable exhibition of children's artwork entitled *The Hundred Languages of Children* has been touring the world for fifteen years with a message of hope that exalts the image and potential of childhood.[11] The drawings reveal an educational system that instills in its young children an abiding sense of their own potential.

The educational system founded by Loris Malaguzzi at the end of World War II is testimony to the exceptional pride and commitment of a city to its young. Developed from a structure of education based on relationships and partnerships, the schools are intricately connected with their surrounding community—its parents and its leaders. Education emerges from an environment that invites children's explorations through actual experience, inquiry, and dialogue in the classroom and in the community. The responsive relationship between children and adults is a cornerstone of the Reggio Emilia approach to early education. Teachers and parents work in teams, maintaining a collegial respect for one another and for their common environment. The special dynamic that exists between children and staff at Reggio Emilia schools is reinforced by a community of caregivers who participate in the growth and development of the school's philosophy.

In this system of early education, the adult plays a central role in activating the competencies and creative energy of the child. The goal is not to teach, but to imbue children with a belief in themselves—to make them aware of their own potential. The adult *nurtures readiness* by delicately seizing moments of inquiry and interest in order to elaborate and interpret the thinking that is *already* occurring within the child.

The environment that surrounds the child is not just a beautiful place to visit; it is a primary resource with infinite potential for learning. It is a canvas of opportunities that continues to grow and change in the creative and skillful hands of its young. In an environment that nurtures readiness, children are given the space and the tools to interpret and develop the many images that stimulate their imagination.

Although art is a very important dimension of the creative process, in reality, the environment provides children with other ways to discover and define themselves, for example, through constructive play, collaborative interaction, cooperative learning, writing, in-depth projects, and through the strong sense of community that is always present to reaffirm and reinforce the child.

A Blueprint for Early Childhood Programs in the Twenty-First Century

The British Infant School, Bank Street, Reggio Emilia, and the Montessori concept of early education are exemplary models for child development. They share in common a belief in the potential of children and a vision of childhood that has stood the test of time. Each program has its own way of blending a child's experiences with the resources that are unique and available to an environment. Children develop interests and competencies as they explore and experience their immediate and surrounding worlds. From meaningful interactions with their social and physical environments, children develop a strong sense of themselves and of where they belong.

A vision and philosophy of childhood must ultimately be translated into a program that teachers can work with and children profit from. The *PLAN* model presented in this book builds on the legacy of earlier approaches and offers a curriculum suitable for the American child at the new millennium. It identifies the fundamental areas of child development as play, learning, the arts, and nurturing. Since play is central to the learning process, the program is in large part shaped by and developed from the natural creativity and nature of the child.

The community is a primary resource for learning in a PLAN environment. A community that is accessible to its young reinforces and acknowledges the dynamic relationship that exists between children and the important adults in their lives.

The challenge for all of us in the field of child care is to progress beyond its custodial image toward a role of shared responsibility and common concern. The Reggio Emilia program is unique to its history and its heritage, but its message is being transmitted around the world. Our challenge is to create developmentally appropriate programs from all of the knowledge that we continue to acquire in order to insure the growth and well-being of children in suburbs and in urban settings where space and resources are limited. On May 1, 1991, after two years of investigation, The National Commission on Children unanimously approved a blueprint for change in early childhood education in the United States:

> The seeds of educational success are sown early, in the prenatal period and the first months and years of life. During this time, children develop basic language and reasoning skills. They also acquire social skills, confidence, and a sense of self-worth, and they come to see themselves as important and competent members of their family and of other small communities in their lives. Children who arrive at school incapable of managing the kindergarten routine can quickly lose confidence in their ability to learn. Traditionally, society's responsibility for educating children began when they entered school. Growing knowledge of child development, however, compels us as individuals and as a society to place far greater emphasis on children's early development to ensure that every child is prepared for school.[12]

It is the responsibility and privilege of child care leaders and workers to preserve the feeling and message of childhood as a time to wonder, a time to play, and a time to grow so children can remember the way it was and carry happy memories into tomorrow's world. The challenge is to progress beyond the custodial image of child care toward a dynamic role of *shared responsibility* and *common concern.*

Where children are concerned, we all are responsible for their safety and well-being, if for no other reason than it is humane and civilized for those who cannot care for themselves. We pick up stray dogs and cats, we feel outrage for animals harmed by greed or used for recreation, we fight to keep trees alive and to clean polluted streams, we are concerned about nutrition and a long life, and we are concerned about the rights of an unborn child. Now we must turn attention and resources to *all* children—to those who have already claimed the right to life.

By so doing, we will preserve the meaning of childhood for generations to come and prepare children for a productive, meaningful life.

NOTES

1. Robert L. Church and Michael W. Sedlack, *Education in the United States* (New York: Macmillan, 1976), p. 271–74.

2. Ibid., pp. 317–19.

3. Evelyn Weber, *Ideas Influencing Early Childhood Education* (New York: Teachers College Press, 1984), pp. 39–41.

4. Frank Newman, "School Readiness and State Action," in *Perspectives on Early Childhood Education,* ed., David Elkind (Washington, DC: National Education Association, 1991), pp. 100–101.

5. Carol Seefeldt and Nita Barbour, *Early Childhood Education: An Introduction,* 2d ed. (New York: Macmillan, 1990), p. 8.

6. David Elkind, *Miseducation: Preschoolers at Risk* (New York: Knopf, 1987), p. 111.

7. Seefeldt and Barbour, *Early Childhood Education,* p. 5.

8. Gail Stout, ed., "Rachel McMillan Nursery School: Deptford, London, England," *Child Care Center* 1(2) (November 1986): 23–26.

9. Veryl M. Short and MaryLouise Burger, "The English Infant/Primary School Revisited," *Childhood Education* 64(2) (December 1987): 75–79.

10. Dorothy H. Cohen, *The Learning Child* (New York: Schocken Books, 1972), p. 92.

11. Lella Gandini, trans., *The Hundred Languages of Children* (Reggio Emilia, Italy: Reggio Children, 1996), p. 20.

12. John D. Rockefeller, *Beyond Rhetoric: A New American Agenda for Children and Families* (Washington, DC: The National Commission on Children, 1991), p. 187.

PART ONE

Child Development

In the broadest sense, [child development] is the process of becoming a fully functioning human being. A child's experience combines with a child's biological givens, and from this mixture emerges an adult person, one who will face the challenges of day-to-day life—as student, worker, friend, family member and citizen. If they are to succeed in these roles as adults, children need to be rooted in the basic skills of modern life. They need to become socially competent. They must come to know who they are. They must have acquired a secure and positive sense of their own identity. In addition, they must become proficient in thinking and in speaking clearly. They must learn to understand the many ways people communicate with one another. It is in the context of this broad conception of the process of child development that we must understand cognitive development.

—James Garbarino

1 Theories and Practices

Now the garden-beds are blooming,
Water-pot in hand we're coming,
All the thirsty plants to sprinkle,
All the buds begin to twinkle,
Scatter now their perfume rare,
They open their petals one by one,
They roll out their cups to the glowing sun,
Rewarding all our tender care.

—From *Mother-Play and Nursery Songs*
by Friedrich Froebel (1878)

Child development is a field of study that examines and interprets human growth and development from conception to adolescence. The principles of child development are derived from systematic, documented research studies that test and validate theories. Theories serve as useful guidelines for understanding the nature, interests, and needs of children at various stages of development. They help us to understand how children acquire and use knowledge and they help us to interpret behavioral characteristics. Most important, from a child care perspective, theories help us to develop strategies for working with children at all levels of development. By understanding the fundamentals of child development, educators can design and implement a child-appropriate curriculum and environment.

Theories Are Guidelines

Educators use theories as guidelines for program development. Theories form a foundation for education. They are intended to shape and direct programs in ways that are relevant to contemporary needs and learning styles. Today's child is socially acclimated and, in many cases, considerably more advanced than were children in Jean Piaget's generation. Most educators agree that children who have been exposed to early enrichment, through quality programs such as Head Start, are at a developmental advantage before entering a formal school experience. All children benefit from a strong learning environment that provides opportunities for language, thinking, and social development.

Adapting Theories

By adapting theories to contemporary knowledge and practices, a child care provider will recognize the importance of meeting the individual needs and developmental patterns of children. She will view the first years of life as extraordinary and critical to a child's lifelong development. A two-year-old can astound a teacher with the rate at which he can process and assimilate information. He can recall and perform routines, discriminate among physical objects, and to some degree, anticipate outcomes. He can pour and mix Jell-o and visualize its solid form if he is familiar with the process. A four-year-old can make associations, generalize information, and begin to form simple concepts. He can identify a dog by its physical appearance, compare it to a cat, and identify them both as members of the animal family. Children who experience positive interactions with people, ideas, and materials at an early age blossom into competent thinkers.

With some basic training in child development, a provider will realize that a two-year-old and a five-year-old will not behave and interact with their environment in the same way; they do not have the same degree of awareness, autonomy, or ability. A two-year-old reacts physically, spontaneously, and emotionally to his or her environment while a five-year-old is beginning to exercise reason and self-control in social settings. A two-year-old grabs or hits in anger while a five-year-old, though still a hitter uses language as a channel for cooperative dialogue with peers. A five-year-old is less controlled by his need for satisfaction and more sensitive to peer feelings. A provider, therefore, will limit the number of choices a two-year-old is given and oversee play activities. She will limit the number and length of formal group activities but will promote cooperative exchanges with peers. At the five-year level, she will increase choices, problem solving, and group interactions in both formal and informal settings (see Figure 1.1).

Knowledge of child development will facilitate optimal development at each stage of growth and learning. A quality environment derives from theories of learning that enlighten and guide leadership in childrearing practices. Children can become fully functioning human beings if they experience a secure and challenging total environment during their formative years. The NAEYC advocates a child development approach to early childhood education:

> The National Association for the Education of Young Children (NAEYC) believes that a high-quality early childhood program provides a safe and nurturing environment that promotes the physical, social, emotional, and cognitive development of young children while responding to the needs of families. Although the quality of an early childhood program may be affected by many factors, a major determinant of program quality is the extent to which knowledge of child development is applied in program practices—the degree to which the program is developmentally appropriate.[1]

Affective Development

Affective education is focused on the emotional development of children. Children's feelings and emotions reflect the way they see, relate to, and respond to their world. A joyful, nurturing teacher generates feelings of happiness in children. In a secure environment, children feel satisfied and unthreatened. They are able to venture forth, test their capabilities, and in the process, find out about themselves.

There is agreement that a child's rate of development is strongly influenced by the quality of family life and the social institutions he has been exposed to. A child behaves as he is treated; he imitates those who surround him. He trusts relationships as long as he can depend on their constancy and predictability. If a teacher who is very important to a child becomes unpleasant or angry, a child will react to the change in mood. If the behavior continues, he will become mistrustful. The teacher's behavior may have nothing to do with the child, but it is the child who perceives and reacts to the change. He doesn't understand why things are different and is not certain how to react. He may act out his feelings by changing his own behavioral patterns—becoming withdrawn, anxious, or hostile. Children are influenced by *how they are treated,* by *what they observe,* and by *what they experience.* They are strongly influenced by *adult role models.*

A child care program should provide *many* opportunities for children to express love and feelings in uncontrived, natural ways. A tender attitude toward

FIGURE 1.1   Developmental Differences between Ages 2 and 5

The 2-Year-Old	The 5-Year-Old

Social-Emotional Characteristics

Is engrossed in his own manipulations of objects.	Includes others in his explorations of the physical world.
Imitates the actions of objects and others as he sees them.	Goes beyond what he sees; invents sociodramatic themes in play.
Spends a lot of his time watching as well as acting.	Is able to pick up a lot of information from a momentary glance.
Self-directive, varies abruptly in his amenability to be influenced by an adult.	Socially tractable, waits for instructions and responds appropriately.
Strong in self-set goals, has difficulty inhibiting an action once initiated.	Can change an intended action in mid-flight at the verbal suggestion of an adult.
His emotional mood changes abruptly, but intensity is often short-lived.	His emotional mood can pervade several situations and is manifested in themes of social play and in approach to materials.

General Cognitive Characteristics

His goals exceed his means; preparing materials sometimes frustrates him as he attempts to reach his intended goal; is sidetracked on means.	Has mastered the simple means of preparing and wielding materials; anticipates definite products.
Has no clear sense of the continuity of past, present, and future, but can anticipate physical consequences of his actions.	Is beginning to see the continuity of his own past, present, and future, but has difficulty generalizing this to other persons.
Treats pictures as static shots of things rather than as momentary freezes of ongoing actions.	Can infer the course of action from a sequence of pictures.
His preferred mode of exploration is manual manipulation combined with observation.	Can visually explore the physical world in advance of manipulation in order to pick up information needed to guide goal-directed behavior.
Has difficulty coordinating his actions with those of other children in group games.	Has no difficulty coordinating his actions with those of others and is beginning to anticipate the meaning of game rules.

Language Characteristics

His sentences omit adjectives and adverbs necessary for explicit communication.	Has more effective ability to express desires and ask questions.
Uses language primarily to express personal desires and immediate needs.	Uses language to gather information about things in general—for example, origins and reasons.
His language is episodic and refers to single events and objects.	His language develops an idea or question, and his sentences build upon each other around a core theme.
His language is quite bound to the spatial and temporal present or to familiar contingencies.	Can use language metaphorically and to invent novel contingencies he doesn't actually see.
Adult's language can be used to activate him if the physical setting is right.	Adult's language can be used to set task constraints and to have him modify the physical setting.

Source: From George E. Forman and David S. Kuschner, *The Child's Construction of Knowledge: Piaget for Teaching Children.* Copyright © 1983 by The National Association for the Education of Young Children. Reprinted with permission from the National Association for Young Children.

animals, family members, friends, and community members will foster nurturance. Children are naturally sociable and friendly. They especially are interested in pleasing the teacher. If she values the environment, they too will become sensitized to the world around them, to its problems as well as its gifts.

According to theorist Erik Erikson, problems and conflicts must be resolved before a child can successfully move on to the next stage of development. A child, lacking meaningful and sustained human contact in the early years, will not conform to normal patterns of behavior. She will not be able to empathize with others, nor will she be able to express her feelings in ways that are healthy and helpful to her development. Her values and perceptions will be distorted by early experiences. A child will need considerable time with adults before being able to exhibit positive, prosocial behavior.

Even a happy child can go through reversals in an out-of-home environment. A child may experience a sense of loss over a mother's absence and not be able to verbalize his feelings. He may become fretful and listless at certain times of the day. In child care centers, teachers and assistants must be sensitive to the moods and dispositions of children at any given time. They must extend themselves by spending personal time with a child in need *while* he is experiencing anxiety or discomfort. This can best be accomplished in an unhurried, nurturing atmosphere.

By assessing each child from a total developmental perspective, a teacher will be better able to design a program. She will know when and how to approach emotional issues such as death or divorce. A young child who has experienced a loss may not know how to deal with expressions of sympathy. An "affective" teacher will know how to connect with a child to facilitate the healing process. She will understand that, at certain times, the best thing to say is nothing at all.

An affective program that acknowledges and cultivates a child's own unique personality while gradually introducing him to his surrounding world is probably the most important "first lesson" for child care providers. As children identify with their immediate environment, they extend their feelings and their perceptions to incorporate their surrounding world. They accept others if they feel accepted and loved. A group is shaped by individual members who gradually develop common interests and points of contact. A group has its own distinct personality and dynamic—there is no one model that can guarantee successful teaching. A model can only create a framework or context for teaching and learning.

A center that does not cultivate the child's own personality is not practicing the principles of child development. Children are individuals before they are members of a group. Early childhood is a time of formation and expression. In the words of the great French educator and philosopher, Jean-Jacques Rousseau, childhood is a time of *unfolding*. It is not a time of *molding* young minds and spirits.

The Work of Erik H. Erikson

In his now famous book *Child and Society* (1963), Erik Erikson developed a comprehensive theory of emotional development that spans eight stages from infancy through adulthood. Erikson's emphasis on psychosocial development from a lifespan perspective was strongly influenced by Sigmund Freud's work in psycho-analysis. Both Freud and Erikson viewed a child's response to distinctive stages of development as crucial to personal development and to personality formation. Unlike Freud, Erikson emphasized the healthy personality affected, but not irrevocably marked, by problems in infancy and early childhood. To Erikson, meeting and dealing with a crisis at the time of occurrence was critical to continued personality adjustment and growth. Under appropriate conditions, people could reorder and adjust their lives before meeting the next conflict. The way in which a person resolves a problem will have a lasting effect on the person's self-image, personality, and view of society.[2]

Understanding and Interpreting Erikson's Stages

Stage 1: Trust versus Mistrust.   During this period (0 to 1 year), the quality of interaction between a parent and child will determine a child's attitude toward other people. According to Erikson, the infant will develop a sense of trust if his basic needs for food and care are met with comforting regularity. He is learning that people and objects exist even though they cannot be seen. The mother figure becomes an inner certainty when the child perceives her presence even though he cannot see her. Under healthy conditions, the child trusts that mother will reappear and will continue to meet his needs. The alternative to trust, mistrust, occurs when children's basic needs are not consistently met—when children cannot depend on the constancy of relationships.

Application to Child Care.   The single, most important person for a young child is the primary parent, or, in a child care environment, an adult caregiver to whom the child transfers his or her security needs and attachment during the absence of the primary parent. If this basic need is threatened, a child will manifest insecure behavior patterns; thumb clutching, nervous habits, physical aggressiveness, fears and anxieties, mistrust, and other signs of dysfunction. Bonding (natural attachment) is a trusting relationship that develops between a child and a caring adult. A child's overall nurturing needs may be met by several adults. But, as is often the case, there will be one person whom a child will single out for comfort and security. Bonding in the form of trust is *essential* to young children in day care centers. Staff members who care for infants and toddlers should be employed with the expectation of a long-term commitment.

Trust is cultivated through continuity and positive relationships. A child care program must strive for consistency in staffing, in behavioral guidelines, and in teaching methods. A child care program that is *trust inspiring* is *loving*. Young children experience love through verbal and nonverbal communication. They want to be hugged and they want to express love to the adults with whom they have bonded. It is difficult to conceive of an affective early childhood environment that is not generous with its affection to young children. Children develop trust when caregivers:

- Show affection—let children know they care and are there for them: to counsel, to comfort, and to participate in their joys and disappointments.
- Emphasize the importance of cross-bonding (child, center, and family) so that children feel a sense of unity among their relationships and their environment.
- Help children understand and cope with negative or anxious feelings.
- Address the child's feelings at the time of occurrence; console the child but do not make false or unrealistic promises.
- Help children learn to trust by providing consistency in communication.
- Promote peer friendships so children can feel secure in their center.
- Plan projects that cultivate nurturing and bonding.
- Help children identify with feelings and attitudes through literature, discussions, fieldtrips, and visual aids.

Stage 2: Autonomy versus Doubt. During this period (1 to 2 years), the child operates in a self-centered world of need gratification. A child's insatiable curiosity can best be satisfied by physical contact with the concrete world—a physical world that is *visible* and *tangible*. The period is essentially egocentric (the child's needs and interests are all-consuming). The child is developing self-control and self-confidence as he makes contact with the environment. He needs to be protected but not overprotected. The alternative to autonomy, doubt, occurs when children begin to feel frustrated because they are no longer in control of their world—when they no longer feel confident in their ability to make choices.

Application to Child Care. Young children exercise autonomy when they are free to investigate and not unduly restricted by the presence of anxious, controlling adults. Children develop confidence by doing more and more for themselves. A child learns how to manipulate and control his environment through *repeated* exposure to positive reinforcing experiences. In the process, the child must take chances and experience a few bruises along the way. If fears have been instilled in a child, he will avoid growth-enhancing experiences that promote mastery and competency. Over a period of time, a child's anxieties may become generalized; more and more things will make him anxious. He may stutter or wet the bed when he feels upset. He may feel uncomfortable with transitions or new situations. The opposite, too much autonomy, may be equally harmful. The adventurous child who knows no boundaries may have difficulty accepting rules designed for his safety. Testing limits, he will continue to have difficulty developing internal control mechanisms. Young children must be trained not only to take chances that are constructive and necessary to their growth but to avoid things that are harmful to their growth. They must learn to practice caution and wisdom *before* they can be entrusted with freedom.

Child care centers should encourage children of all ages to become independent. They should be expected to care for their personal belongings, to keep their cubbies tidy, and to cooperate with their classmates in maintaining and caring for their rooms. Jobs and chores should become a natural part of classroom routines and management. Every child should understand the value of good hygiene, good eating habits, and overall cleanliness. When they are participants in self-care and center care, they will be able to transfer their good habits to other situations outside the center. They will become more cooperative at home and in their communities. They will become trustworthy. Children will develop autonomy when caregivers:

- Reinforce their need to explore and investigate their concrete and surrounding world on their own.
- Select appropriate materials for them to play with and learn from.
- Help them develop self-control by understanding that some behavior is acceptable and some behavior is not tolerated—like being unkind or hurtful to others.
- Help them understand consequences (cause-and-effect relationships).
- Encourage them to make choices when selecting activities.
- Help them develop self-management skills within their developmental level (zippering, buttoning, folding sheets on a cot, unpacking a lunch box).
- Help them develop caution in physical and social play.
- Encourage them to take responsibility.
- Encourage them to develop coping mechanisms to help them deal with stressful encounters and disappointments.

Stage 3: Initiative versus Guilt.   During this period (2 to 6 years), children must be given opportunities to test their capabilities. Erikson believes that initiative is the "willingness to undertake, plan, and attack a task for the sake of being active."[3] This is an exciting period when children begin to test their skills and, at times, to challenge authority. During this critical period, children begin to develop formative skills and concepts that will lead them toward higher levels of thinking. On the other hand, guilt occurs when children feel unsupported and unchallenged by their environment. They will begin to doubt themselves when they do not experience positive reinforcement or acknowledgment and when they fail to exert initiative.

Application to Child Care.   In order for children to develop confidence, they need reinforcement from the important people in their lives. They must be free to explore and observe in order to develop self-awareness and competency. By interacting with people, children begin to develop a sense of identity. As they discover their world, children seek role models for reassurance and reinforcement. These are the people who help the child believe in himself. A child who is confident will exercise initiative. When children do not receive positive messages from their surrounding human environment and when they are not supported by parents, adults, and friends, they will lose confidence in themselves and in others.

A child with initiative has a built-in sense of responsibility. She is a role model and a budding leader. She becomes a teacher's helper by natural selection because she is reliable and responsible. This is a child who is helpful to others; who can quickly locate a missing mitten and button a jacket. Her take-charge attitude is pleasing and unpretentious. She comforts children when they are sick or hurt, cares for younger children on fieldtrips, and carries the bag of snacks on and off the bus without complaining. She holds hands, listens, and respects authority. Unfortunately, she is not a typical day care child.

Teachers are often agitated about the unwillingness of children to exercise responsibility. Coaxing and cajoling doesn't always work when children have an antiwork, negative mindset. For these children there's always an excuse for not picking up and there's always someone else to point a finger at for not doing his or her fair share. Some children will go to the extreme of not playing in order to avoid work. Their attitudes are unmistakably negative. Projecting toward second or third grade, these are the same children who storm into day care, slam back-packs on tables, and start the afternoon complaining about too much work. When behaviors are instilled early on in day care environments, children do not need to be reminded about their responsibilities. When everyone does his or her fair share, it is truly difficult to distinguish work from play. Usually, when teachers are initi-ators, children display initiative. A teacher who cheerfully models cooperative behavior by sharing in pickup time will quickly have a following.

Initiative involves taking risks. A child should be able to anticipate and accept failure on her journey toward self-mastery. She should be willing to risk the toppling effect of an unstable building when she places one more block on the top. The last block on a wobbly, vertical structure is a breath-holder even for a child who can cope with unwelcomed consequences. The less mature child might get angry or throw a block when she sees her building destroyed. The more mature child would probably pick up the pieces and start all over again. In the more pos-itive mindset, the child is becoming *self-actualized* (increasing awareness and com-petency); he has instinctively accepted that the *process* is more important than outcome. It is important to:

- Avoid setting up roadblocks to self-development by discouraging making decisions and taking risks.
- Avoid making children so dependent that they cannot assert their indepen-dence.
- Avoid overprotecting children through negative feedback: "You see, I told you not to climb on the bars; now you've fallen and dirtied your clothes...next time you'll listen to me!"
- Encourage children to become self-starters and self-managers so they can function independently and competently.
- Allow time, space, and flexible time for children to fully engage in classroom activities.
- Praise their quality time and their positive efforts toward socialization and good citizenship.
- Help children identify and build on strengths and interests.

Stage 4: Industry versus Inferiority.   During this period (6 to 12 years), children are beginning to see the relationship between doing a job and feeling good or not good about the outcome. They are moving into a less defined world that offers more choices and opportunities. Children begin to feel more competitive and goal oriented. They begin to display initiative toward their schoolwork. They are learning about values, responsibility, and rules of conduct. The opposite of industry, inferiority, occurs when children feel unimportant and unaccepted. No longer self-directed, an unhappy child becomes unmotivated. She is reluctant to try new experiences because she is fearful of outcomes. She avoids people who make her feel uncomfortable, preferring to be an onlooker rather than an active participant.

Application to Child Care.   An industrious child applies herself to a task-at-hand with perseverance and pride. She pays attention and knows how to allocate her time in order to complete a task and is not easily diverted or distracted. The amount of effort a child puts into tasks and the precision with which she performs her tasks tells a lot about the child. A little child painstakingly pastes one piece of paper onto another. With equal care, a school-age child glues together a model airplane, carefully wiping off excess glue as he strives for perfection. At both levels, a learner is occupied in productive work that requires patience and perseverance. Both children would be well served by reinforcement. A "good job" comment by the teacher symbolizes appreciation and recognition to a child. To help the child internalize the satisfaction, a teacher's comment might be: "You must really be proud of yourself for doing such a good job today." More than likely this brief but positive interaction will motivate a child to continue pleasing her teacher and satisfying herself.

There are some children who appear to be natural taskmasters; they apply their preference for order at work and at play. Blankets are meticulously arranged around dolls, homework is carefully organized and executed, shoes are always tied, and clothing in place. For most children, however, industry needs training and reinforcement *from the beginning.* If children are expected to be industrious, they will soon tire of escape mechanisms: "I can't," "My mother doesn't care if I don't do my homework," "I'm too tired, I'll do it later." Teachers can cultivate incentive by helping children recognize the importance of taking responsibility and becoming positive members of a group. . . . The little red hen worked very hard to make bread but her children were not very cooperative . . . and what happened? Lazy chickens and lazy children don't always get to enjoy the good things in life! Industry will develop when caregivers:

- Help children develop confidence and self-belief.
- Present tasks that are within the range of capability and avoid giving children too many steps and too many instructions.
- Make agreements with children regarding classroom chores and responsibilities.
- Have children evaluate outcomes and participate in decision making.

- Plan activities that encourage children to organize and implement classroom and community projects.
- Develop strategies for positive reinforcement.
- Develop a buddy system with child helping child—to cut, assemble, and tend to personal needs.
- Provide materials and activities to encourage self-development and re-sourcefulness—magazines and books, board games, community visitors and leaders with whom children want to identify.
- Reward children for good works (small but important symbols of appreciation like ice cream floats, handmade bookmarks, a trip to a park, a pencil, an "I had a great day" note).
- Teach children self-pride so they can feel that they are appreciated and accepted.
- Work with parents for cross-bonding, emphasizing the importance of recognizing and rewarding industriousness and initiative.

The Work of Lawrence Kohlberg

Lawrence Kohlberg (1927–1987) is recognized for his work in moral development. Expanding on Jean Piaget's work, Kohlberg conceived of moral reasoning as taking place in six sequential stages. The first two, moral reasoning and moral independence, are quite similar to those developed by Piaget; the next four represent more sophisticated levels of moral thought found in adolescents and adults. At the earliest level of moral reasoning, the child accepts rules as givens—rules come from adult authority figures; they are unchanging and not to be challenged. As the young child's thinking matures, he begins to adapt rules to fit his needs, exercising moral independence. He interprets rules according to his own perceptions and experience. The way an individual reasons through a dilemma determines his level of emotional maturity. In Kohlberg's schema, each stage is qualitatively distinct, building on knowledge and understandings from previous stages.[4]

Understanding and Interpreting Kohlberg's Stages

Premoral Levels.   During the first two stages, referred to by Kohlberg as the *premoral levels,* children abide by externally imposed rules categorized by right and wrong responses to their behavior. Their actions and reactions reflect their desire to avoid what is unpleasant (punishment), to serve their own needs and interests, and to please adults. They see rules as unchanging and having a reality of their own.

Conventional Levels.   The next two stages, referred to as the *conventional levels,* reflect children's need to conform to social norms. Children can take the perspective of others and begin to think through the consequences of actions. There is a moral code from which to operate that is determined by a conventional social order. The child is gaining moral independence but still demonstrates compliance and respect for moral truths.

Principled Levels.   In the final stages, *principled levels,* moral values reside in principles and standards that can be shared. The dominant motives are a sense of obligation to a social contract and the belief in universal principles. Children become attuned to societal values and expectations.[5]

Application to Child Care

Young children incline toward self-satisfying, pleasure-seeking behavior that is often imitative in nature. Rules of behavior can confuse children if they are not consistently applied and enforced. When children observe unkind and inappropriate behavior among peers, they begin to challenge the values they are practicing in classrooms. They observe how peers avoid punishment by stretching or distorting the truth. As they begin to identify with a group, they learn their own messages about personal conduct—messages that may undermine family values and affect children's character development—messages that need to be corrected.

As children mature, they can understand the difference between appropriate and inappropriate behavior. They are able to make moral judgments: "It is wrong to disobey the rules," "She didn't mean to do it, it was an accident." Sometimes, truth can be distorted by what a child wants to believe or by what a friend wants her to believe. Children need help in sorting out their feelings, in responding to personal and moral dilemmas, and in understanding the nature and consequences of making choices.

Moral training has traditionally been a family-centered responsibility whereby children are raised according to certain codes and principles that are passed from one generation to another. The church, synagogue, and school counselors also have served as exemplary conduits for guiding children toward a moral consciousness. However, moral training is no longer identified exclusively with home and religious training. Given a change in family structures and in family relationships, moral development is increasingly perceived as a *shared* responsibility between families and childrearing systems.

There is a growing sense that, in its efforts to protect diversity, the United States has neglected training in commonly accepted universal values that affect conduct and define our obligations as citizens. These values might include respect for human dignity, the cultivation of personal character, and the exercise of responsible citizenship.[6]

Most caregivers would agree that child care training should include moral training, yet they are not certain how to define moral training. When working with young children, it is best to generalize commonly accepted values in words that children can identify with: Children should be kind to all living things, they should be good friends, they should be good helpers, they should always tell the truth, and they should respect adults, friends, and their environment.

On a deeper level, caregivers may be called on to discuss moral issues that cannot be comfortably communicated to young children. Many, if not most teachers, feel inadequate and unprepared to discuss commonplace issues such as street violence, unwed mothers, child abuse, drugs, and divorce. Before discussing moral issues that do not fall under accepted family values but appear to be important at a given time, teachers need to consult with parents so that there are no misunderstandings about what topics are to be discussed and how to present them. In cases where parents appear irresponsible or unconcerned, teachers may have to assume a greater responsibility for moral training. On issues where parents hold strong convictions, however, avoid or delay discussing them until an agreement is reached on the proper approach to use.

A value-conscious environment will help children clarify their feelings and attitudes in prosocial ways. There are many ways—through drama, music, movement, or by rereading favorite storybooks that encourage children to make observations about characters—teachers can create a moral climate for children. Should Goldilocks have helped herself to the three bears' breakfast and left a broken chair on the floor? What would have happened if she'd knocked on the door and had been invited to have breakfast with the bears? What would have happened if she'd waited for the bears and told the truth about the chair? A nurturing program will encourage children to develop strong moral values. They can learn to make healthy choices with regard to their own conduct when caregivers:

- Encourage young children to make healthy, appropriate choices.
- Encourage children to anticipate consequences before making choices.
- Help children develop internal codes of conduct that will develop strong character.
- Encourage manners and practical life training.
- Select literature to foster moral development.
- Provide opportunities for children to extend their kindness to others less fortunate or handicapped.
- Help children cope with feelings of failure and inadequacy.
- Help them release negative feelings, understanding that everyone experiences doubt, frustration, and anger at times.
- Give children freedom to discover and define themselves.
- Help children develop social consciousness and compassion toward all living things.

The Work of James L. Hymes, Jr., and Daniel A. Prescott

In recent years, much of the work of educators James Hymes and Daniel Prescott has been devoted to continuing and expanding the child development point of view. Their focus on mental health and affective learning has strongly influenced contemporary education. Prescott believes that an emotional climate that affirms children through loving relationships is the key to wholesome, healthy development. He describes the value of living in a loving environment:

- Being loved can afford any human being a much needed basic security;
- Being loved makes it possible to learn to love oneself and others;
- Being loved and loving others facilitates belonging in groups;
- Being loved and loving in return facilitates identification with parents, relatives, teachers, and peers by which the culture is internalized more readily and organizing attitudes and values are established easily;
- Being loved and loving facilitate adjustment to situations that involve strong unpleasant emotions.[7]

Application to Child Care

There are many opportunities to communicate caring feelings in environments that nurture children. Children may be affirmed through direct contact and guidance. Training children to care for themselves and others is a loving message. Promoting the conditions conducive to their growth and development is a loving message. Helping them to extend their potential and to reach for new heights is a loving message. Letting children know relationships are not conditional on behavior or performance but grounded in love, may indeed be the most important message one can give a child.

A loving environment is a nurturing environment. In his candid and refreshing book, *Teaching the Child Under Six*, Hymes (1989) expresses these thoughts:

> Today's young children are headed toward an increasingly interdependent world. The speed of transportation, the ease of communication, the interlacing of economies, the ever-present threat of universal destruction make this world one shrinking planet, one tight family of man. For children's self-protection, the capacity to care for others must be nurtured—for people we know, for people we have never seen; for people like us, for people very different, for people near at hand, and for those far out of sight. This sense of caring must be nurtured just as much for our children's self-fulfillment, so that they can grow into the deepest potential of their humanity.[8]

Cognitive Development

Cognition is the process by which children acquire knowledge. Knowledge occurs naturally as a child actively constructs, interprets, and transforms his environment. At the early childhood level, knowledge consists of concrete information and a growing awareness of one's surrounding physical and human environment. A child acquires knowledge by the quality of verbal interactions with adults and by direct observation. A theory that views knowledge as an active interactional process between the child and the environment would prioritize activities that fully engage the child. Such activities might include those that encourage questioning, reasoning, problem solving, and self-regulated learning.

A young child acquires knowledge as she interacts with and manipulates physical objects, gradually comprehending why and how things work. An older child consolidates and extends her base of concrete operations through tasks and skills that require inquiry, experimentation, reasoning, problem solving, and critical thinking. A curriculum that values children's thinking does not limit or stifle opportunities for self-discovery that may have the potential for higher levels of awareness and understanding. A child's best tools are her own *need to know* and her own *desire for mastery.*

Even though stages differ qualitatively, development is a continuous process. The child is always growing, from the early stage of one phase to the later phase of the same stage and from one stage to the next. He absorbs and modifies information in order to accommodate new learning. He reasons as he experiments and makes choices as he plays: This will work, this will not work. He makes predictions and observes consequences: A flower dies when it is not watered, a child gets hungry in mid-afternoon if he doesn't eat his lunch. He tests himself and his sense of boundaries as he creates, makes changes, and moves forward. It is through testing, guidance, and by applying reason, that a child constructs his own base of knowledge. In the process, the child experiences *insight* (the sudden perception of new relationships) and *motivation* (the desire to acquire more knowledge).

Cognitive theorists believe that learning is the result of an individual's attempt to understand and to master his world. The way a person perceives and experiences the world influences what he will learn. What a child learns is related to *what* he has learned, to *how* he processes new information, and to the *quality* of his experiences. The quality and appropriateness of early childhood environments will strongly influence a child's ability to learn. John Dewey's (1938) pedagogical principles illustrate how important environments are to the educative process:

> A primary responsibility of educators is that they not only be aware of the general principle of the shaping of actual experience by environing conditions, but that they also recognize in the concrete what surroundings are conducive to having experiences that lead to growth. Above all, they should know how to utilize the surroundings, physical and social, that exist so as to extract from them all that they have to contribute to building up experiences that are worthwhile.[9]

The Work of Jean Piaget

Jean Piaget (1896–1980), a major force in developmental psychology, began investigating children's thinking in the 1920s. It was not until the 1960s, however, that his work received major recognition in the United States. Piaget investigated cognitive processes from infancy through adulthood. His theories have produced both praise and criticism among contemporary educators, but as a theoretical framework for cognitive development, his work is unparalleled in depth and scope.

According to Piaget, cognitive abilities progress in four sequential stages. Each stage is invariant (in a fixed order) representing a different organization of knowledge and experience but linked to the preceding stage. Continuity of mental growth is assured as each structure "results from the preceding one, integrating it as a subordinate structure, and prepares for the subsequent one, into which it is sooner or later itself integrated."[10] As the child forms new cognitive structures, he is able to think at higher levels. Each stage represents a different organization of experience, information, and knowledge.

For Piaget, the child develops intelligence as he spontaneously acts on and experiments with his physical world. Though the stages are constant, a child's learning is influenced by developmental factors such as maturation, social interaction, experience with objects, symbolic thought, language, and moral judgment. Along with these factors, it is necessary to consider the factor of *equilibrium*—a fundamental aspect of growth and development.[11]

In Piaget's developmental schema, children naturally progress from concrete levels of operation to more abstract, complex levels of operation. They draw on and reconstruct prior learning in order to reach new levels of maturation and understanding. In the process of acquiring knowledge, the mind is constantly active. Through the process of assimilation, children internally absorb information that is continually being processed in an external environment. As a child continues to think, he accommodates new information to his ever-expanding base of knowledge. In the process, the child seeks *equilibration*—a sense of balance and harmony between his internal and external world. Piaget's recognition of the active role children play in their own learning is best reflected in a child-centered learning environment.

Understanding and Interpreting Piaget's Stages

The Sensorimotor Stage (0 to 2 years).   Piaget used the term *egocentricism* to describe infancy and young childhood. For infants, this is the inability to distinguish between the self and the external world; for a toddler it is the inability to see the world from another's perspective. In both instances, the "I" is the dominant motivating force. The child's understanding of his world is initially limited by what he experiences: by human contact, by his surrounding environment, and by sensory experiences. During the first months of life, the baby's movements are uncoordinated, and his actions are spontaneous. Within a few months, the growing child learns to coordinate movements by reaching for objects or turning to look for the source of a sound. By further integrating sensorimotor information, the infant begins to discover the various properties of objects.[12]

When the child begins to crawl or walk, he becomes more and more fascinated with manipulating objects. As he satisfies one interest, he moves on to another—to what he can put in his mouth, bang around, grab, or throw. Though his movements are awkward and his behavior still appears unfocused, his intentions are quite clear: He wants what he wants! He is coordinating what he has learned with what he wants or with what is already familiar. He goes to a door and reaches for the handle that will open the door. He carries a shoe and puts it near a foot. He pulls glasses off his caregiver and attempts to replace them. To Piaget, the young child is demonstrating the beginnings of intelligence and problem solving by actively experiencing and experimenting with his environment.

The significant development during this stage is what Piaget refers to as *object permanence*, which occurs at around 8 or 9 months. This is a higher level of operation by which a child can understand that objects and familiar people can exist *apart* from himself. He senses that even though he cannot see a familiar object, it is present. For a two-year-old, this means that a teddy bear may not be in his chair, but it can be found somewhere else in the room. The rudiments of thought and memory are gradually developing.

Application to Child Care.   The growing child operates primarily in a sensorimotor world of concrete objects. Central to this world is her dependence on primary adult figures. She enjoys exploring her world and imitating increasingly complex movements and sounds. She begins to coordinate body movements, sounds, and language. If she is introduced to favorite songs, such as *Ring Around the Rosie,* she will need little prompting to go into her act—turning around, making beginning sounds, and even falling down. (For a little child the best part of a song is a surprise ending that is accompanied by unexpected movement.)

Learning cannot be separated from a child's physical and human needs and from his basic desire to explore. The young child develops self-awareness as he touches, makes observations, and reacts to the people who occupy his space and who satisfy his needs. The young child's primary modes for learning are through *self-initiated experiences* that satisfy his curiosity, and through *adult-child interactions* that satisfy his need for comfort, affection, and attention. Learning, for the young child, is experiential, active, and dynamic. His relatively small world is a huge repository for hands-on experiences. The role of the adult or teacher is to guide him safely, securely, and confidently toward competency.

Learning takes place as the child discovers on his own, and as he interacts with his environment. In order to make discoveries, children need an unhurried, tension-free environment. They need many hands-on experiences such as riding on trucks, playing on mats, and digging in the dirt. Young children are very curious—a new object on a science table will immediately attract attention and curiosity. A bird's feather may become a focal point for a group experience—examining the feather under a microscope, identifying its source (a bird), going on a bird-watching trip, making a nest for a window sill. Adults provide stimulation, challenge, and support by selecting activities, materials, and experiences that will enhance learning.

The Preoperational Stage (2 to 7 years).   Around age two, the child begins to develop *symbolic thought*—"the use of mental images and words to represent actions and entire events that are not present."[13] He is beginning to internalize experiences and to think about people and objects that are not present. He makes pictures that resemble familiar and important objects: the sun, a flower, a boat, or a plane. Children's thinking processes are still immature and limited to momentary experience, the most pervasive characteristic of this age being *preoperational egocentrism.* Piaget believed that children are unable to take the point of view of others, which causes them to interpret the world from their own impressions.[14] Nor did Piaget think preschool children were capable of *reversibility*—a logical operation that enables a child to reason a problem through and reverse direction.[15]

Preoperational children are *perception bound:* They are deceived by the appearance of objects based on their limited perception. Two glasses of equal amounts of water may be perceived as quantitatively different by a young child if one glass is tall and thin while the other is short and wide. Piaget referred to this operation as *conservation.*

Application to Child Care.   Children learn through play. Play enables children to make connections and extend conceptual understandings. A child's play world often represents his real world. The child incorporates features and memories of his experiences into play schemes. He uses objects symbolically: Two blocks may become a plane, a vertical block may become an air traffic control tower. As children play imaginatively, they *recreate* their world in their own terms, applying logic, thinking, and problem solving to the task at hand.

Children can begin to understand the concept of change at the preoperational level. By observation and experience they learn that some things remain constant (a stationary object) while other things, like seasons and weather, change. They can explain ways that people and nature adjust and adapt to changing seasons, and they can activate change themselves: making ice from water, applesauce from apples, a snake from play dough. As a young child experiments with objects and art experiences, her perceptual field widens. She begins to discriminate among shapes and textures, to classify by common attributes, and to perceive spatial relationships.

During the preoperational stage, the preschool child is beginning to think about actions and perceive consequences. He begins to use problem solving as a way of managing his world. Language becomes an increasingly useful tool for communicating needs and ideas. Language enables a child to translate thoughts into words: to negotiate, to clarify, and to question. It helps him to develop the social skills that will enable him to *decenter*—to take the perspective of others. Through language production, a child learns how to negotiate and how to express his thoughts. He becomes aware that if he chooses the right words, he can influence outcomes.

A child-centered program will maximize opportunities for children to make observations and discoveries through *self-initiated learning.* At the early childhood level, *play* is the primary medium for learning. Children construct as they play, they learn social skills as they play, and they develop thinking and reasoning powers as they play. Play encourages children to make connections and to try new combinations. As they play, children naturally begin to sort and arrange objects. Sometimes they have a plan and sometimes a plan grows from an activity. As they play with toys, children become aware of spatial dimensions—when things don't fit, adjustments must be made.

A child-centered program also will provide children with many opportunities for socializing with peers. Children enjoy sharing experiences. If, for example, the bird feather became a topic of interest for group circle, the teacher might read a story about a little bird that gave away his golden wings to help others (*Tico and the Golden Wings* by Leo Lionni). To extend understanding, the children may write bird stories, make real bird feeders, and visit the birdhouse at the zoo.

The Concrete Operational Stage (7 to 11 years).   Piaget viewed this stage as a turning point when children's thinking begins to resemble adult thinking. The basic characteristics of this stage is that children recognize the logical stability of the world, the concepts of transformation and conservation, and the fact that changes can be reversed.[16] The growing child begins to apply reason, to solve problems, and to predict outcomes. She is interested in acquiring and applying new information to her cognitive structure. New ways of thinking enable the growing child to understand cause-and-effect relationships and to think conceptually. Though the child still operates on a concrete level, she is developing perception as she adapts to a more challenging world.

Application to Child Care.   The growing child is becoming more and more self-reliant and knowledgeable. She uses reflection and reason to direct her actions and to influence her decision making. She is curious to discover why things work and motivated toward self-directed learning. Influenced by what she observes and experiences, the child continues a building-block process of applying new learning to previously acquired knowledge.

The Work of Jerome Bruner

Whereas John Dewey and Jean Piaget saw the child as qualitatively different from the adult, Jerome Bruner viewed the child as a little scholar. Children, he believed, are capable of mastering subject matter at a far younger age than traditionally acknowledged if material is presented in its simplest form. Bruner's *spiral curriculum* theory became the backbone of the discipline-centered curriculum reforms of the 1960s. The theory is based on the model of the learner who is capable of thinking by means of a process of inquiry–discovery.[17] Bruner believed that a massive transfer of knowledge can take place when children are given the opportunity to apply new understandings to previously learned material. The basic tool for gaining knowledge and insight is language. This process of inquiry and discovery is based on the scientific method.

Understanding and Interpreting Bruner's Stages

Enactive.   At the first level, children learn by doing, by observation, and by reacting to what others do.

Iconic.   At the second level, children begin to form images of objects.

Symbolic.   In the third stage, children represent their world through the use of symbols.[18]

Progression of Learning.   In his learning-through-discovery approach, Bruner believed that learning proceeds inductively from simple to complex levels of understanding. The basic tool for learning is language. As children learn to apply basic knowledge, they can perceive several options at one time. An idea can become a catalyst for higher levels of development. If, for example, children are learning about animal homes, a teacher may begin by introducing a simple one-to-one problem-solving activity (draw a line from the animal to its home). As children gain more information about animal homes, they begin to identify animals with specific settings: an alligator with a swampy area, a deer with a woods, a whale with a large body of water. They are making generalizations and building concepts about the unique patterns and characteristics of animals—understandings that go way beyond a teacher's first lesson. Within a short period of time, they may be able to make their own animal/home book, identifying pictorially where animals live with the structure and materials of their homes.

Bruner's theory reorganized curricula across grades. By simplifying fundamental subject matter and challenging children to think and solve problems, children were able to master complex forms of learning at far younger ages than previously believed possible.[19]

Application to Child Care.   In a discovery environment, children should be exposed to information and ideas through simple, yet challenging experiences that generate thinking. The simplest project can become a catalyst for concept building. Number concepts, such as more, less, equal, unequal, can become a focus for a science discovery center. Learning the letter *B* can become an opportunity for expanded learning throughout the week: making a *b*irdhouse and a *b*ird's nest from natural materials, planting *b*ulbs, making *b*inoculars for a *b*ird-watching hike, making a *b*ig *b*ook on *b*locks, *b*aking a *b*ig cake with *b*lue candles to celebrate *B* day. A culminating project may be a *B* word list that incorporates all of these experiences. With ideas and information provided, in part, by a teacher, children can proceed on their own using the scientific method to gain mastery.

The Work of Lev S. Vygotsky

Of Russian background, Lev S. Vygotsky was a contemporary of Jean Piaget. In 1962, his book, *Thought and Language,* was translated into English. Vygotsky believed that knowledge is created by society and transmitted to individuals by society. Individuals vary in the way they respond to various kinds of cultural stimuli. When development is perceived as socially induced, major cultural trends, such as television, computers, and fads, tend to affect the way people perceive the world and themselves.[20]

Increasingly, the premise that all mental functions have social origins has gained credibility among contemporary child psychologists and educators. In order to understand the psychology of childhood, one has to understand the pervasive impact society has on human growth and development, even at the earliest stages of life. Young children who have had group experiences at a young age will be socialized early on. They have been defining their personality and developing their own sense of identity as they interact with peers and supervising adults throughout most of their waking hours. Their world is not just one of family, but of group, community, and all of the impressionable experiences that influence behavior. The quality of an environment is clearly a powerful influence on developing personalities.

Understanding and Interpreting Vygotsky's Theories

A Social Interactional Theory. Like Bruner, Vygotsky differed with Piaget about the importance of language to child development. Piaget believed that language patterns of the young child were primarily self-centered and immature due to the fact that the child lacked the capacity for meaningful communication. A child's monologues and utterances were not seen as significant indicators of mental awareness or development. In contrast, Vygotsky believed that language developed from social exchanges between a child and another person. Early monologues or babbles (referred to as private speech) were seen as meaningful functions in a child's quest to understand and relate to the immediate world.

Adult Guidance. Whereas Piaget stressed the importance of peer interaction to language development, Vygotsky emphasized the importance of adult guidance in facilitating communication and comprehension. His term, *zone of proximal development,* was identified as a level of learning in the young child that required adult assistance.[21] The underlying premise was that tasks within this zone are too difficult for a child to handle alone. Under adult guidance, a child can perform better when he has direction and monitoring before he begins a task. As a child becomes adept at understanding and processing tasks, he requires less and less instruction. He is increasingly able to direct and self-regulate his learning.

Application to Child Care. With regard to group learning, a teacher can initiate inquiry and problem solving by structuring an experience in a creative way. For example, if children are making a bird's nest, a teacher might attempt to keep their focus by planning a nature walk to gather materials for the project. She gives each child a small bag to discourage children from gathering large objects, such as stones or debris that are not related to the project at hand. By structuring and restricting choices, the teacher is promoting concentration, memory, and concept development. As they gather materials, children are *thinking* about what they need, the kinds of materials they want to work with, and the probable shape and size of the nest. Some may begin to think in terms of a specific nest for a specific bird. To expand the experience, a teacher may want to introduce children to various kinds of birds, their building styles, and nesting habits.

When a teacher explains the purpose of an activity, she is helping children to begin the activity. She is providing useful information that will facilitate understanding. When teachers provide a setting for learning, they are encouraging children to develop good work habits: to pay attention, follow directions, concentrate, and apply one's self to a task at hand. Under proper guidance, children gradually become less dependent on teachers and better able to work independently. By helping a child to self-start, a teacher is helping a child to accelerate the learning process and to gain confidence in her ability to complete a task. When a child experiences fewer obstacles, she has more incentive to direct her own learning.

Although most activities at early childhood levels should not be teacher-directed, teacher-initiated learning is valuable as long as it does not overshadow children's need for independent, self-initiated learning. There are some circumstances, however, that do require direct teacher intervention. Students who are slow learners, easily distracted, in poor health, or who have emotional problems need help in applying themselves to a task and in completing it. Young children with physical deficits, such as poor motor control or visual perception deficits, will need direct assistance in cutting and pasting. Teachers who work directly with children on a one-to-one basis must always encourage, praise, and reinforce children's work regardless of the outcome.

By setting up clear guidelines at the beginning of the year (on the first day), a tone will be set for the whole year. A positive, productive work/play climate will require less and less of a teacher's personal time. Children will begin to help each other, they will become self-reliant, considerate members of a group. Teachers will have more time to interact with children on a personal basis that is not task oriented and supervisory.

A Developmental–Interaction Approach

This approach may best be described as an open, integrated concept of learning in which development is seen as a *dynamic interplay* between the learner and the environment. It is basically the *total child* operating within the *total environment*.

Every child has a uniquely endowed personality with the potential to develop and function as a caring and competent human being. In the maturation process, a child's internal world of thought is in constant interplay with her external world of experience. Affective and cognitive factors influence a child's behavior and development. The interaction that takes place between a child and her environment may be growth-enhancing or growth-restricting. A growth-enhancing environment recognizes the vital interplay that takes place between a learner and her environment by setting up conditions that encourage positive and constructive interaction such as involving children in community projects and in projects that take them beyond their immediate environment.

When children experience themselves as unique and capable learners, they begin to conduct themselves like caring and responsible members of a group. In an environmental-interaction approach, children are both *shaping*, and *shaped by*, their surrounding world. Cognitive and affective domains are interrelated and reinforcing. Jean Piaget wrote: "There is no behavior pattern, however intellectual, which does not involve affective factors as motives. . . . The two aspects, affective and cognitive, are in the same time inseparable and irreducible."[22]

The Work of John Dewey

The developmental–interaction approach is personified by the turn-of-the-century writings of philosopher and theorist John Dewey. Dewey's panacea for educational reform envisaged an active learner working in harmony with his environment. Dewey's key hypothesis was that life itself, particularly the occupations that serve social needs, should be the focus of a curriculum. A second hypothesis is that freedom of expression is a necessary condition for growth, but that such expression must be guided by a teacher. In this context, Dewey perceived freedom and open learning as a means to intellectual development and not as ends in themselves.[23] Dewey believed that the child and the school were a unit—organically connected and inter-supportive. Denouncing traditional approaches that prevented a child from experiencing active learning, Dewey conceived of a classroom as "a microcosm of democracy in which children are active participants and learning encompasses moral as well as intellectual goals."[24]

In progressive schools, children are given ample opportunities to engage in scientific thinking. A worthwhile activity is one that gives children a chance to test and evaluate their own work through problem solving. In this respect, the child, endowed with natural resources, is seen as central to the educative process. An active learner, he views school as intellectually stimulating and challenging. He develops skills and competencies in practical life tasks, in reasoning skills, and in social skills. Dewey's theories are identified with the open classroom, learn-by-doing approach referred to as progressive education.

> I believe that the school is primarily a social institution. Education being a social process, the school is simply that form of community life in which all those agencies are concentrated that will be most effective in bringing the child to share in the inherited resources of the race, and to use his own powers for social ends. Education, therefore, is a process of living and not a preparation for future living. The school must represent life, life as real and vital to the child as that which he carries home, in the neighborhood, or on the playground.[25]

Application to Child Care.   Today, educational reformers are increasingly looking to Dewey's classroom as a model for the future. They are recommending a developmentally appropriate approach that encourages child-initiated learning, individualized learning, multicultural curriculums, learning centers, open classrooms, cooperative interaction among peers, group projects, and the scientific method. Of equal concern to reformers is moral training. Educators and adults, concerned about the lack of moral training that children exhibit, are recommending a social consciousness that is similar to Dewey's ideal society. Children are now being encouraged to identify with and participate in their larger community.

Child care centers are miniature societies—small versions of a bigger world that has common interests, needs, and points of view. In a miniature society, children learn by doing and by acting on their physical environment in cooperative ways. Children are *affectively, cognitively,* and *socially* connected to peers by shared experiences and common goals. Each child contributes something unique and special to his or her center/society. Children seek companionship and support from one another in a play/work environment that is challenging, nurturing, and growth-enhancing. In an open, organized classroom, the child and the environment form a unit.

The Work of Uri Bronfenbrenner

Uri Bronfenbrenner is credited with developing an ecological model of child development that, in many ways, complements and expands Dewey's interactional model. An ecological model emphasizes the interconnection between a child and society. Bronfenbrenner's model begins with the child and extends to a *microsystem,* consisting of family, school, day care center, peers, neighborhood play area, church, and health services; an *exosystem,* of extended family and community services consisting of neighbors, legal and social services, family friends, schools, and workplace; and finally a *macrosystem,* that encompasses attitudes and ideologies of the culture at large.[26]

Application to Child Care.   In this context, child care is seen as a dynamic, interactional system of shared responsibility in the raising and nurturing of young children. Bronfenbrenner emphasizes the importance of community support for working parents that includes paid maternity and paternity leave, sick leave, as well as support for unemployed and disadvantaged families who feel isolated from the exosystem.[27] When a system functions at all levels of society, it will function for children, too. There will be more cross-generational participation in promoting a quality environment for children and staff. A system of shared responsibility provides an excellent role model for young children in child care environments who need to see themselves as not only important in their own right but as vital members of a larger society.

A developmental–interactional approach should begin at an operational level in a child care center. A miniature community is one that extends itself to all of its members: children, staff, and parents. It is connected to a larger community with equal interests and concerns. A program designed for children will generate its own sense of family. Everyone will become an integral and important member of a group. Barbara Biber and Edna Shapiro recognize the potential inherent in a developmental–interactional approach:

> It is a basic tenet of the developmental–interactional approach that the growth and cognitive functions—acquiring and ordering information, judging, reasoning, problem solving, using systems of symbols—cannot be separated from the growth

of personal and interpersonal processes—the development of self-esteem and a sense of identity, internalization of impulse control, capacity for autonomous response, relatedness to other people. The interdependence of these developmental processes is the *sine qua non* of the developmental–interactional approach.[28]

The Work of Loris Malaguzzi

The founder of the Reggio Emilia early childhood schools in Northern Italy was Loris Malaguzzi, a man who dedicated his life to the education and care of young children from the depressed period following World War II until his death in January, 1994. In 1991, *Newsweek* magazine recognized the Reggio Emilia Schools as one of the ten most outstanding school systems in the world.[29] Malaguzzi's image of childhood and teaching has established a lasting foundation for early childhood education.

The program developed in Reggio Emilia, Italy is strongly rooted in community support and family involvement. Parents are required to participate in making and evaluating school policies, program development, and other educational concerns. The collaboration between the schools and the surrounding community is carefully organized and constructed around the child.

Drawing from the theories of Dewey, Vygotsky, Piaget and others, Malaguzzi and his colleagues have created an environment that is becoming a point of reference for early educators throughout the world. This environment is organized around the theory that the child learns best when he is encouraged to inquire, and given the tools to satisfy his inquiries.

In a community of inquiry, learning evolves with the child. The child actively constructs knowledge as he makes discoveries and interprets his findings. The dynamic between the child and the environment is reinforced through projects, art, play, and, most importantly, through dialogue. When learning is viewed as a joyful and challenging interactional process, teachers assume an active role in guiding children's interests and development.

Application to Child Care

Young children are most receptive when they are learning to interact with people and materials in constructive and challenging ways. When they feel supported and valued, children become the source of their own creativity.

The only way children can experience a total environment is to have a close and continuing relationship with the people who are important in their lives. This requires a commitment to children that extends beyond an immediate environment. It requires that teachers extend themselves beyond their contracted hours; parents participate in a center's program; and a community values its children enough to become *actively* involved in their education.

Building a viable child care community requires a philosophy of childhood and a strong work ethic; it requires the same brick-by-brick energy that empowered Loris Malaguzzi to construct the first community-based school in Reggio Emilia at the end of World War II.

The Work of Howard Gardner

In *Frames of Mind* (1983), Howard Gardner, professor of education at Harvard University, presents a cognitive theory of multiple intelligences that suggests the wisdom of reassessing the way we look at children and work with children. His theory is premised on the belief that children evidence strengths in many domains of development that have not traditionally been identified with intelligence, such as art, music, and movement. In Gardner's view, if a child's intellectual profile is identified at an early age, it should be possible to channel specific talents in ways that enhance a child's educational opportunities.[30] In contrast to traditional definitions of intelligence, Gardner's theory presents a broad view of human cognition that suggests the importance of early training in many areas of development, some of which have not been given serious attention.

Gardner has identified the following seven intelligences:

- *Linguistic.* Ability to use and enjoy language as well as to communicate effectively
- *Logical–mathematical.* Ability to exercise critical thinking, to engage in complex operations, to organize and assemble materials and objects, to make observations, and to solve problems
- *Spatial.* Ability to work with objects in space, to construct and create from one's own perceptions, to modify and make changes, and to develop concepts
- *Musical.* Ability to identify melodies and instruments, and to gain musical competence through training and exposure
- *Bodily Kinesthetic.* Ability to perform physical tasks, to develop strong and fine motor skills, and to participate in organized group sports or activities
- *Interpersonal.* Ability to empathize, take the perspective of another, and to show leadership
- *Intrapersonal.* Ability to feel comfortable with one's self, and to have a sense of self-esteem and comfort with others[31]

Gardner has recently identified an eighth form of intelligence which is called the *naturalist* intelligence.[32] This area of intelligence is promoted in quality preschools where children are given quality time to investigate their surrounding world in their back yard, science centers, nature centers, and museums.

Application to Child Care

In 1984, Howard Gardner, David Feldman (Tufts University), and colleagues launched Project Spectrum at the preschool level. Its purpose was to establish a framework from which to identify distinctive intellectual strengths in young children. The premise was that if teachers could be trained to identify specific strengths and interests and adjust their programs accordingly, children, and especially at-risk children, would be less likely to experience failure.[33] Among the many advantages of working with young children in this way is the certainty that children will increase in self-esteem and confidence. Furthermore, children engaged in an activity that holds meaning for them, have the possibility of truly experiencing and building on their natural potential, interests, and abilities.

The concept of opening opportunities for learning beyond routine skills and activities may pose a problem for some early childhood teachers. Methods of teaching and learning will need to be examined, materials and opportunities for extended learning evaluated, and far more effort will be required. There may also be a concern that by identifying and nurturing distinctive strengths, a teacher may be depriving the young child of the opportunity to develop competencies that may not appear evident at a given time.

For many teachers, however, this approach will serve to affirm what is already known and practiced. An insightful teacher recognizes the value of providing children with activities and experiences that expand their interests and extend their learning. For teachers who feel inadequate or unable to work with children in a multiple intelligence framework, a director might choose to schedule specialized classes in sports, music, movement, the arts, and science. He can utilize the skills and talents of his existing staff and parents or he can budget for specialists in the community.

Summary

Children's development is integrally connected with their attitudes, training, perceptions, and environmental experiences. In a growth-enhancing environment that provides a myriad of creative opportunities for self-development and social development, children naturally flourish.

In a child-centered environment that encourages children to be inventive and industrious learners, children are eager to connect with peers. Language and thinking are natural accompaniments of a cooperative society (a miniature community). The beginning of social consciousness occurs when children share cooperative experiences that promote good feelings and goodwill. If, as educators, we believe that children emulate the values they are consistently surrounded by, we must begin to turn our attention to the "program" component of child care: How can we translate what we know about child development into a workable program for the contemporary young child in a child care environment?

A developmental–interaction system of education provides an appropriate model from which a whole-child curriculum such as PLAN can be developed because it encourages the child to make important connections between his immediate and expanding world—a world that is increasingly stimulating his awareness, imagination, and desire to know more.

NOTES

1. Sue Bredekamp, ed., "NAEYC Position Statement," in *Developmentally Appropriate Practices in Early Childhood Programs Serving Children from Birth through Age Eight* (Washington, DC: NAEYC, 1987), pp. 1–2.
2. As cited in L. Hoffman, S. Paris, E. Hall, and R. Schell, *Developmental Psychology Today,* 5th ed. (New York: Random House, 1988), pp. 31–35.
3. Erik E. Erikson, *Childhood and Society,* 2d ed. (New York: W. W. Norton, 1963), p. 255.
4. As cited in Zick Rubin and Elton B. McNeil, *The Psychology of Being Human,* 3d ed. (New York: Harper & Row, 1981), pp. 321–25.
5. Hoffman et al., *Developmental Psychology Today,* pp. 302–304.
6. *Beyond Rhetoric: A New American Agenda for Children and Families* (Washington, DC: National Commission on Children, 1991), p. 346.
7. Daniel A. Prescott, "The Role of Love in Preschool Education," in Margaret Rasmussen, ed., *Readings from Childhood Education* (Wheaton, MD: ACEI, 1966), pp. 59–60.
8. James L. Hymes, Jr., *Teaching the Child Under Six,* 3d ed. (West Greenwich, CT: Consortium Publishing, 1989), p. 66.
9. John Dewey, *Experience and Education* (New York: Collier Books, 1938), p. 40.
10. As cited in Evelyn Weber, *Ideas Influencing Early Childhood Education* (New York: Teachers College Press, 1984), p. 160.
11. As cited in James D. Quisenberry, E. Anne Eddows, and Sandra L. Robinson, eds., *Readings from Childhood Education* (Wheaton, MD: ACEI, 1991), p. 19.
12. Rubin and McNeil, *The Psychology of Being Human,* pp. 372–75.
13. George E. Forman, *The Child's Construction of Knowledge* (Washington, DC: NAEYC, 1983), p. 73.
14. As cited in Laura E. Berk, *Child Development* (Boston: Allyn and Bacon, 1989), p. 238.
15. Ibid., pp. 238–39.
16. As cited in Anita E. Woolfolk and Lorraine M. Nicholich, *Educational Psychology for Teachers* (Englewood Cliffs, NJ: Prentice-Hall, 1980), p. 58.
17. As cited in Daniel Tanner and Laurel Tanner, *Curriculum Development* (New York: Macmillan, 1975), p. 121.
18. As cited in Woolfolk and Nicholich, *Educational Psychology for Teachers,* p. 66.
19. Ibid., pp. 209–12.
20. Hoffman et al., *Developmental Psychology Today,* pp. 43–45.
21. Ibid., p. 44.
22. Weber, *Ideas,* p. 168.
23. Tanner and Tanner, *Curriculum Development,* p. 237.
24. Berk, *Child Development,* p. 678.
25. As cited in Ronald Gross, ed., *The Teacher and the Taught* (New York: Dell, 1963), p. 144.
26. Berk, *Child Development,* p. 22.
27. Ibid., p. 23.
28. Weber, *Ideas,* p. 186.
29. As cited in Carolyn Edwards, L. Gandini, and G. Forman, *The Hundred Languages of Children: The Reggio Emilia Approach to Early Education* (Norwood, NJ: Ablex, 1995), Introduction.
30. Howard Gardner, *Frames of Mind: The Theory of Multiple Intelligences* (New York: Basic Books, 1991), p. 10.
31. Howard Gardner, *The Unschooled Mind: How Children Think and How Schools Should Teach* (New York: Basic Books, 1983), p. 15.
32. Elizabeth F. Shores, "Howard Gardner on the Eighth Intelligence: Seeing the Natural World," *Dimensions of Early Childhood* (Summer, 1995):5–12.
33. Jie-Qi Chen, Mara Krechevsky, and Julie Viens with Emily Isberg, *Building on Children's Strengths: The Experience of Project Spectrum* eds., Howard Gardner, David Henry Feldman, and Mara Krechevsky (New York: Teachers College Press, 1998).

CHAPTER

2 The Child

The native and unspoiled attitude of childhood, marked by ardent curiosity, fertile imagination, and love of experimental inquiry, is near, very near to the attitude of the scientific mind.

—John Dewey

Characteristics and Needs of Childhood

Development occurs in a number of different ways in the maturation process. At birth, the child already is endowed with basic characteristics that will influence his growth. As the child matures, his development is affected by his physical and human environment. The quality of his experiences and of the people around him strongly influence his development. Development tends to occur in stages that are basic to childhood regardless of environs; for example, children crawl before they walk and progress from simple to complex functions. Life circumstances also affect development in significant and less predictable ways; for example, poverty restricts development because children are not getting their basic needs met. Within these parameters children progress at their own rate and in their own way. Development cannot be hurried, nor can it be defined exclusively by ages and stages. This is particularly true given the diverse backgrounds in a pluralistic society. Most of all, development evolves in ways that cannot be readily observed or anticipated. It is directly influenced by external factors in the environment and society, but in large part, it is an *internalized* process unique to each individual.

Children are . . .
- always adapting to an increasingly complex environment.
- active, often spontaneous, in their work and play.
- initiators and architects of their play world.
- flexible, creative thinkers.
- curious and inventive.
- by nature: empathetic and caring, innocent and loving, self-centered, sensitive, and vulnerable.
- resourceful problem solvers.
- forming habits and values that will influence and direct their lives.
- interested in people and in developing friendships.
- physically oriented.
- engaged by concrete objects and tasks.
- attracted to sensory stimuli.
- oriented to music and movement.
- stimulated by books.
- users of language.
- imaginative and expressive.
- not bound by time and space.
- immersed in the here and now.
- ever expanding their perceptions and understandings about how and why things work.

Children need . . .
- to feel in control of their environment.
- consistency and trust in relationships.
- loving, authentic relationships.

- interaction with important adults in their lives.
- to observe and learn from adult role models.
- a sense of balance and routine in their lives.
- praise and guidance from adults.
- limitations and appropriately administered discipline.
- a healthy balance of freedom and structure.
- freedom to play without interruption; make choices; express themselves; and test their environment, themselves, and others to discover their potential.
- training in self-management and self-care, foundational skills, social skills, and human relationships.
- outlets for creativity and self-expression.
- to develop:
  — skills and concepts through integrated learning experiences;
  — their own resources;
  — talents and interests;
  — initiative;
  — competencies in many areas;
  — self-control;
  — good work habits;
  — good citizenship.
- to discover and invest in their total environment.
- to experience their own indoor and outdoor play world.
- to shape and construct their own learning.
- to become:
  — responsible, caring members of society;
  — self-directed and self-disciplined;
  — problem solvers and critical thinkers.
- to take the perspective of others.
- to experience the wonders and innocence of childhood.
- to be surrounded by people who care about them and who want to participate in their upbringing.
- to value and treasure every day.

A Profile of the Young Child in Child Care

An Active Discoverer

The young child needs to touch and manipulate everything within reach. She will become fascinated by common objects: a dry leaf, a piece of cellophane, a toilet bowl, a light switch, a cricket, and a multitude of tiny objects. She is a whirlwind of activity—climbing, running, patting, pulling, pushing and jumping, tasting, smelling, listening, looking, and sometimes, crying. As the child explores and interacts with the people and objects in her environment, she develops awareness and confidence. She learns by doing, by discovering, and by experimenting with objects. Not everything works, not everything fits, and not everything is easy. It is through struggle and some risk-taking that children gain control of their environment.

An Explorer

Through exploration, the child begins to assimilate and order his physical world. He finds objects that go together, he rearranges these objects, and he tests ideas. His ideas do not always coincide with his buddy's ideas—sometimes it takes a strong push or pinch to make a point or solve a problem. The explorer soon finds out, however, that this behavior will not sustain friendship or attract new friends. The adaptable child learns the art of persuasion and accommodation, as well as the power of reconciliation. Though easily frustrated, the emotional young child is quick to recover his sense of balance.

The curious child thrives in an environment that encourages investigation and active learning. Children need areas for imaginary play: huts, caves, castles, forts, or tents. They need centers for imagination and discovery that stimulate exploration and open space for physical play. They need digging equipment, riding equipment, and climbing equipment. They need things they can move around as they create play themes: backpacks, binoculars, and compasses for hiking; kits and tools for exploring nature; and maps of their backyards with places to bury treasures. They also need to venture beyond their immediate environment to visit duck ponds, nature centers, and parks.

To a young child who delights in the ordinary, a walk around the block is a big adventure filled with novelty and wonder. Children need to stretch their bodies to reach new physical heights: climbing, balancing, skipping, hopping, running, and jumping—energy and movement are the beats of childhood. The growing-up child shows considerable initiative as he moves across handbars and finds new tricks to perform on a tumbling mat. He enjoys the pleasure of accomplishment for its own sake, but he also enjoys the favorable comments he receives from others. He needs praise and reinforcement when trying new activities but also needs to be reminded to exercise caution. The physical energy of the young child at play knows no bounds. Rest is tolerated but usually unwelcome. Rest time is particularly difficult unless, of course, a friend is nearby.

A Taskmaster

The child has an innate need to manipulate and master his world. His goal-seeking behavior requires endless amounts of physical energy and patience. Simple tasks like putting on a shoe or a mitten can become major undertakings for the young child. Loading and unloading a lunch box, handling bathroom needs, or organizing a cubby are not easy tasks for little fingers. Children who are given time and encouragement to complete simple operations do not feel frustrated or bored by routine tasks—they enjoy play/work and, most important, it is through daily contact with familiar objects and routines that children become competent taskmasters.

By the time a child is between four and five years of age, he has mastered many of the basic routines involved in self-management. He is ready for more complex levels of operation. He already knows how to count to ten—now he is experimenting with number concepts in his everyday world. Though still at a basic level, he has little difficulty sorting, grouping, and arranging items in patterns. Similarly, he already knows many of his letters and some familiar words—now he is experimenting with printing them in his own way. He no longer listens quietly to a story; he thinks about the story as the plot unfolds and identifies with its characters and its message. At this level of mental functioning, the child is processing and using knowledge—he is exploring and trying out his impressions.

A Learner

Learning is a dynamic child-centered process. The child is *central* to the process. The teacher is a guide. She promotes learning by exposing children to ideas and by organizing activities that reinforce and build on their level of knowledge and awareness. She may present, point out, ask questions and help children organize and extend their thinking; but the teacher should avoid making statements, giving children answers, or interrupting their thought processes. Most of the time, a learning child will want to express her thoughts and ideas as they occur. Group conversations should reflect the natural flow of children's language and thinking. A child who has to wait her turn or raise her hand will probably forget what she had intended to share. A teacher can encourage courtesy and taking turns without placing unnecessary obstacles in the way of self-expression. As the child continues to develop mental competencies, she will be better able to hold on to ideas, wait her turn, and to organize her thinking.

With each new experience the child continues to acquire knowledge and mastery. She can understand cause-and-effect relationships (a balloon pops when it gets too much air), and she can make logical assumptions (a lion can't find his tail because he is sitting on it, a flower needs water when it hangs its head, a caterpillar eats to get fat before it sleeps to become a butterfly).

Learning experiences often are presented in group circles. These are informal gatherings that take place in a designated area. Children sit around their teacher. Group circles are a means for teachers to develop social skills, language skills, and thinking skills. They are sometimes organized around a theme, a creative activity, or a specific learning experience (e.g., a science experiment); other times they are spontaneous get-togethers with no particular theme in mind (often children's favorites).

The time of day, the temperament of children, and the activity presented also influence group outcomes. A skillful teacher will bring out less verbal children by inviting participation: "I think Mary knows how to take care of plants; her mommy told me she has her very own garden at home." Mary will probably smile, nod her head, and maybe even say a few words. By the end of a semester, Mary may be speaking in sentences. A skillful teacher will *limit* her objectives and her time frame when she is conducting a circle for an entire group. In smaller gatherings, a teacher will *extend* her objectives and her time frame to encourage participation. When children interact in small groups, they are far more attentive to what is going on and far less intimidated by peers. There are more opportunities for hands-on experiences and for spontaneous communication.

A Language Maker

Language is an empowering tool for a young child. Children listen to one another intently and somehow manage to communicate the near-words that constitute early language development. Children love language in all of its forms: listening to language, making conversation, experimenting with sounds, and mastering the elements of speech—that is, discriminating sounds, recognizing words, using sentences, asking questions, and writing. They use language to express their thoughts and to communicate with one another. In the second and third years of life, children's ability to communicate dramatically increases. An open, play-oriented environment promotes language by supporting language. In play and in group experiences, children use language as a medium for communication and for peer acceptance. In its natural form, language is an extension of the child. If a child cannot find a word, he invents or makes up a word. Children become language users as they build on language experiences. They begin to organize their thoughts into sentences. They become fascinated with books and with the pleasure literature brings. Young readers get to choose a book, turn its pages, look at illustrations, figure out words, recall favorite parts, and sometimes, they get to read with a teacher. To a young child, the process of selecting, opening, and "reading" a book is totally absorbing and exciting. Favorite books are read and reread until the child discovers another book. Favorite stories may be tucked away and worn away, but like *The Velveteen Rabbit,* they are never forgotten. Language is rooted in familiar experiences that generate feelings of wonder and identification in young learners.

A Creator

Creative expression can be a never-ending source of satisfaction for a young child. She delights in the process and in her natural, unedited productions. She creates when she plays with blocks, when she arranges a play center, and when she assembles a collage of dried flowers and lace doilies. She creates when she makes pictures, when she arranges clothes on a doll, and when she arranges a tea set on a table. She creates when she interprets picture books through oral language, art, and original writings.

In order for a child to be creative with everyday experiences, she must instinctively feel that her environment is *creative.* A teacher who endorses and encourages a creative environment does not get concerned about spills or messes. She does not scold a child, and she does not punish a child by making her clean up her mess. A child who feels that she has done something wrong is not learning anything from a teacher's directive: "I told you to be more careful; get a sponge and clean up the mess immediately." A sensitive teacher will keep a bucket of water close by and clean up herself without drawing attention to the child, or, she may ask the child to help her clean up at the end of the project. In a positive mindset, children love to clean and take responsibility for their room. They especially love to be helpers and good friends.

Teachers should make time to sincerely recognize children's artwork but need not lavish them with praise (children already feel good about their work). She encourages children to try ideas—to design and create using many textures, mediums, and materials. The child creates as the child experiments with materials. Unlike the school-age child, the young child tends not to be concerned about finished products. He is absorbed in using materials in inventive ways. In the untrained eyes of the child, everything is beautiful—especially his own work. It is an adult who can introduce self-doubt: "Why don't you add a little yellow to your picture? I think it would make it prettier, don't you?"

A Person Who Delights in the Ordinary

A day flows naturally and comfortably for children when there is not too much stimulation. Children are already stimulated by the variety of people and colors in their day. In his delightful book, *Frederick*, Leo Lionni captures the natural glow of childhood. As other field mice busily prepare for winter, Frederick spends his time storing the rays of the sun, the colors of fall, and writing verse. Though not a practical mouse, Frederick is special in his own way. When food becomes scarce, it is Frederick who entertains his friends through the long days of winter. It is Frederick who gives them hope when their food supply is running out.

A teacher who recognizes children's delight in the ordinary does not rush them through early childhood. She will give them time to absorb their environment in their own way. She will find opportunities to capture special moments. Children may become sky watchers, bird watchers, pond lovers, and elves in a forest. They may follow an ant or a worm to its destination, catch the wind, fly like a butterfly, or wonder about a robin's journey southward or a seagull's preference for a cold, windy, wintery day. An ordinary world becomes quite extraordinary for children when they can *see*, *touch*, and *investigate* their natural world. When children are given time for quiet observations, they are gathering and storing experiences that will continue to shape their personalities.

A Homebody

Children respond to environments in unique ways. Young children become personally attached to a classroom. A friendly, cozy atmosphere helps children feel comfortable and secure. A room should contain many soft colors that are interrupted occasionally with bold, bright colors and eye-catching objects—a bright area rug, a colorful flowering plant, an orange tree, a teddy bear in a rocking chair, windchimes, and window ornaments. Children enjoy looking at familiar pictures and photographs and they love looking at their own artwork. They enjoy experiences of discovery like matching textures, pouring water from one container to another, or looking through a magnifying glass at objects they have gathered: a dead bug, a piece of glass, a rock, a leaf. They enjoy quiet moments, soft lights, and music. They love new things and old things, and they particularly love surprises.

Children especially enjoy a room that invites play. They respond favorably to a room that is organized around activity centers. Children tend to see objects in relation to other objects. They perceive common attributes among play objects and their purpose. They realize that a paint center functions differently from a block center, a housekeeping unit functions differently from a listening center, and that a table area is used for sit-down finger and hand activities like eating or pasting. As they play in centers, children intrinsically develop organizational and discriminatory skills. They begin to identify favorite things, favorite activities, and favorite ways to spend their time.

Within a familiar organizational framework, children love to use open play areas and to move objects from one place to another. They love to try new arrangements adding and subtracting items as they play. At the end of each play period, however, they enjoy seeing the familiar restored. This constant, repetitive process of playing, making choices, picking up, and restoring an environment, only to take it apart again, is fundamental to their learning. Through repeated actions, children gain self-confidence and mastery over their environment.

A Member of a Group

Children are natural friends. They enjoy and learn from one another. They like parallel play; close enough to enjoy companionship yet not too close to get in one another's way. As children mature, they seek playmates. They enjoy the comfort and companionship of dramatic play and of circle time. Even though a two-year-old cannot sit but a short time, she enjoys interacting with an adult friend. Group time provides opportunities for children to greet one another, to share, and to make observations and choices about their play world. Ideally, young children should experience several small group teacher/child gatherings throughout the day. During these brief intervals, a teacher can observe basic skill levels and language development. Through communication with a teacher, children gain knowledge about people, their environment, and themselves, and teachers gain knowledge about children.

As the child nears the latter stages of preschool development (four to five years of age), she can participate in group activities for longer periods of time. She has increased her attention span and language usage and is curious about learning and about playmates. She enjoys experiencing herself in a group context, selecting words to express ideas that she is eager to share. Sometimes these ideas will enliven and reinforce a subject being discussed; oftentimes they will not. Given a young child's limited attention span, distractions may end a circle quickly. Within minutes, a conversation may be disrupted by a sneeze, a bug, or an unusual noise. A preschool teacher must be ready for the unexpected, and be flexible. She must know when the children have lost interest and when it is time to make a transition. Despite the unpredictability of group interactions, they are invaluable to children's overall development. When children are active learners, they tend to become absorbed in a teacher-initiated experience and less likely to wander off the subject. Some ideas for group participation might include the following range of ideas.

> *Language Development.* "Today it is raining, let's sing our rainy day song. . . . Do you think it's a good day to read about the mushroom in the rain? A mushroom is something like an umbrella, isn't it? Who can remember what happens to mushrooms when it rains? Do you remember all the friends who came to sit under the mushroom on that rainy day? Who are they? What happened when it stopped raining?"

> *Social Awareness.* "Did you know Matthew has a new puppy? Can you tell us what its name is, Matthew? Can you use your hand to show us how big your puppy is? What does your puppy eat? Do you think you can bring him to school?"

> *Discrimination Skills.* "If you listen carefully, you will hear many different sounds. What are some of the sounds you can hear, Jenny? Let's take a listening walk today. What do you think you'll hear? Should we take our tape recorder? Do you think we'll frighten the cricket? We certainly don't want to do that! How can we be absolutely quiet listeners so that we don't disturb nature's little creatures?"

> *Recall.* "Who can remember what Hansel had in his pocket? Do you think the birds ate all the bread crumbs? Who else would eat bread crumbs? Do you remember our trip to the duck pond? What did we feed the ducks? That's right—birds and ducks like bread. What kind of bread do you like? Where does bread come from?"

> *Manners.* "I think we are forgetting our manners. Is it hard to hear when people are shouting? What happens when two people talk at once? Do you think it's a good idea to take turns? Can anyone think of a time when everyone uses their voices at once? Good thinking—when we sing and when we play games outside. Would you like to play a whisper game? Let's pass a message around the circle and see if we can remember the words?"

Beginning each day with a welcoming circle will set a positive, friendly tone for the day. A circle *anchors* a day for a child; it provides a sense of routine and organization. A brief circle at the end of a session provides continuity and closure.

A Growing Child

Clinging to childhood, but challenged by growing up, a preschool child can be unpredictable and changeable. This is a volatile, high-energy period of development. One day a child wants to be a baby, thumb in mouth. Another day she is industriously washing tables, being the big sister in dramatic play, asserting her will, and probably sounding very much like her mother or primary role model. In the process, a child is constantly testing relationships and her own powers. She can be self-centered and often disagreeable when she wants her way. For the growing-up child, however, frowns become smiles within minutes. A child who can express feelings without hurting others is on her way to maturation. It is important to *acknowledge children as they really are,* not as adults think they should be.

Gradually, a child builds confidence, and with confidence, self-esteem. She learns how to negotiate and when to compromise. Sensitive to peer relationships, she releases some of her self-centeredness for group acceptance. She becomes a cooperative partner in the games that are played; sometimes a winner, sometimes a loser, but nearly always a friend. In the process, she is discovering something about leadership although she doesn't really understand what it means. What she does understand is that children are attracted by her and make her feel special. She begins to use her sense of importance to extend leadership—she volunteers to be the teacher's messenger or an arbitrator in playmates' disputes. She is quickly chosen as a lead character in play plots: a queen, a mother, a fairy godmother, a strong, but gentle lion. Watching a child at play provides a momentary glimpse of the child grown up. The patterns of childhood continue into the future; leadership is developed during the early years.

A Role-Player

Pretend play peaks during the latter stages of early childhood. Dramatic play is a primary channel for expressive development. Children will cooperate during dramatic episodes even if it means compromising. More than anything, they want to be accepted by playmates. Pretend play stretches imaginations and expands creative thinking. Children vacillate between fantasy and reality. They discuss and solve problems and quickly transform into the characters they have chosen for themselves. As plots grow, dramatic play becomes more directed and absorbing. Children become the characters and role models whom they are familiar with or identify with; interpreting the world through their own eyes and their own experiences.

A Friend

Growing children are very sociable. Relationships are constantly examined and adjusted by young playmates. Leadership roles are implicitly and explicitly defined. Instinctively, children move toward friends whom they find attractive and fun to be with. Once chosen, they quickly become best friends. Best friends act alike, think alike, and often tire of one another. Close friendships create problems for the children who are not included in an inner circle. They promote an "in" or "out" mindset. Children who do not fit a peer's role model are often teased or ignored. Children can be very hard on one another especially if a child appears physically "different." Children also can be unkind and exclusive in their play patterns especially when they have peer support and reinforcement. When children bond in less than healthy ways, their behavior changes. They place unfair restrictions on unwanted playmates, such as only boys or only girls can join. A child's teacher must be attentive to the kinds of play that close friends are engaging in and monitor and intervene as necessary.

The desire to be independent and the need for companionship move a child toward peers. Peers become an extension of self for many children. They influence behavior in both subtle and direct ways. Observing and listening to peers causes a child to assess herself. Often a child will imitate negative behavior. She makes adjustments that enable her to fit in. If she is grounded in values that contradict such behavior, the child will go through a sorting out process until she reaches equilibrium that will accommodate both worlds. She may, for example, attempt to influence a playmate's behavior or she may avoid situations that she knows would be unacceptable to those whom she loves—her family and her teachers.

Conversely, a child who is not guided by values may become vulnerable in peer interactions. Seeking peer approval, he may gradually change his behavior over a period of time. He may ignore or talk back to his playmates or his teacher. For an unhappy child, a teacher may begin to symbolize restriction and a child care center may symbolize an unwanted home. It is important for a teacher to give children emotional support while recognizing their need for independence. Educator Barbara Biber writes:

> In order to supply the child with the kind of psychological support which he needs, it is necessary that adults take his drive for independence for what it is really—the first steps in the difficult job of constructing one's own personality. The child still needs, together with his freedom to grow away from grownups, the confidence that they will stand by.[1]

A Risk Taker

To practice and refine their capabilities, children must engage in some risk taking. Taking risks requires an environment that encourages initiative and reinforcement as well as the importance of good judgment. In planning and equipping children's activity centers for age-appropriate play, safety is a primary consideration. Even in child-safe environments, however, children have accidents. Testing bodies and endurance, showing off, feeling confident, the developing child has difficulty anticipating outcomes. A teacher's role is to supervise without being obtrusive. Preventive measures might include cautioning children, standing near children, redirecting dangerous play, and periodically reviewing guidelines for playground safety.

A Member of a Larger World

The growing child is becoming a part of a broad social system that demands more from her than earlier environments did. She now views herself in relation to others—to what peers are doing, to what turns them on, and to what displeases them. As a child sifts through environmental influences, she hopefully will reaffirm her unique personality and values. As she becomes self-affirmed, a growing child's interests will turn outward toward the larger world. Its concerns will become her concerns. When a child identifies with the larger world, she becomes aware of the interconnectedness of human relationships and needs. One of the best rewards a child care provider receives is the knowledge that a child will leave a center with a strong foundation, a sense of self, and a commitment to one's larger community.

A Child-Centered Environment

A child-centered environment must instill in children a foundation for *lifelong learning* that enables them to function effectively and efficiently as individuals and as members of society. Foundations are established during the formative years of development. Attitudes also are established in early environments. A child's natural quest for knowledge is influenced by his total surroundings: the attitude of adults, the philosophy and objectives of a program, the atmosphere and design of an environment, the activities and materials that stimulate curiosity, the mood and feeling that prevail throughout the day, and the continued presence of love.

Each child must be given appropriate amounts of freedom to learn and discover, to question and challenge, and to practice and perfect talents. Continued exposure to quality experiences and to special caring adults will establish a framework for a happy, creative, and productive life. In a child-centered environment, adults should:

- Be attentive to children's needs and growth patterns.
- Set the stage for later learning by encouraging children to learn how to learn.
- Encourage the development of good life skills and positive attitudes.
- Give children honest and consistent messages.
- Provide opportunities for children to express creativity and develop self-confidence.
- Establish a nurturing environment that fosters compassion.
- Give children freedom to develop their competencies and talents and to experience the satisfaction that accomplishment brings.
- Provide personal time for children throughout the day.
- Encourage children to experience their total environment: to discover new things, to investigate their surroundings.
- Train children in practical life skills that can become useful adult skills.
- Help children to distinguish between positive growth-enhancing and negative growth-inhibiting behavior.

When a good teacher is in a truly child-centered environment, there is great reward and satisfaction in experiencing the unfolding of a child.

A Developmental–Interaction Model

A developmental–interaction model reflects the importance of opening boundaries and the wisdom of integrating knowledge across the disciplines (see Figure 2.1).

Characteristics of a Whole-Child Model

A developmental–interactionist approach stresses the importance of connecting children's school life with their greater community by engaging them in *authentic*, first-hand learning experiences. The information derived from interactions becomes a take-off point for extended learning. When children experience little pieces of their community in depth, they are gaining knowledge that can be understood and represented in follow-up activities. Through direct experience, children are making observations, sharpening their senses, and awakening their imaginations. Learning deepens from the dynamic interaction that is taking place as the child makes discoveries. In the right hands, this can become a total or *whole-child* experience. A developmental–interactionist teacher integrates knowledge across the disciplines by doing the following:

- Establishing an environment that nurtures and builds on children's strengths, interests, abilities, and desire for acceptance
- Acknowledging the importance of self-initiated learning through choices, problem solving, and positive reinforcement
- Acknowledging the crucial relationship between teaching and learning
- Acknowledging the interactive, *dynamic* relationship between play and learning

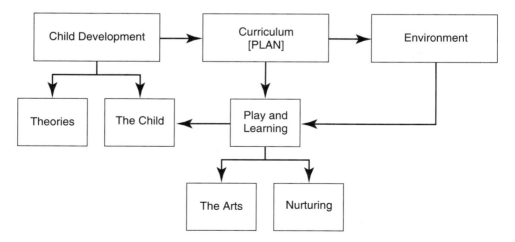

FIGURE 2.1   Developmental–Interaction Model

- Perceiving the arts as a critical bridge that connects a child's internal world to his external world
- Values the importance of nurturing in relationships, training, and *affective* development
- Guiding children by challenging developmental projects that promote and extend learning beyond the classroom
- Being responsive to children's diverse backgrounds, individual needs, and prior experiences
- Giving children time and space to discover their environment, their strengths, and themselves
- Documenting children's progress from a whole-child perspective, so that parents can identify with and share in their child's development

The PLAN Curriculum: Play, Learning, the Arts, and Nuturing

A developmental–interaction model appropriate to all age levels and environments must be constructed from a whole-child foundation that reflects and gives equal importance to *all* facets of early childhood development.

The PLAN Curriculum has been developed from a developmental–interaction whole-child model. While the four primary components of PLAN are conceptually separate, they are integrated and interdependent during most interactions that take place between the learner and his environment. In a child-centered environment, learning is play and sometimes work, play is learning and sometimes work, art is an empowering bridge between a child's internal and external world, and nurturing is as natural as the rain, feeding and nourishing the basic needs of children.

The model is premised on an environment that is nonhurried, noncompetitive, appropriately structured, carefully designed, purposeful and challenging, creating and inviting, and essential to the needs of childhood.

Play

When children play, they acquire self-sufficiency and mastery. They become inventive, resourceful, and self-reliant. They define and accomplish their objectives when they can play without interruption for long periods of time. The systematic play strategies children use as they interact with materials are identified with creative and cognitive development. The absorption and intensity that characterize children at play demonstrate the need for self-direction and exploration. Whether play is solitary or social, children work through ideas and express feelings as they play. They transfer their ideas onto an environmental drawing board—a mound of dirt, a sandbox, an arts and crafts table, a block center, a dramatic play center.

Motivated by a desire to interact with materials, children direct and control their play projects. They design and create interesting plots for pretense as they organize, evaluate, and make changes. Serious play requires planning, concentration, determination, and when playmates are involved, cooperation.

The function that play serves in child development can be both pleasureful and therapeutic. Children are happy when they play—they smile frequently and interact with confidence. When children play, they focus more on a project and playmates than on themselves. As they play, children reveal themselves. They act out feelings, attitudes, and real-life themes that may need to surface. Spontaneous play facilitates mental health. It employs energy in productive ways. Everything a child creates involves body movement and control, be it modeling clay, painting, pretend play, moving objects in a play yard, collecting play items, pounding wood, or building free-standing objects. When a child is physically and mentally absorbed in something he likes, he loses his sense of time and place.

Play creates feelings of happiness. For a happy child, life is a playground filled with objects and people that attract and motivate natural curiosity. A child moves at her own pace as she discovers how to function in a challenging yet wonderful world. In the hands of a child, something ordinary becomes a small wonder: a stone, a bug, a wildflower. Play engages children permitting them time to grow, to think, and to let their thoughts wander through the fields of discovery.

Learning

In challenging, creative environments, learning is a natural function of childhood. The learning child is a curious child who questions and learns through active, self-initiated channels. On a less abstract level, learning skills are integrated into a child's full day through direct and indirect experiences that stimulate thinking and develop competencies. In an open learning environment, children perceive relationships as they connect ideas to concrete experiences. A teaching unit on transportation may be extended to include large-motor play, an art project, a cooking experience (cookies shaped like little autos), and a language activity, thereby enabling children to participate in a whole-learning experience.

For example, a group of children may take a seeing walk in their backyard, noticing specific features that identify their play environment—equipment, grass areas, trees and shrubs, extended surroundings. They record their observations, drawing what is important to them. They talk about and compare the items and features they remember. They begin to see a difference between a natural and an unnatural environment. They talk about caring for nature and caring for property. Later the same day, children may take another seeing walk, this time making a picture of their school. Shapes, colors, and materials are identified, windows counted, and friends added. A hands-on, sensory experience may even motivate children to write a story about their very own backyard.

A skillful teacher knows how to direct and extend the learning processes that are already at work within the child. She encourages investigation, questioning, and reasoning. She generates ideas and concepts through natural, spontaneous dialogue. A teacher encourages children to discover things for themselves.

The Arts

When children are encouraged to express themselves, they sharpen their senses and expand their level of awareness. They interpret the world as they paint, paste, build, and engage in dramatic play. They use their eyes to study intricacies, their bodies to experience pleasures, their hands to explore and investigate features, and thereby construct a base of knowledge from personal, hands-on experiences. A child, for example, may paint a butterfly after observing its movements outside. She reproduces the features that stood out in her memory. She remembers its design and the shape of its wings. She adds flowers and personal touches to the picture—a picture that is uniquely hers.

Through various media children continue to develop and explore their creativity. They connect feelings and ideas through sensory experiences that help them to communicate with their environment. They use their imagination to become the characters they are interpreting, finding words, props, and apparel to authenticate their role-playing. Children who express themselves creatively begin to take notice of little things that are not usually apparent. They become attentive to their environment—its changes, nuances, and potential.

Nurturing

When children are exposed to a nurturing environment, they develop attitudes that foster trusting relationships and good character. As in any family structure, child care relationships are built on communication and cooperation. The teacher, like the parent, establishes and cultivates a climate conducive to growth and learning. She encourages responsibility to one's self and to one's group. She helps children to become culturally conscious and sensitive to the diversity that surrounds them. She provides materials that strengthen children's backgrounds and identities. By developing core values, the teacher is encouraging lifelong habits that will enable children to function as competent and caring adults.

Nurturing builds the bridge between what a child accomplishes and how he feels about his accomplishment. Without nurturing, an organism languishes; both the flower and the child begin to tire.

For a happy child, gardens can grow even without watering cans. When given the opportunity to fully experience, the child will cultivate seeds of wisdom.

Objectives for the PLAN Curriculum

The following objectives relate to specific areas of development that require ongoing observation and documentation in keeping with a whole-child philosophy.

Social and Emotional Development.   Children are encouraged to:

- Play and learn cooperatively.
- Interact without a competitive, demanding attitude toward others.

- Value and care for property.
- Value and support friends.
- Share with and care for others.
- Become active learners with agile minds.
- Communicate problems and tensions before they escalate into major confrontations.
- Develop self-control.
- Find ways to express anger that are not hurtful to others.
- Respect and honor rules of conduct.
- Express feelings and moods without inhibition.
- Develop positive values.
- Feel good about themselves, their center, and their friends.
- Participate in making agreements and in establishing rules of conduct.
- View their center as an extended family and its members as friends.

Reasoning and Thinking Skills.   Children are encouraged to:

- Engage in hands-on learning and play.
- Make wise choices and accept the consequences.
- Explore, investigate, and solve problems.
- Practice critical thinking as they play and work.
- Learn to be flexible in attitude formation and creative thinking skills.
- Learn to communicate thoughts and ideas in ways that can be understood and respected by others.
- Develop interests and talents fully.
- Become a self-manager, an initiator, a motivated student who does not require rewards for a job well done.

Language and Communication Skills.   Children are encouraged to:

- Become active, responsive listeners.
- Communicate ideas and feelings.
- Develop comprehension skills.
- Read books.
- Develop and enrich language skills.
- Practice creative writing in learning and play centers.
- Learn language skills through creative experiences.

Physical Development.   Children are encouraged to:

- Develop and coordinate body movements.
- Be physically active during indoor and outdoor play.
- Develop fine-motor and gross-motor skills through materials, equipment, and special activities designed for various stages of growth.

- Engage in a wide variety of group games and activities.
- Develop social skills through cooperative games, play, and projects.

Creative Development.   Children are encouraged to:

- Express themselves through art, drama, music, crafts, play, literature, and other arts-related experiences.
- Develop sensory discrimination.
- Develop talents and interests.
- Use self-expression as a way of understanding and interpreting one's world.
- Develop aesthetic appreciation.
- Take the time needed to experience and investigate their natural world.
- Take pride in the accomplishments.
- Appreciate process over product; effort over outcome.

Practical Life Skills.   Children are encouraged to:

- Learn to care for and about themselves.
- Develop good hygiene and habits when caring for their bodies.
- Identify appropriate behavior and avoid inappropriate behavior.
- Develop standards of conduct that ensure well-being.
- Develop good eating and resting habits.
- Learn to regulate activities so that there is time for quiet and active play.
- Learn to organize and care for personal belongings—clothing, lunch boxes, cubbies, toys, back packs.

Teaching Methods

A Guided-Discovery Approach to Teaching and Learning

An effective method for teaching and learning in a PLAN environment is one of guided discovery. A guided-discovery method recognizes the importance of self-initiated learning, as well as the importance of partnering with children. In a whole-child environment, a teacher is a friend and role model who is very present and active in the growth and development of her young children. She directs without being directive, supports without stifling, and challenges without domineering. Realizing the value of giving children materials and activities for independent learning, she is equally ready to extend opportunities for extended learning.

Roles and Responsibilities

In a typical day with young children, a teacher assumes many roles that cannot readily be categorized. There are three distinct roles that occur during most classroom interactions: *initiator*, *partner*, and *observer*.

Teacher as an Initiator

In this role, teachers extend learning opportunities by interacting with children in small groups or in a group circle. Teachers initiate when they plan a unit, organize skills and activities for children's enjoyment, and work with small groups to facilitate developmental skills. Teacher-initiated experiences are especially crucial at the early stages of development when skills and concepts are forming and when children have more need of adult guidance. As an initiator, a teacher:

- Establishes herself as a primary and caring role model in a classroom
- Develops and sustains a creative learning environment that builds on children's strengths and interests
- Provides materials and opportunities that encourage children to construct their own knowledge
- Helps children to integrate learning experiences through selective, hands-on activities that promote exploration and discovery
- Assists children in making choices and in decision-making issues without stifling a child's own resourcefulness
- Assists children in organizing and consolidating information
- Creates an open, nonhurried atmosphere for children, recognizing the importance of balancing a day within the context of a total environment
- Provides a loving, secure, and safe environment from which children can develop important values and understandings
- Designs and implements a program that recognizes the diversity of talents, interests, and needs in a particular setting
- Identifies children's experiences, interests, and available resources before selecting themes and projects; encourages their participation in soliciting ideas and in making decisions
- Documents and displays key activities, photographs, and children's work; keeps a portfolio on each child
- Constructs centers of interest that enable children to fully engage in independent play, investigation, cooperative learning, and reflective (less active) activities
- Builds on classroom activities using props, imaginative ideas, and inventive tools to activate learning
- Promotes literacy through independent and cooperative activities that capture a child's interest, imagination, and desire to learn
- Assesses children from a whole-child perspective, communicating their progress, needs, and emerging interests to parents on a regular basis

Teacher in Partnership with Children

In this role, teachers interact with children as friends and role models. Teachers are partners with children whenever they spend personal time enriching their lives or sharing experiences. During these periods, teachers are facilitative, nondirective, and nonjudgmental as they interact with children. Often, they are next to a child, saying little but adding comfort, guidance, and support to a child at play. Teachers also may use this concept of partnership to redirect or change inappropriate behavior. As a partner, a teacher will:

- Share personal time with each child every day.
- Reinforce appropriate behavior in ways that can be understood and appreciated by the child.
- Train children in self-care and manners.
- Help children develop self-control.
- Help children cope with problems and develop prosocial behavior patterns.
- Personalize and individualize relationships so that children can feel secure and confident in their environment.
- Work independently with children who have special physical or emotional needs.
- Comfort and help children through their adjustment process.
- Share and help develop children's interests and skills.
- Support and enhance children's creativity.
- Help children connect a center to a home and a teacher to a parent.

Teacher as an Observer

In this role, teachers are noninterventionist unless children require attention or assistance. Reasonable limits and expectations already have been set by adults and children. Children understand and, for the most part, respect agreements. The environment has been designed for independent play, exploration, self-management, and safety. Children are encouraged to use their time constructively and to be attentive to one another's needs. Even though there is minimal interaction, staff is always attentive to where children are and what they are doing. Objectives for teaching with an observer method are as follows:

- Notes children's dispositions, strength's, problems, and preferences in play and in group interactions
- Notes children's relationships with adults and with peers; especially noticing peer-to-peer relationships such as a child's sensitivity to and acceptance of physical, cultural, or mental differences
- Observes children's self-management and independence in practicing routines such as buttoning, eating, rest patterns, and handling bathroom needs
- Observes children's communication skills, particularly, listening skills, and language development
- Observes children's characteristics such as humor, flexibility versus fastidiousness, patience versus impatience, ability to share, levels and expressions of esteem, curiosity, and disposition for learning
- Observes children's points of frustration and impatience; when and why there is an occurrence
- Observes the emergence of self-expression, imagination, and pretense through symbolic play and creative experiences

- Observes how children think, follow directions, approach a task, and complete a task
- Observes children's abilities to perceive cause and effect, to discriminate, to differentiate, to solve problems, and to make or to anticipate conclusions
- Observes children's understanding of spatial relationships in physical-motor activities, at play, and in the expressive arts
- Observes how a child behaves in an out-of-context situation, such as on a field trip or at a special event
- Records information and examples of children's work in order to maximize opportunities for continued growth and development, and most importantly, to personalize early education
- Keeps an ongoing student file that may be shared with parents and with relevant members of a staff (see Developmental Checklist for PLAN in the Appendix)

Summary

A program that is designed for a child's total development must address the central issue of how children learn and develop according to their own unique potential. A *PLAN* approach supports a child-centered, homelike environment for *all* children raised in a child care community. It is premised on the belief that a child's emotional and social well-being plays a critical role in a child's ability to learn and to adapt within his or her immediate community and within the greater society. An *affective* environment provides opportunities for self-growth and social development, creative and cognitive development, and moral and practical life-skills development. It views a child's world as unified, balanced, and challenging and endorses a *developmental–interactional* (whole child) approach to learning and teaching. This approach requires a supportive and compatible relationship between a center and a child's primary home environment.

In a child-centered environment, children are not hurried into experiences that are not appropriate and do not serve the needs of childhood. Rather, they are given time and space to discover their world and themselves. A *guided-discovery* approach recognizes the critical relationship between teaching and learning by acknowledging the importance of values, play, self-expression, and children's feeling. This approach encourages interests and talents and places the child at the center of his or her own learning experience.

An environment must be loving and supportive if children are to experience happiness and security. It must be sensitive to cultural differences, learning rates, and backgrounds. The environment should discourage unhealthy competition that makes children feel inadequate. An individualized program acknowledges the specialness of each child. As children become confident, they reach out toward others. They perceive their child care center as something like a home—rich with possibilities, filled with friends, and ripe for learning.

R E S O U R C E S

The Developing Child Series (Cambridge, MA: Harvard University Press)

Child Abuse, by Ruth Kempe and C. Henry Kempe
Children Drawing, by Jacqueline Goodnow
Children's Friendships, by Zick Rubin
Children's Talk, by Catherine Garvey
Daycare, by Alison Clarke-Stewart
Distress and Comfort, by Judy Dunn *Early Language,* by Peter A. de Villiers and Jill G. de Villiers
Early Language, by Peter A. de Villiers and Jill G. de Villiers
Early Literature, by Joan B. McLane and Gillian D. McNamee
Learning Disabilities: A Psychological Perspective, by Sylvia Farnham-Diggory
The Perceptual World of the Child, by T. G. R. Bower

The National Education Association Early Childhood Series (Washington, DC: National Education Association)

Activity-Oriented Classrooms, by Milly Cowles and Jerry Aldridge
Behavior Management in K–6 Classrooms Cooperative Learning in the Early Childhood Classroom, by Harvey C. Foyle, Lawrence Lyman, and Sandra A. Thies
Developmentally Appropriate Teaching in Early Childhood, by Dominic F. Gullo
Educationally Appropriate Kindergarten Practices, ed. Bernard Spodek
Learning Centers for Child-Centered Classrooms, by Janice Pattillo and Elizabeth Vaughan

Multicultural Education in Early Childhood Classrooms, ed. Edwina Battle Vold
Parent-Teacher Conferencing in Early Childhood Education, by S. Dianne Lawler
Perspectives on Early Childhood Education, ed. David Elkind
Play's Place in Public Education for Young Children, ed. Victoria Jean Dimidjian
Problem Solving in the Early Childhood Classroom, by Joan Britz and Norma Richard
Multicultural Education in Early Childhood Classrooms, ed. Edwina Battle Vold

Early Childhood Education Series, ed. Millie Almy (New York: Teachers College, Columbia University)

Island of Childhood: Education in the Special World of Nursery School, by Elinor Fitch Griffen
The Joy of Movement in Early Childhood, by Sandra R. Curtis
Diversity in the Classroom: A Multicultural Approach to the Education of Young Children, by Frances E. Kendall
Making Day Care Better: Training, Evaluation, and the Process of Change, eds. James T. Greenman and Robert W. Fuqua
Ideas Influencing Early Childhood Education: A Theoretical Analysis, by Evelyn Weber
Young Children Reinvent Arithmetic: Implications of Piaget's Theory, by Constance K. Kamii

N O T E

1. Babara Biber, "The Five to Eights and How They Grow," in *Readings from Childhood Education,* ed., Margaret Rasmussen (ACEI: Wheaton, MD, 1966), p. 73.

PART TWO

The PLAN Curriculum

By adapting theories to contemporary knowledge and practices, a child care provider will recognize the importance of meeting the individual needs and development patterns of children. She will view the first years of life as extraordinary and critical to the child's lifelong development.

—Ellen Cromwell

CHAPTER

3   Play

"Play" is a small word, only four letters long. Children may be playing when they manipulate objects, climb walls, or tumble in autumn leaves. Yet philosophers debate its meaning, researchers study its forms and functions, and teachers ponder its place in the curriculum. In play, children solve self-imposed problems. Some are social and some are material; some are imitative and some are original. Even though researchers distinguish particular forms—functional play, pretend play, and games—one form often blends into another.

—Greta G. Fein

P_{lay} is the universal language of childhood. It is a natural and necessary activity through which a child communicates with himself and with his surrounding environment. No one need persuade a child about the value of play. When a parent asks, "What did you do in school today?" the child readily responds, "I played." The parent may wish for a more elaborate response, but for the child this message has considerable substance. It means he had a happy day, though he may be unable to explain why; it means he was pleasantly occupied, but he may not recall the details; it means that he made discoveries, though he may not understand their importance. He does know he wants more of whatever "it" is.

Play is a child's way of meeting, greeting, responding to, and mastering his world. It symbolizes pleasureful and purposeful activities that are natural and necessary to growing up; activities that reinforce, and shape childhood. Most importantly, play generates a desire for continuation—for more of whatever it is that is engrossing and challenging to a child at play.

The challenge for early childhood teachers is to effectively integrate play into a curriculum without changing its spontaneous, pleasureful nature. This requires blending children's interests with complementary activities and materials. In a child-centered program, there is a symbiotic relationship between a child and his environment. Like the child, the environment is a living, changing organism. It influences children's thinking and behavior. A child-welcoming environment works to connect the inner child with his external world in ways that enhance growth.

Weaving play into a curriculum requires the skilled and subtle hands of a creative teacher who affirms the value of play. In a play-centered classroom, teachers give children more opportunities to choose and to experiment with their surrounding environment. Play stimulates the learning process by promoting independent thinking and problem solving. In a play-centered environment, active learning is balanced with reflective opportunities for personal growth. By creating such an environment, teachers establish an ideal foundation for child development.

Characteristics of Play

Play influences all aspects of development. It unites body, mind, and spirit in ways that are self-enhancing and self-rewarding.[1] Catherine Garvey identifies the primary characteristics of play:

1. Play is pleasurable, enjoyable. Even when not actually accompanied by signs of mirth, it is still positively valued by the player.
2. Play has no extrinsic goals. Its motivations are intrinsic and serve no other objectives. In fact, it is more an enjoyment of means than an effort devoted to some particular end. In utilitarian terms, it is inherently unproductive.
3. Play is spontaneous and voluntary. It is not obligatory but is freely chosen by the player.

4. Play involves some active engagement on the part of the player.
5. Play has certain relations to what is not play.[2]

Through play, children may synthesize previous learning, develop creative thinking and aesthetic appreciation, and expand their experiences in novel ways that generate inquiry and imagination.

Why Children Like to Play

By its very nature, play allows a child to feel successful and in control. Wherever there are objects to manipulate and space to explore, children will spontaneously gather and envelop a play space. Each play experience has its own special meaning to a child. It may or may not begin with a plan and it may or may not end with a product. In all of its complexity and challenge, play consistently absorbs and challenges children more than any other early childhood experience. Play enables children to:

- Meaningfully connect child to child and child to group.
- Take risks and experience autonomy even when things don't always work, and when people don't always cooperate.
- Feel free from external expectations and rules.
- Make choices, predict and accept consequences.
- Seek answers to questions that occur during play.
- Challenge themselves and others.
- Construct and build on knowledge.
- Take the perspective of others.
- Place themselves in a larger community.
- Use pretense as a pathway for self-expression and imagination.
- Exercise judgment without concerns for failure.
- Experience success without praise or rewards.
- Open imagination, stretch boundaries, and claim themselves as unique and special people.

How Play Benefits Children

Play Satisfies Children's Need to Explore

A simple object such as a new rubber tire in a playground captures a child's eye. Initially, the child acquires information about the object drawing on prior experiences. He looks at its location in space, its features, its properties and surrounding objects, then steps inside the tire. As he begins to identify with the object, he sees it as more than a tire. Reinforced by peers, the tire becomes a boat; oars are added, a sail is hoisted, food is gathered, a captain is appointed, and the children prepare to sail. When interesting objects are available to children, and when children are encouraged to use materials creatively, exploration leads to dramatic play.

When children anticipate that a play opportunity is forthcoming, their disposition changes from one of passive involvement to arousal to active participation. Motivated by the anticipation of play, they become more companionable and find new ways to communicate with one another. They gather materials and make decisions about the use of space and the friends who will occupy it. Preparing for dramatic play can require considerable forethought, collaboration, energy, and organization. Selecting a theme, assigning roles, and choosing props require agreement among the players. (Children don't think of play items as props—they create an environment by using things that convey an impression they can relate to.)

Play Requires Planning and Industriousness

Play incorporates voluntary or spontaneous movements that may appear random and unfocused. In reality, children are preparing for play. They are play/working as they choose a play theme and gather supporting materials. Young children do not distinguish between play and work if they are in control of the process and if they enjoy the work. Most of their efforts require self-directed activity and attention to a task at hand. A child play/works when he gathers sticks for a pretend cook-out, connects tracks, peals apples for a pie, or moves large blocks from one area to another. He play/works when he negotiates roles and makes agreements that clarify the rules of play at each moment of decision making.

Play Encourages Experimentation with Ideas and Language

In early childhood, play is primarily identified with *fantasy* or pretense. During play, children experiment with language in novel and exciting ways. As a child disengages from the known world of rules and regimes, she communicates from her imagination the ideas and memories she has internalized. Language flows naturally because her mental processes are activated by the desire to play.

Play Is Mentally Challenging

In deep imaginative play, a child experiences a heightened sense of awareness and imagination as her creative and logical instincts are awakened. Symbolic, or make-believe play requires the child to substitute objects for those that are unavailable. She seeks ways to express herself nonliterally. She may transform herself into a character who holds special significance or a special memory for her. She may express her role verbally and in nonverbal communication. She is challenged by the process of a play activity which may require industry: sorting, building, modifying, and experimenting. Her attitude is playful but intense, her mind is alert, and her senses stimulated.

Play Instills Life-Long Memories

The Reggio Emilia schools emphasize the importance of early childhood memories to child development.[3] As children play, they collect and document memories of teachers, friendships, and important events. Although some play experiences may appear inconsequential, they may be integral to a child's development. A small gift, a whispered secret, or a symbolic gesture of affection may become moments for memories.

These memories may be stimulated later through images, projects, words, or photographs. Retrieved memories may help a child interpret a current experience. Teachers who nurture children's memories find meaning and value in all of the precious experiences and emotions of childhood. The sharing, the caring, the humor, and the occasional pain of growing up in a wholesome, child-centered environment provide memorable and enriching moments for both child *and* teacher.

Play validates childhood as a time to:

- Express, act on, and engage in unconditional fantasy.
- Enjoy all of the wonders and challenges of childhood.
- Try on and try out being "me."
- Find out about others.
- Take risks, reach out, and experience autonomy even if things don't always work and even if people don't always cooperate.
- Be free from external rules.
- Investigate and discover.
- Be autonomous.
- Make choices and exercise decision making.
- Open imagination and thinking, stretch boundaries, and claim one's self as a unique and special person.

Challenges Posed by Play

Creating a Play-Friendly Environment

A curriculum that values play as a unique and essential framework for early childhood development will be communicated throughout an environment. A play-centered environment opens space and removes barriers for children by limiting and consolidating activity centers in developmentally appropriate ways. Children require a specific use of space for large and small motor play, imaginative play, project work, and quiet, less active experiences such as reading, writing, painting, or listening to music.

Designing a classroom for play requires understandings from its members. In an atmosphere of cooperation, children value and respect freedom. A teacher can facilitate appropriate choices by setting up guidelines for child-initiated play at the beginning of the year. Children should understand:

- Which objects or materials they may move between activity centers (e.g., may children use markers in a dramatic play center or bring dolls and dress-ups into a construction center?)
- How much freedom they have to make choices (e.g., may they move between activity centers whenever they choose?)
- How long and how frequently they may play in one center
- What play is not acceptable indoors and outdoors (e.g., superheroes, karate, playing ball, using blocks or sticks as weapons, or playing doctor)
- What language is prohibited or discouraged
- When noise levels become uncomfortable
- When play becomes chaotic and unproductive
- What materials and equipment are not available to children

Maintaining Play's Value as Children Develop

Traditionally, play has not been an integral part of early childhood curricula. Too often, nursery schools have paid disproportionate attention to academics, sometimes at the expense of overall childhood development. They have essentially adopted a school-age classroom approach for preschool-age children. Of equal concern, excessive attention has been given to routine, time-consuming responsibilities required of child care workers. Practitioners in both academic and custodial environments may perceive a loss of control in a play-oriented curriculum. Neither has adequately endorsed the constructive role of play as essential and formidable in child development.

The PLAN approach posits that a formal, institutionalized school-like setting is inappropriate at early childhood levels. It further maintains that nurturing a child's emotional and social needs provides a healthy balance between custodial and academic objectives. Young children require a challenging, organized environment in order to process information, construct knowledge, and form friendships. Basic to this environment is the opportunity to learn through play.

The transition from a play-friendly environment to a more structured environment occurs at the kindergarten level of development. This transition can be jolting for a child nurtured in a whole-child environment, requiring special sensitivity from the teacher. Kindergarten bridges the gap between the pretend world of childhood and the real world of growing up, therefore, it is a particular challenge for a kindergarten teacher to ease and connect this critical time of transition.

Regrettably, once children reach elementary school, play is usually relegated to an afterthought or reward in curricula. Play and learning are separated from each other. As play becomes perceived as a reward rather than a self-justifying accomplishment, school-age teachers will be challenged to continue providing meaning and opportunities for learning through play.

Teachers will affirm the value of play when they appreciate its many contributions to children's lives. Teresita E. Aguilar describes a playful atmosphere as one that:

- Increases a sense of freedom
- Provides an outlet for self-expression
- Encourages people to "play with" ideas rather than "work for" solutions
- Allows for physical manipulation
- Provides risk/challenge in varying degrees
- Encourages problem-solving activities
- Incorporates the arts (music, dance, drama)
- Is flexible
- Minimizes or eliminates negative consequences for playful behaviors
- Allows for escapism, fantasy, and imagination
- Encourages and demonstrates good humor
- Allows for experimentation/exploration[4]

How Children Play

Play patterns and preferences reveal different cultures, experiences, and backgrounds among children. Some children prefer to play alone or with a single playmate most of the time, while others view play as primarily a social experience. It is not unusual for young children to hold on to play patterns and playmates for extended periods of time. During play time, a child might move quickly to a favorite construction center or to a dramatic play center, once again dressing for the occasion by selecting her favorite costume or garment. In an environment that structures play by assigning children to centers, there is less opportunity for children to choose and fully experience their play space. Children who are unable to continue their play themes and interests over a period of time, feel incomplete about a play experience.

From Simple to Complex Levels

Most children tend to progress from simple levels of *object-centered* play, to *cooperative play,* to more complex levels of fantasy or *imaginary play*. Within this spectrum, children's play generally evolves from solitary, to imitative, to various forms of social/cooperative play. As children mature socially and intellectually, the structure and style of children's play becomes more diverse and complex.[5] Higher levels of play require higher physical, cognitive, and socioemotional maturity.[6] Assessing the quality of play can assist teachers in evaluating children's needs and development (see Table 3.1).

Observer/Participant

Young children enjoy observing and imitating the actions of peers at play—filling, dumping, and endlessly arranging and rearranging objects within reach. At some point, an observing child becomes a participating child. He is fascinated by an

TABLE 3.1   Play: From Infancy to Age Five

Age	General Development	Social Play	Physical Play	Cognitive Play	Age-Appropriate Toys	What You Can Do
Infants to 18 Months	■ Major advancements in physical development (walking) ■ Major developments in language (talking) ■ Is learning about the world, especially through taste and sight	■ Plays alone and with no regard to other babies ■ Laughs during play ■ Enjoys looking at self in mirror ■ Peek-a-boo and pat-a-cake are favorite games	■ Baby is gaining control of body: crawling, standing, trying to walk ■ Follows the movements of objects with eyes ■ Hits, holds, and drops objects ■ Baby is exploring her environment	■ Baby repeats banging and sucking movements ■ Imitates sounds and facial expressions ■ Learning characteristics of toys ■ Baby plays with one toy at a time and can control it	■ Rattles and mobiles ■ Bars to hold onto when learning to walk ■ Pots to bang ■ Mirrors ■ Water toys and soft blocks (with holes) ■ Light ball between 8" and 24" in diameter ■ Plastic containers	■ Give baby lots of crawling room ■ Spend time playing with baby ■ Provide different types of sensory stimulation ■ Facilitate baby's self-awareness with mirror and peek-a-boo games
18 Months to 3 Years	■ This age group is *very* curious ■ Walking is a new means of independence and a great way to explore everything ■ Experimentation with the joys of language—especially the word *no* ■ Temper tantrums	■ *Parallel play:* Children play with similar toys—like pails in the sand—but don't interact while playing ■ Play on their own ■ Will not share ■ May take toys from others	■ Stands, walks, and turns pages of a book ■ Uses large and small muscles ■ Kicks and rolls a ball, pulls a wagon, and rides a small trike or big wheels ■ Chases other children	■ *Functional play:* Child's play is thought through—ordering, gathering, and dumping objects/materials ■ Children use more than one toy at a time ■ Trying out new roles and situations through fantasy play ■ Pretend themes	■ Balls ■ Books with cloth pages ■ Toy phones ■ Wagons ■ Beads to thread ■ Unit blocks ■ Play corner and simple play props	■ Encourage children to play together ■ Allow children to make choices about what they wish to play with ■ Provide lots of small and gross motor toys ■ Encourage children to play out fantasies

Age						
3 to 4 Years	■ Like to please adults ■ Very independent and begin to assert independence ■ Still some tantrums and the need to say "no!" ■ Interested in other children	■ *Associative play:* Children play together, talk to each other while playing, and engage in a common play activity ■ Play intentions are still different ■ Sharing is still a difficult behavior	■ Children like to balance and tiptoe ■ Love moving to music rhythmically ■ Climbing steps and small ladders ■ Kicking a ball, and catching a large ball are favorite activities ■ Jumping is fun	■ *Constructive play:* The child builds structures ■ Uses materials such as blocks, paints, and clay to make things ■ Children engage in pretend play—taking on the role of a familiar person such as mom or dad	■ Dress-up props of familiar people for dramatic play ■ Unit blocks, duplo blocks, and snap blocks ■ Balance beams and slide and ladder structures ■ Play-dough, crayons, sand ■ Dolls	■ Encourage children to experiment with creative materials ■ Allow children to make choices ■ Encourage and support fantasy play ■ Allow lots of physical activity
4 to 5 Years	■ Ask lots of questions ■ Children at this age are extremely egocentric—they view things only from *their* perspective ■ Imaginary friends are big with this age group ■ Very active; often destructive	■ *Cooperative play:* Children play with others and can wait their turn ■ Three or more children play together ■ Sharing is a common behavior ■ Children may have a common play goal	■ Enjoy chasing games and obstacle courses ■ Ride small bikes with training wheels ■ Can button shirts and tie shoes ■ Skip, hop, run, skip rope, and do puzzles	■ Involvement in constructive play more than 50 percent of the time ■ Role-playing is based on more complex and less familiar people and situations (often based on fiction such as superheroes, ghosts, etc.) ■ Complex structures are built (blocks, clay)	■ Blocks, Legos, sand, water, and wood work ■ A bike with training wheels and scooters ■ Climbing structures ■ Fantasy play props ■ Tape recorders and musical instruments ■ Puzzles and dolls	■ Use props and stories to encourage fantasy play ■ Avoid gender-role stereotyping in fantasy play ■ Help children share and take turns ■ Provide choices rather than "you must"

Source: From *PRE-K TODAY*, Issues from 1987 and 1988. Copyright © 1987, 1988 by Scholastic Inc. Reprinted by permission of Scholastic Inc. All rights reserved.

73

activity or a peer, and wants to participate. By adding something to a simple construct, the child gains approval. This, however, is still a relatively immature level of interaction that occurs spontaneously and is not readily sustained. Young children have short attention spans and even less patience. They do not share easily and cannot be counted on to sustain moments of cooperative behavior. At the beginning levels of socialization, the young child is more interested in short-term imitative friendship than with a long-term playmate relationship.

Parallel/Associative Play

Children often gravitate toward favorite areas of a room such as an arts and crafts table, a water table, or a light table organized around novelty items that engage the senses and challenge imaginations. This attraction often brings one child near to another child in a side-by-side relationship. This brief but pleasureful encounter may be understood as an extended form of solitary play or the beginnings of associative, companionable play.

In parallel/associative play, children gradually apply their beginning social skills to pleasing a playmate in subtle but important ways. Parallel/associative play enables children to comfortably function somewhere between solitary and cooperative play. They are not alone, yet they are not together.

It is not unusual, however, for young children in a quality, play-centered environment to engage in relatively mature levels of play at an early age. Teachers can promote social play by encouraging children to become friends. A two-year-old, for example, can call a friend by name, follow a friend around, learn minimal social courtesies, and enjoy the warmth and intimacy of friendships. She is already in the process of practicing rules and values that are being taught and reinforced daily. She can show empathy when a peer is hurt and even give up a treasured toy (at least for a little while). She is learning about appropriate and inappropriate behavior through satisfying exchanges with playmates and teachers.

A teacher of a two- or young three-year-old should encourage cooperative behavior when she observes children expressing friendship. Young children often act the way they are expected to act. If a teacher promotes and models cooperation, children tend to become sociable and surprisingly empathetic. If a teacher exudes love and kindness, children will respond with similar feelings. They will progress steadily toward prolonged intervals of cooperative play.

Rough and Tumble Play.   Rough and tumble play is a physical form of parallel/associative play. Young children (particularly boys) love to engage in jumping, rolling, or other kinds of imitative play that may begin innocently with a pile of leaves or an inviting hill. Unfortunately, rough and tumble play can quickly get out of hand if it is not carefully supervised. Children in child care centers move toward rough and tumble play when they are tired or required to wait for long periods during transitions.

The game of chasing that is common at four and five years of age correlates with rough and tumble play, although it tends to be less random and more directed. When children are allowed to run around playing chasing games, they release energy in companionable and satisfying ways. Children adore the movement, the physical contact, and the outcome that accompanies games such as freeze tag and hide-and-go-seek, but as with rough and tumble play, chasing can get out of control when children become overly physical or aggressive.

Solitary Play

Solitary play is no longer considered a noncommunicative level immature of development. To the contrary, in solitary play, children communicate their feelings and thoughts in quiet but meaningful ways. When children exercise the language of thought (inner speech), they are developing insight and knowledge about themselves and their environment. In a prolonged, reflective play mode, the child is probably operating at a high level of concentration and creative thinking.

Solitary play can be extremely beneficial to a child in a full-day care environment. Brian Sutton-Smith posits that while it resists traditional categorization, solitary play may be more wholesome than social play.[7] It is incumbent on teachers to provide young children with outlets for personal time—places where children may experience their inner selves without intrusion or distraction. The value of solitary play is revealed while observing children when they are peacefully and happily absorbed in an activity, and not dependent on others for satisfaction. Children who experience most of their early years in overcrowded and understaffed child care centers are in critical need of time alone.

Solitary play often begins with exploration. A little girl chooses to play in a discovery center. She becomes fascinated by a mother mouse and her new litter of ten babies. The child begins to identify with the mother: busy, protective, alert. Every now and then the little girl stops watching the mother and attempts to count the babies. When her finger gets too close to the mouse heap, mother mouse gets upset and flitters around. Sensing the mother's anxiety, the sensitive child momentarily backs away. After a while, she continues her vigil, watching in quiet fascination. She'll remember the experience later that day. She will recall details that suggest her level of concentration; patterns of behavior, the mother's attentiveness to her babies, the size of the babies. The child has had a *personal* and *pleasant* experience that has significantly enriched her life. Solitary play often ends abruptly when a child's attention is diverted.

When the little girl tires of her mouse vigil, she shifts her attention to playmates. Joining friends in a housekeeping center, the child redirects her focus to a dramatic play theme already in progress. In a brief period of time, the whole gamut of human relations may be dramatized by the child/actor—a child/mother scolds a peer/kitten for spilling milk on a clean floor. A child/father reminds a peer/child to get busy and stop fussing. Two little ponies in an open field frolic and giggle unabashedly in a secure world of make-believe that is momentarily unaffected by right and wrong, yes and no, and the many conflicting messages of childhood.

Social/Cooperative Play

Two types of social play, *constructive* and *dramatic,* predominate throughout the preschool years until the age of six or seven, when games with rules become significant in children's play.[8] Constructive play is identified with manipulating objects such as playing with blocks, play dough, or puzzles, and is probably the most common form of play at age three to five. It is important to note that constructive play often triggers pretense in a young child, particularly in a creative environment. Dramatic play is identified with *fantasy* and *pretense* and peaks at around five years of age. At this age, children are mentally able to represent the perspectives of favorite characters, and coordinate these impressions with their own understandings.[9] The ability of the growing child to think symbolically and abstractly poses a challenge to the kindergarten teacher, particularly those who associate children's readiness exclusively with the development of specific, concrete skills (cutting and pasting, table work activities, dittos, etc.).

In *Childhood and Society,* Erikson states that child's play is the infantile form of the human efforts to cope with experience by creating model situations to master reality by experiment and planning.[10] In cooperative play, children put into operation all that they have absorbed and experienced in a short lifetime of experiences. They organize their play with materials that may be present or symbolically represented through similar objects. They assign roles and negotiate understandings about how a game or theme should be played.

In most cooperative experiences, there are dominant players—children who have gained recognized stature as leaders or as problem solvers. These are children who may be particularly verbal, easy to play with, and generous in their support of others.

In cooperative play, a child relinquishes some of his autonomy (and toys) to his playmates. For a project to continue, there must be compromise and respect for each other's positions. Playmates must be willing to engage in reciprocity by *decentering* or empathizing with others.[11] They thus acquire many important social and moral skills such as taking turns, sharing, cooperation, and the ability to understand other people's feelings and emotions.

Children benefit from plentiful opportunities to work together in partnership with a teacher and peers. Collaborative interaction facilitates good citizenship, group identity, moral and social development, empathy, compassion, positive attitudes, outlets for physical and mental energy, development of interests, communication skills, and identification with the world beyond the classroom and play yard. Play/work cooperatively organized projects should be:

- Enjoyable and productive
- More process oriented than goal oriented
- Community oriented
- Within the control of the child
- Affectively carried through to completion
- Reinforced by recognition and small rewards

Examples of cooperative projects are making a garden, raking leaves, washing windows, making a mural or a sculpture for a central hallway, baking and cooking for holiday gifts, sending flowers and special tokens of appreciation to members of a staff, writing notes to friends who are sick, setting a table for snack, washing and sorting toys, making doll's clothes, mending stuffed animals, caring for live animals, watering plants, staging a puppet show or a fairy tale for the center's youngest children, visiting senior citizens, and sponsoring a child-in-need project.

Reinforcements Should Be Simple yet Meaningful. Shells, decorated stones, magic feathers, walnut turtles, magnets, a small book of poems, marbles, memorable note paper or photographs, balloons, clothespin dolls, and old stamps or coins, are examples of token gifts that express recognition of children's accomplishments. Assorted gifts can be stored in a box labeled "Memories" and brought home at the end of a school year.

Stages of Cognitive Play

In his comprehensive theory of cognitive development, Jean Piaget views the mind as developing mental structures that enable it to adapt to its environment, achieving a progressively better adaptive fit with experience.[12] As it develops these structures, the mind of the child is very active. The child learns through maturation and experience, reflecting a sequence of stages that strongly influence developmental outcomes.

Although Piaget was less interested in its affective functions than in its cognitive functions, play is crucial to his theory of how children learn. Piaget believed that through play the child seeks to imitate and accommodate to complex adult actions and speech, gradually reshaping and reconstructing received information. Piaget's three broad sequential stages of play that reflect a child's level of cognitive functioning are *practice/sensorimotor play, constructive/symbolic play,* and *games with rules.* Within this framework, patterns of play reflect a child's growing capacity for increasingly complex mental activity.[13]

Practice (Early) Play

According to Piaget's findings, at the earliest toddler level, children's play tends to be solitary and functional. The child is self-centered and object centered. A child's perceptions and understandings are shaped by *sensorimotor* encounters between himself and his immediate, known environment. A young child's limited attention span and skills do not permit sustained social interaction or communication. This does not, however, inhibit a child from observing peers or from reciprocating gestures of friendship. Young children are absorbers. They are keenly aware of what is happening around them. They know when a familiar face enters a room and when a new face enters a room. Sensorimotor play does not disappear with the advent of symbolic play, but remains as the foundation for more complex kinds of play.[14]

At the beginning stages of play, the child relates to his world through experiences that satisfy and stimulate curiosity and exploration. Movements dominate his actions. They appear to be repetitious and nondirected. What appears to be of little consequence, however, is actually the child's way of discovering and mastering his world. The child is experiencing the functions and pleasure of play through sensory interactions with objects (touching, feeling, tasting, observing, and investigating). He manipulates and rearranges objects repeatedly (e.g., stacking, dumping, and restacking). He is fascinated with the shape, texture, function, and challenge of objects.

Piaget believed that a child's choice of play objects and capability for imitation are excellent indicators of advancing intellectual development. The young child constantly modifies his perceptions of reality to accommodate new information. Through trial and error, he gradually figures out what works and what doesn't work. Through imitation, he models (or mimics) observed behavior and develops his personality, disposition, and awareness. Within a reservoir of opportunities, the young child is developing and perfecting knowledge of himself and his environment. He is becoming a learning child.

The young child gradually replaces functional, nongoal-oriented play with focused, directed play. He begins to organize his objects and actions in time and space. He uses familiar gestures modeled from adults (a cup is for sipping, a spoon is for tasting, hands are for clapping). These are the beginnings of pretense. Piaget believed that thought began long before language. Sensorimotor activities provide the cognitive foundations for language, just as they make possible the emergence of imitation and make-believe.[15]

Constructive Play

Children are always constructing, assembling, ordering, and organizing a play space. As children make the transition into constructive, cooperative play, they must learn to reconcile conflicting feelings and points of view as they interact with peers. This learning can be a source of friction and frustration.

Because constructing something is a focused, goal-oriented activity, children are sensitive to the need for collaboration to achieve the desired outcome. They are knowledgable about the size and number of blocks, accessories, and the key pieces that make a difference in assembling manipulatives. They are adamant about the rules of space and the distribution of items. Language tends to be more receptive than expressive, particularly at the beginning stages of building and constructing when children are less confident about their needs. Children can quickly change from a receptive, congenial disposition, to an authoritative disposition as the constructive play experience progresses toward a climax.

In constructive play, children use organizational skills, perceptual/motor skills, and natural instincts to complete a project. A project advances under each child's capable and creative attention to detail and design. In the process of construction, children experiment with shapes, textures, volume, and space. They investigate how and why objects move, perceive whole–part relationships and anticipate cause and effect relationships.

Sometimes a child will have a plan before he starts building, but more often a construct grows under a child's control and imagination. As a project expands, imagination expands: Lincoln logs are used as a rocket launcher, a paper towel roll as the body of a spaceship, and marbles symbolize shooting stars. Within moments, a freestanding object becomes a launching pad for dramatic play: A spaceship is airborne, props are added; a cube becomes food for the astronauts; and a yellow bristle block becomes a light beam that guides the ship while in flight. Language becomes more imaginative and expressive as children are less constrained by the discipline that is required at the initial stages of construction.

Children who engage in constructive, cooperative play become increasingly aware of what each can contribute to a pretend theme. They listen to ideas and adjust their play themes to accommodate one another. When children plan and play cooperatively, they usually experience a successful outcome, particularly if there is adequate space and materials for building vertically and horizontally.

Dramatic Play

Children love to be surprised. They love teachers to take something out of context and transform it, enabling them to interject, correct, or elaborate. They adore humor, challenge, and especially, the unexpected.

In many ways, this is how children perceive and engage in dramatic play. Pretense happens because it is triggered by something that fires a child's imagination. While some children who are literal thinkers are uncomfortable engaging in fantasy, in a playful environment, most children will break through barriers and become creative, divergent thinkers.

What Is Symbolic Play?

When a child imitates reality (what is familiar) by substituting one object for another (what may become familiar), she is engaging in early forms of pretense. Jean Piaget identified pretense as a crucial aspect of children's cognitive development. Through symbolic play, the child may imitate adult actions and speech, gradually reshaping what he learns from the external world and applying it to what he knows in his limited range of memory.[16] In the process of "making believe," a young child shifts from self-referenced to other-referenced actions. The child appears to have abstracted the basic qualities of known experiences and is able to apply them in pretend play.[17]

At the earliest level, a young child may pretend to be sleeping, or play peek-a-boo, or answer a phone. She is imitating behaviors that have been learned in her environment.

At a later level, around two years of age, the child begins to include others in make-believe actions. She holds a cup (or something like a cup) for her teddy bear and she pats her doll to sleep. The child has begun to transition from simple *self-centered pretense* to *object-centered pretense*. She is able to transform objects into elements that represent a theme or event that is familiar and interesting: Clay becomes a cookie; a spoon and pan a drum.[18]

In "Pretend Play in Childhood," Greta Fein summarizes the criteria for symbolic play:

1. Familiar activities may be performed in the absence of necessary material or a social context.
2. Activities may not be carried out to their logical outcome.
3. A child may treat an inanimate object as animate (offer food to a teddy bear).
4. One object or gesture may be substituted for another (a block becomes a pot).
5. A child may carry out an activity usually performed by someone else (pretending to be a doctor).[19]

Make-believe play becomes less object dependent as children move into deeper levels of fantasy. As children become more inventive and creative in their use of props, they distance themselves from known representations. They become facile in improvising representations to communicate a message or activity that holds meaning; a scarf becomes a cloud or a bird.

The young child's interest in make-believe play is accompanied by feelings of pleasure and well-being. The spirit of childhood is never more evident than when a child is immersed in fantasy. As the child experiments with new modes of imaginative expression, she is affirming herself.

Many educators believe that children are at their highest level of social and cognitive functioning during dramatic play. Pellegrini found that kindergarten children who engaged in symbolic play activities were better able to comprehend words and stories than children who did not have such exposure.[20] Both Piaget and Vygotsky view pretend play as instrumental to the development of internal systems of representation that gradually expand children's awareness from the here and now to objects and events that are not immediately present.[21]

In advanced levels of pretend play, children make assertions about earlier experiences that may be real or imagined depending on the momentary disposition of the child. Maturing children are able to recreate memories through imagination, asserting that objects and people in their immediate play space are other than what the child knows them to be.[22] They become inventive thinkers who are continually reshaping their recollection of prior experiences to accommodate to a play space, playmate, or play theme.

When children engage in serious drama, they pretend to be something or someone that has particular meaning to them, adding their own individuality to their characterizations. The fairy is good or bad depending on the child's perception and feeling about fairies or about himself. As children engage in dramatic play, they make rules to fit the occasion. They employ strategies that sustain play and reinforce their perceptions of how things ought to be. They decide how a plot is to be structured and portrayed. If necessary, they promote and defend their feelings by using language inventively and imaginatively.

In the process of role-playing, children become skillful at negotiating and manipulating a theme in order to maintain their position. They learn to listen to the language of others, adding new words to their steadily increasing vocabulary. They learn to compromise with others to sustain a play theme, seeing friends as a necessary and pleasant part of their play world.

Children borrow ideas for role-playing from their real-world experiences and from their immediate environment. Cultural trends, television, literature and peer influences are often reflected in children's pretend play. Pretense may become an enactment of typical family situations such as when a child gets sick and goes to the doctor, a mother and daughter go shopping, or a father is working. By changing costumes, children change their identity: A frog prince becomes a growling, hungry lion, or a swan becomes a princess. Although little boys typically may favor heroic, larger-than-life roles while girls prefer nurturing, compassionate roles, such preferences become less discernible when dramatic play and construction centers are designed to attract both sexes.

To function independently in dramatic play, children must become *self-starters* and *self-managers*. Unrehearsed dramatic play demands language facility, planning, and above all, cooperation. Children must be able to communicate well enough to interact with peers and to function independently for reasonable periods of time. Eager to please, children recognize that they must reconcile differences and reach accommodation or they will lose their friends to an activity across the room.

How Do Children Select Play Themes?

A play theme may be inspired by a favorite fairy tale, a favorite television show or movie, a field trip, or a holiday such as Halloween. It may be a reenactment of typical family situations: A child gets sick and goes to the doctor, a mother and daughter dress for the theatre, a husband and wife go shopping or fishing, and, of course, everybody goes to the supermarket. Often children will replay the same theme over and over, changing roles to add variety.

Children become amazingly facile in dramatic play. They button, snap, and improvise with aplomb. They combine objects that are functionally related (e.g., cups and saucers) and transform objects into inventive combinations that have meaning only to the child at play (a carpet square becomes a sailboat). For the imaginative child at play, what is real is pretend and what is pretend is real. As inanimate objects take on new meaning, children's imaginations soar. Noise levels increase to reflect play themes (children can't play in quiet voices). From time to time, communication becomes argumentative and challenging. In pretend play, children have to stand up for themselves—there is no one to solve their problems, but they instinctively know there is always someone to take their place. A child in the background may be an eager and ready understudy.

Prancing in high heels, pushing a stroller, and carrying a shopping bag require agility as well as imagination. Children extend themselves to "fill the shoes they are wearing." Friends become an extended version of self as the child moves from *me* to *we*. Children's dramatizations are not unlike real-life drama. One of the reasons dramatic play is so valuable to children's development is because they get to practice being grown up. They get to express themselves without inhibition and constraints. They experience being free and independent, and they love their sense of importance.

Sociodramatic Play

Dramatic play becomes sociodramatic play when children engage in *cooperative theme* or *script building.* As children represent themselves in more imaginative ways, play themes become more intricate. Therefore, children must be relatively mature and linguistically competent to function at an effective sociodramatic level.

At this stage of sociodramatic play, children are challenged by creating roles that require them to stretch their imagination more so than when they adopt conventional roles with defined characters and plots. When children create their own characters, they are operating at high levels of pretense. Increasing levels of fantasy require props or objects that are *not* well defined and therefore do not constrain the imaginations of children.[23] As children elaborate on play, they become more inventive in their use of language and more divergent in their thinking. With the increasing complexity of role characterizations and the demands of a script, children may even assume more than one role at a time. Children's representations reflect intricate systems of relationships and responsibilities as they work through roles and scripts in dramatic play.

Sociodramatic play is a vital outlet for children's creative resources, enabling them to:

- Develop confidence and self-control.
- Satisfy their natural desire to perform.
- Experience their own creativity.
- Work through problems.
- Connect with others in meaningful ways.
- Develop leadership skills.
- Express themselves through many mediums of communication.
- Cultivate and gain knowledge about the arts.
- Appreciate multiple points of view.
- Become innovative, original thinkers.

In sociodramatic play, children draw from a wide variety of resources and interests. They must be able to engage in thematic fantasy play (enter into a pretend play space), role-play (I am Beauty), make believe with playmates (I know! You be the Beast) and with objects (This can be your magic ring), reenact remembered experiences, use language, engage in symbolic substitution (a pipe cleaner becomes a magic ring), and persist in role-playing so a plot can be played out without a great deal of disruption or confusion.

Some researchers believe children should be trained in sociodramatic play. Extensive research conducted by Sara Smilansky (1990) supports the importance of teaching children how to play. She believes that pretend play can be promoted by training and exposure to direct experiences such as a teacher participating in dramatic play, or by exposing children to experiences that facilitate role-playing. Smilansky's findings indicate that adult participation is particularly effective when working with underprivileged children. In her pioneering research with Israeli children in 1968, Smilansky found that socially disadvantaged children rarely exhibited social pretend play because, unlike in middle-class homes, such play was not modeled or encouraged by adults.[24] As important as these findings are, they must be kept in perspective. Children will often stop playing or become inhibited when an adult is present or intervening in a child's space. As long as children appear to be actively engaged in role-playing with friends, adults should remain at a comfortable distance.

Teachers can enhance and enrich children's dramatic play in other ways such as through themes and projects. As children's themes change, teachers should change play centers. A log cabin can become a home for early settlers, an igloo, or the witch's cottage in *Hansel and Gretel*. A puppet theatre can become a bank, a small supermarket, or a check-in point for departing planes on a favorite airline. A dress-up rack can stimulate imaginative interest in dramatic play. Toys, novelty items, and prop boxes invigorate dramatic play. One change can be pivotal. It can become the starting point for a theme that, in the hands and imagination of children, may continue for days.

Games with Rules

Children acquire basic rules of play through training, and generalized rules through experience. It is not uncommon for four-year-olds to make up rules as they play with simple games or with manipulatives. They learn from older siblings or other peers. They may not know every aspect of the game, but they can extrapolate from experience and improvise sufficiently to maintain the game. The challenge for young children who are not rule bound is to play cooperatively rather than competitively. The quality of experiences children share through early play equips them for more formidable and competitive challenges later in life.

As children engage in higher levels of thinking (around five years of age) and as they become more socially cognizant, they enjoy playing games that are skill oriented and physically challenging as well as competitive in nature. When children engage in competitive play, they are building intellectual, social, and personal skills. They are strategizing and learning to think logically in order to win a game or win others to their position. Competitive play may be challenging and enjoyable, but in excess, it can become unhealthy for children who identify themselves as winners or losers. Children who measure their popularity by success in competitive peer play are frequently disappointed by outcomes. They rarely can be satisfied when winning means holding on to one's position and losing means adjusting to an ego-deflating situation (I didn't win, I never win!).

A major developmental aspect of this age is the development of conscience and an increasing awareness of moral conduct and codes. Fairness and following rules become an absolute condition for participating in group games and for being expelled from group games. Teachers in child care environments find it beneficial to encourage young school-age children toward cooperative play with fewer rules as a way of encouraging prosocial behavior and avoiding altercations. They also look for alternative ways for children to develop and practice affective behavior rather than competitive, goal-oriented behavior—forming community or service-oriented clubs; tutoring peers; collecting and distributing food; scout groups; forming a drama club, a tutoring club or a "friends of the community" club.

Play Centers

Play centers are activity areas that encourage both independent and social play, ideally with minimal supervision. They encourage children's independence and decision making within environments that reinforce their need for imaginary and constructive play. All play centers should hold the potential for *cognitive* and *affective* growth.

Play centers are defined by purpose, materials and imaginative potential. Many early-childhood centers distinguish between construction and dramatic play. In constructive play, manipulative (small motor) play and physical (large motor) play are separate but reinforcing play components. In dramatic play, children are encouraged to create their own play experiences from assorted materials and from the projects that are being studied. Excessive structuring of play centers, however, inhibits children's need to determine and control a play experience. Opening play centers to children's innovative ideas and use of materials requires an understanding of how children conceive and construct play.

Activity centers vary in their developmental challenge. Some, such as construction and dramatic play centers, encourage active, imaginative, and cooperative play. Others, such as an art or a discovery center, require a more reflective, internalized approach that is equally important to the growth of a young child. In a whole-child environment, both forms and functions of activity centers are important to a whole-child curriculum.

A Construction Center

At age two and three, a construction center should contain materials that facilitate small- and large-motor control as well as imagination. Props and accessories may be added from time to time in order to expand play experiences. They require space for push, pull, and riding toys; play structures such as steps, bridges, and small crawl-throughs; and two-level structures that encourage early forms of constructive, imaginative, and cooperative play.

At age four and five, a construction center should include a complete set of wooden blocks, a variety of multishaped and interlocking blocks, building sets, and manipulatives. Visuals highlight, while play props reinforce and extend themes and projects. Favorite themes that can be imaginatively integrated into a construction center include transportation, farm animals, the zoo, a construction site, a pond, community friends, a park, a circus, homes people live in, and homes animals live in.

A Dramatic Play Center

At age two and three years, a dramatic play center should look like a real home. It should offer furnishings that convey a message of family, familiarity, and caring. Toys and furnishings should be selected for imaginative and social play. A small sofa, a doll's bed, a carriage, puffy valances, nurturing pictures, hands-on books, puppets, and stuffed animals create a sense of connection between a child and his environment. Mirrors, visuals, an area rug, and a lamp add warmth and personality to a dramatic play setting. A two-level playhouse encourages children to re-create a home environment that is both satisfying and fills their need for continuity and security.

At age four and five, a dramatic play center should contain a basic family unit as well as creative opportunities for extended play: dress-ups, novel materials, a playhouse, a sectional rug, pillows, a puppet theatre, a book shelf, and space for children to enact themes and projects. In a child-challenging environment, prop boxes should be available for extended thematic play. A puppet theatre can become an all-purpose set for extending projects and imaginary experiences such as the creation of a flower stall, a bank, a travel agency, or an entrance to a county fair, circus, or sports center.

Teachers can prepare children for dramatic play through direct experiences such as telling or acting out stories; encouraging creative writing and expression; promoting the arts through music, dance and drama; setting up projects that are under the control of the child; taking children to dramatic performances; and inviting specialists to share their talents and their interest in the arts. They can also prepare children for dramatic play through sensory experiences that invite exploration and imagination, such as nature walks, cloud watching, kite flying, bubble blowing, or bird and butterfly watching.

Teachers should be very attentive to how they equip and maintain a dramatic play center. Materials should maintain a balance between low-realism open-ended props and realistic props that children routinely play with (see Figure 3.1). Teachers should perceive a dramatic play center as a point of departure rather than arrival. It should be an evolving space that is open for imagination and exploration and always evolving.

FIGURE 3.1   **Props for Various Types of Sociodramtic Play**

Restaurant

Cookbooks
Chef's hat
Apron
Dish towel
Dish cloth
Hot pads
Rolling pin
Cookie cutters
Doughnut cutter
Cookie sheet
Muffin tin
Gingerbread man pan
Heart-shaped pan
Cake pan
Bread pan
Pitcher
Mixing bowl
Measuring cup
Measuring spoons
Tablecloth
Timer
Funnel
Scoop
Spatula
Pastry brush
Whisk
Large mixing spoon
Cake knife
Recipe file box
Recipe cards
Pencils
Sifter
Egg carton
Cupcake liners
Play dough
Plates
Saucer
Glasses
Cups
Salt shaker
Pepper shaker
Ladle
Cake server
Egg beater
Pot

Laundromat

Toy washer
Toy dryer
Laundry basket
Clothes
Bleach container
Detergent box
Measuring cup
Children's clothes hangers
Clothespins
Open/Closed sign
Hours of operation sign
Toy money

Farm

Toy farm animals
Apron
Work gloves
Shovel
Hoe
Bucket
Wagon
Seeds
Toy barn
Toy tractor
Toy trailer
Visored hats
Toy computer
Toy cellular telephone

Camp

Tent
Rope
Blanket or sleeping bag
Fishing poles
Toy fish
Toy axe
Compass
Flashlights
Backpack
Walkie-talkie
Telescope
Canteen
Stew pot
Mess kit
Wood for campfire

Field guide to birds
Field guide to insects
Ice chest
Toy food

Airplane Travel

Camera
Travel brochures
Toy money
Captain's jacket
Steward's apron
Serving items for meals
Suitcase
Paper
Pencils
Pens
Stamps
Pilot's hat
Magazines
Maps
Seatbelt
Airplane ticket

Veterinarian Clinic

Toy animals
Hypodermics
Scratch paper
Folders
Pencils
Clipboard
White shirts
Bandages
Brush
Towel
Plastic tub
Washcloth

Fire Station

Firefighter's helmet
Firefighter's coat
Firefighter's pants
Firefighter's boots
Rubber hose
City map
Telephones
Goggles

FIGURE 3.1   Continued

Baseball Park

Baseball shirts
Baseball pants
Baseball bat
Baseballs (or softballs)
Gloves
Baseball hats
Candy boxes
Hotdog containers
Napkins
Toy money
Sunglasses
Sunscreen
Cups
Mustard container
Ketchup container
Relish container

Hat Play

Straw beach hat
Necklace
Ladies' dress hat
Stetson hat
Straw hat
Army officer's hat
Motorcycle helmet
Suitcase
Safari hat
Visored cap
Baseball cap
Scarf
Goggles
Ski cap
Safety helmet

Office

Stickers
Stamps
Pencils
Colored markers
Stamp pad
Rubber stamps
Eraser

Diary
Typing paper
Stationery
Invitations
Postcards
Thank-you notes
Notepads
Birthday cards
Pencil case
Pencil sharpener
Notecards

Nursery

Doll
Doll blanket
Changing pad
Baby clothes
Bib
Bonnet
Bottle
Serving dish
Baby spoon
Pacifier
Bath sponge
Baby lotion
Powder
Diapers
Fresh wipes
Teething ring

Boat

Toy or real boat
Fishing poles
Worms
Flag
Oars
First-aid kit
Life jacket
Towel
Water
Fishing net
Toy fish
Bucket

Shovel
Sand
Sunglasses
Sunscreen
Beach toys

Garden

Seeds
Water jug
Harvesting basket
Gloves
Watering can
Shovel
Rake
Hoe
Toy lawn mower
Sprinkler
Garden hose
Toy or real wheelbarrow
Vegetables
Sunscreen
Plant food
Hats

Grocery Store

Food containers
Shopping basket
Apron
Newspaper advertisements
Coupons
Checkbook
Checks
Toy money
Wallet
Pads of paper
Pencils
Pens
Toy or real cash register
Price tags
Nametags
Sale signs
Brown paper bags
Produce

Source: From *A Right to Play,* September 1992, Southern Early Childhood Association, Little Rock, AK: 1993, pp. 52–53. Reprinted by permission.

Developmental Advantages of a Play-Centered Curriculum

Play and Social/Cognitive Development

Children both shape and are shaped by their social and physical environment. Constructivists believe that children construct their knowledge and values from interactions with, and actions on, the physical and social world.[25] Through qualitative interaction, children develop attitudes toward the individual and the group, and toward their larger sociocultural environment. Through play, children build concepts and affirm understandings as they interact with their physical and social environment.

Imaginative play symbolizes a gradual change in a child's thinking processes from concrete operations to abstract levels of reasoning. To make the transition from simple stages of pretend play to more elaborate forms of pretend play, a child must be able to consolidate knowledge and replicate (or reproduce) reality. She must have acquired a mental image of the appearance and function of objects in order to find substitutes. A child demonstrates mental growth when she combs a doll's hair with an object that represents a comb, pushes a block and pretends it is a car, or pours pretend tea into a small cup. She is recalling objects and their functions, and using them imaginatively.

Play stimulates mental development. It is particularly important during the early years, when children's language and thinking processes are developing. Through exploration and imaginative play, children form impressions and understandings about their world. Mental playfulness generates a desire for continued learning. In her book, *Ideas Influencing Early Childhood Education*, Evelyn Weber writes:

> Play is a child's way of making sense out of the world. The child's active manipulation of objects, his repeated activity with people and things, leads to a growing awareness that objects have properties, and that they can be viewed along different dimensions. Through continual use of materials—lifting, sorting, arranging, building—the child comes to note similarities and differences to work out his own imagery.[26]

Imaginative play promotes social interaction. As children observe peers at play, they are attracted by feelings of companionship. A child pulls a friend in a wagon all the way to Disneyland. Other children are patiently waiting to get on board. Pretend tickets are passed out and gas is needed. The adventure grows. The lead child derives pleasure from the attention he is getting from peers and his sense of importance. He works harder, exerting more and more physical energy.

Nearby, two friends are swinging side-by-side looking for interesting cloud images. Some clouds look like huge, threatening animals while others look like peaceful, soft pillows. The two friends feel a sense of intimacy that is like sharing a secret.

As children progress in cooperative play experiences, they become inventive. A small rug may become a magic carpet and a scarf a distant mountain top, hand-painted by little gnomes. As children mature, they are less bound by gender and are willing to try multiple roles in dramatizations. In creative environments that support imaginative play, children are less inhibited in their choice of roles and characters—they are willing to step beyond stereotypical casting that makes a flower a girl or a tree a boy. Less bound by convention, a boy may become an Annie and a girl a Peter Pan.

Maturation affects the quality of children's pretend play. Children who are socially mature are capable of sustained levels of play. Little, if any, teacher intervention is required when children are playing positively and cooperatively. Without cooperation, however, feelings get hurt. In some instances, a teacher may need to intervene on a child's behalf. She may have to help children get a plot underway, and she may have to oversee its progress until children are able to sustain cooperative play.

Serious play requires collaboration and compromise. When children prepare for a play theme, they brainstorm, problem solve and make choices. They assume role-taking tasks with competence and confidence. As they develop themes, they consolidate what they have learned with what they are learning. Positive and negative feelings are worked through without the need for adult intervention. When children see value in collaboration and cooperation, they are able to put aside differences and preferences. By applying social rules and etiquette to a play production, they can feel reasonably assured of a positive and self-affirming outcome.

Children's social/cognitive development is influenced by their:

- Knowledge of the social world
- Ability to communicate with peers
- Willingness to compromise and share
- Adaptability and flexibility
- Motivation and interest levels
- Ability to extend themselves to others
- Ability to negotiate and solve problems
- Ability to be patient and supportive
- Readiness to contribute to a plot or play theme
- Capability and resourcefulness in beginning and sustaining a play theme

As with adults, children's social/cognitive levels of functioning vary from day to day. Children's play is affected by internal factors such as emotional stress, prior experiences, and general patterns of attitudinal functioning. Children's play is also affected by external factors such as the quality of the environment, the availability of toys and materials to facilitate play, teacher expectations, and the ages and sexes of peers. The social/cognitive benefits of play are never more apparent than out-of-doors where space and activities are less confined and conditions are conducive to inventive, imaginative play.

In *The House of Make-Believe,* Singer and Singer summarize the social and emotional long-term value of imaginative play:

> Imaginative play serves important purposes in the emergence of the psychologically complex and adaptable person. Individual differences in the frequency and variety of such play seem to be associated not only with richer and more complex language but also with a greater potential for cognitive differentiation, divergent thought, impulse control, self-entertainment. Emotional expressiveness, and, perhaps, self-awareness. Imaginative play is fun, but in the midst of the joys of make believe, children may also be preparing for the reality of more effective lives.[27]

Play and Sociomoral Development

One of the greatest challenges in creating a child care environment is to transform a physical environment into a human environment.[28] An environment, like its children, acquires unique characteristics over time. At best, it provides a setting from which children can develop a sense of belonging and intimacy that is validated through daily encounters with the people who are important in their lives. If these encounters are systematically positive and reinforcing, children begin to feel a sense of community, identification and security in practicing their own ideas.[29]

Play and Problem Solving

In play, children continually solve problems and create new problems to be solved. The experimental nature of play invites divergent open-ended thinking, particularly when children challenge themselves by challenging others. When children do not feel intimidated by excessive rules or by adult reprimands, they frequently show amazing agility and adeptness in their ability to control and master a play experience.

Complex levels of thinking become operational when children use a variety of nonrealistic objects and materials with inventive ideas to represent an imaginary play theme. Aware of the seriousness of their task, children in deep play use language, creative thinking, and negotiating skills to work through problems and to find solutions (see Figure 3.2). Children at play negotiate problems as they:

- Develop fluency in expressing ideas.
- Experiment with trial and error reasoning.
- Experiment with cause-and-effect relationships.
- Explore, validate and accept their outcomes.
- Affirm and challenge perceptions and understandings.
- Listen to and learn from playmates.
- Use inventiveness and creative thinking.
- Apply new information to knowledge already acquired.
- Learn how to control and master their play environment.

Goal

To develop competencies in reading, writing, and mathematics

Abilities Necessary to achieve goal	**Concepts and Skills** Experiences required to develop abilities	**Means (Play)** To develop concepts and skills

- Visual memory
- Auditory memory
- Language acquisition
- Classification
- Hand-eye coordination
- Body image
- Spatial orientation

- Configuration
- Figure-ground relationships
- Shapes
- Patterns
- Spatial relationships
- Matching (shape, size, color)
- Whole-part relationship
- Arranging objects in sequence
- Organizing objects in ascending and descending order
- Classification
- Verbal communication
- Measurement
- Solving problems

- Blocks
- Cubes
- Pegs
- Finger paint
- Brush paint
- Dough
- Clay
- Water
- Sand
- Wood

FIGURE 3.2   Learning through Play

Source: S. Swedlow, "Children play—Children learn," in J. S. McKee, ed., *Play: Working Partner of Growth*, p. 33. Reprinted with permission of S. Swedlow and the Association for Childhood Education International, 17904 Georgia Avenue, Suite 215, Olney, MD 20832. Copyright © 1986 by the Association.

Play and Language Development

It is primarily through play that language is practiced and developed in early childhood. In play, children use language practically, as a tool for communicating and fulfilling their needs, and descriptively, to express themselves and their feelings in the context of play. Lev Vygotsky, a contemporary of Piaget, emphasized the importance of language to cognitive development.[30] He believed that all higher mental functions have social origins, stressing the central role of social communication in the development of children's thinking. Crucial to the development of language is what Vygotsky referred to as a *zone of proximal development*—that critical moment of intervention when a child seeks or requires assistance from a teacher in order to extend learning. At such time, the teacher should provide only enough assistance to enable the child to continue.

Language development is fostered by teachers who are skillful in promoting literacy through a variety of verbal and nonverbal exchanges. A teacher may encourage conversation during informal play experiences and during structured experiences designed to enrich language development. She may facilitate language development by interacting with a child, playing with a child or supporting a child's desire for conversation.

Sociodramatic play centers encourage children to express language through social interaction and inventive thinking. When children can't rely on physical props to convey their play meaning, they realize a need for language.[31] Thematic play provides opportunities for children to experience and enrich their own language facility. As themes change, language expands. Children use language to communicate knowledge about key events in their play world. As children play in project-oriented activity centers, they practice all the language arts.

Language is enriched by teachers who value children's literature. Teachers read with maximum impact when they take the time to understand and share with children the meaningful messages within a story. The messages that are not immediately obvious are the most fun to explore—the *why* and *what if* messages that stimulate creative thinking and language development. A story may be told and retold. Children never tire of hearing favorite stories that over time become old and dear friends.

Play and Creativity

Increasingly, play and the arts are regarded as complementary companions in the creative process. *Children at play are artists at work.* The visual images that are constructed in children's play creations are not unlike the symbolic images expressed in their paintings. In both forms of expression, children work with incongruencies as they experiment with materials. They construct, explore, and experiment as they organize and eventually (but not always) synthesize the parts into a whole.

When children play spontaneously, they are creating from new perspectives and new levels of awareness. Sometimes, a child at play will reenact real-life experiences and interests: A doll is a baby brother or sister, a stuffed animal is a real pet, steps are an escalator, a box is a car. Other times, a child will create plots that are highly original and not readily identifiable. They will reenact favorite stories, such as Cinderella and Peter Pan, changing story lines, adding characters, and embellishing plots with childlike fantasy and humor. As children mature in their play, their levels of thinking and imagination become more elaborate, more abstract, and more skillful.

Children bring their individuality to every play experience. Within minutes, children at play can create something from nothing using odds and ends in resourceful and innovative ways. The level of intensity that generates creative play suggests a need not only to express, but to control and transform an environment. Nothing is fixed in creative play; children constantly sort through and select items while they set up a play scene.

Divergent (open-ended) thinking is associated with creativity. Flexible, original thinking automatically accompanies spontaneous play. A child absorbed in play uses improvisation and forethought to accomplish immediate goals. Concerns (something that doesn't fit or match a child's expectation) necessitate problem solving and creative solutions. A child at play must clothe and equip herself according to the character she is playing; she must find a way to fasten oversized garments, to negotiate for an item she needs, and to manage her role within a very short time. While she is busy at her tasks, her playmates are also scurrying for favorite dress-ups. A frenetic atmosphere often prevails when children prepare for dramatic play.

Preparing for dramatic play is an all-consuming, challenging experience for a young child. A setting must correspond to a theme. With few materials available, a child must be inventive in the way she selects and arranges play objects. When setting a table, a child will use what is available and create the rest. A small basket filled with acorns, "borrowed" from a science center, becomes a centerpiece. The child hurriedly makes place mats and places dolls in appropriate sitting arrangements. Some objects are realistic and some bear only a slight resemblance to known objects. Her thinking is open-ended; a sense of freedom and excitement enables the child to think and act intuitively, to become her character.

Children use their senses imaginatively and inventively as they play. Sensory awareness is essential to the creative process. As they play, children taste, smell, and listen. Dinner is served, coffee is poured, and the baby is crying for a bottle. They select from dress-up fabrics that please and attract them—feathers, lace, fur, leather, velvet. They become familiar with textures as they physically interact with materials.

Sensory stimulation through pretend play is equally important to school-age children. Children who rarely experience their artistic culture or express feelings of creativity miss a vital dimension of child development. They are unwilling or unable to express themselves in original ways that enhance their development. Unchallenged by literature and the arts, these children experience a cultural vacuum that may never be filled.

Elliot Eisner asserts that by neglecting the arts in American education, we are depriving children of sensory experiences that are vital to intellectual and creative development. "Sensory forms of representation found in such activities as poetry, the visual arts, music, and dance can provide the conceptual basis for meaning that will be represented later in the oral and written language codes."[32]

Play and Personal Development

Watching a young child engaged in pretend play is like watching a home movie that is filled with vignettes of movement and expression passing before one's eyes too fast to be absorbed. Energetic whirlwind movements, emotive chatter, and a wonderful sense of aliveness radiates from children's play.

The child at play is expressing an inner world; a real, unedited script that portrays the child/actor. Where do children get their scripts? Mostly, children act out what they have experienced and what they are familiar with. When children play, they can cause things to happen or change things. They can express moods and emotions that are inside, feelings that suddenly may be triggered by play. Expression is a form of release especially when it comes spontaneously from the child at play.

Play promotes confidence and self-validation. A child is better able to express her ideas and feelings in nonthreatening pro-social settings than in group-controlled settings. She can practice and validate the standards of behavior that are expected in her real world. She can care for a kitten, rock a baby to sleep, iron a scarf, and set a table with an unlikely combination of food. She can schedule an appointment, make a shopping list, clean the house, and make dinner before going to the office. She can become a homemaker, a career woman, and if she wants to, she can turn herself into a fairy godmother. Everything is possible during dramatic play when children are free to be themselves and express themselves in a pretend world.

Playful people are able to find fulfilling interests and hobbies throughout their lifetimes. They are self-motivated and rarely bored. This is borne out when, at the age eighty, a woman gathers tiny shells or pine cones, imagining an arrangement that reflects her nature and continuing desire to create. The fingers may not be as nimble as they once were, but the imagination is still in full gear. Originality and imagination are shaped in childhood. Creativity challenges a person to move beyond conventional levels of thought, to open and travel the corridors that lead to a fulfilling life.

Play and Nurturing

Play can cultivate an appreciation for nature. Environmental consciousness in children can begin early. Children who play outdoors are sensitive to changes: the passing of fall, the excitement of a first snowfall, or the budding of an early spring.

Children may be introduced to nature through play. They should be allowed time to investigate little pieces of their surrounding world such as wildflowers, worms, slugs, and ant colonies. An egg fallen from a nest can trigger a nurturing reaction that becomes a script for a pretend play experience. The child shares her discovery with a friend who suggests that they build a nest for the baby bird that they believe to be inside the egg. They become excited as they find and select materials that they believe a bird would use. Drawing from experience, the children place the nest in a protected setting inside a bush. They worry about mother bird not finding the nest. When they agree on a location, they shift from concern to practical application; they carefully roll and shape worms for the baby, suggesting that there may not be a happy ending to this drama (i.e., the nurturing children are preparing for the possibility of mother bird not returning).

Play and Movement

Children at play are extremely active, developing muscle control, refining motor skills, practicing eye–hand coordination. Through movement, they recognize

> their position in space, their relationship to the space around them, and the relationship between three-dimensional and two-dimensional space. They develop a sense of laterality (two-sidedness) and dominance (one side is the dominant side) and kinesthesia (knowing the location of a part of the body in relation to space and other external stimuli). They refine other skills such as large- and small-muscle control, eye–hand coordination, and the increasing ability to change the focus of eyes from near to far or from far to near.[33]

As children play, they become aware of themselves in relation to their physical environment. They use their bodies resourcefully to claim their play space and, if necessary, to change their play space. They become skillful and adept at negotiating space and managing themselves in many different settings—a small loft, a large activity center. Teachers who allow children to make choices and move freely within their environment are promoting both mental and physical development. Early childhood educator, Clare Cherry writes:

> Children's entire orientation to the world develops through movement. Through play, their understanding of the world is enhanced. Wholesome play involves movement of all kinds. It provokes the reception of accompanying sensory information and brings about an awareness of feelings and thoughts. Every action of a child at play relates to learning, self-image, self-awareness, and self-esteem.[34]

Large- and small-motor play releases energy, develops coordination, and empowers children with a sense of accomplishment. A simple trike ride or a walk on a balance beam engenders both skill and imagination in children. A child uses his hands to assemble manipulatives, to hammer a nail into wood, to pound dough, to play a drum, and to finger paint. He uses his imagination to transform a simple activity into a creative experience. For the child at play, motor skills are rarely divided into small- and large-motor categories. The child who is in constant motion uses his total body when he plays. In order to master movement and skills, he needs both defined and open play parameters.

Specific motor skills can best be developed through teacher-initiated activities such as tumbling, cutting and pasting, bar work, rhythm and movement activities, follow-me games, and so on. The frequency and range of physical activities children are exposed to will affect their large- and small-motor development. The manner in which teachers initiate and present activities will influence a child's degree of participation (see Table 3.2).

TABLE 3.2 Physical Development: From Infancy to Age Five

Age	Developmental Milestones	Large-Muscle Development	Small-Muscle Development	Sensory Development	Creative Movement	Relaxation
Infants to 18 Months	*Large muscles* ■ Rolls over (3 months) ■ Sits unassisted (9 months) ■ Creeps forward (9 months) ■ Walks alone (13 months) *Small muscles* ■ Reaches for toys (6 months) ■ Fills and empties containers (9 months) ■ Feeds self (6–9 months)	■ Put a toy just beyond baby's reach to stimulate mobility ■ Provide large safe areas for exploring ■ Provide push-pull toys ■ Provide climbing structures, bouncy swings, and ride-on toys for toddlers	■ Provide rattles, squeeze toys, and cradle gyms for infants to swipe at and grab ■ Provide stacking and nesting toys, pans with lids, and a pounding bench for older infants ■ Play pat-a-cake ■ Provide small plastic blocks and balls	■ Provide textured toys for mouthing and teething ■ For water play: provide cans with holes, plastic containers, and bath toys; place baby walker in shallow puddle ■ Attach mirrors to cribs ■ Provide food experiences for tasting and smearing	■ Carry child while dancing to music and pat out rhythm on child's back ■ Playfully roll child into different positions for fun ■ Show children ways their bodies can move as you talk about them	■ Help babies relax by rocking, cuddling, and singing to them ■ Stroke or rub babies's backs while singing softly to them ■ Help babies relax with soft rhythmical music or the burring sound of a fan
18 Months to 3 Years	*Large muscles* ■ Climbs up and slides down low equipment; climbs stairs (19 months) ■ Jumps and runs (20–21 months) ■ Kicks ball (24 months) *Small muscles* ■ Scribbles with crayons (18 months) ■ Uses scissors (3 years)	■ Provide climbing gym, moderate slides, (no pumping), and tricycles ■ Provide bouncy mattresses for jumping ■ Provide balls for kicking and rolling ■ Encourage older children to march to music	■ Provide markers and crayons for scribbling ■ Allow plenty of time for easel and finger painting ■ Provide simple puzzles with frames ■ Provide containers with twist-off / on tops ■ Encourage sandbox play (spooning and filling)	■ Provide manipulative materials like dough and clay ■ Set up beginning cooking experiences; allow time for tasting, smelling, and feeling ■ Substitute cornmeal or seeds in sand table ■ Allow for water play	■ Use props and dress-ups to encourage movement ■ Have children dance like a bear, hop like a bird, etc. ■ Ask, "How little can you make yourself?" ■ Have children ride rocking horses to music (vary tempo): two horses together are fun	■ Provide soothing activities such as swinging or rocking in chair ■ Allow for water and sand play ■ Stroke or rub children's backs at naptime

3 to 4 Years	*Large muscles* ■ Climbs readily ■ Runs, hops, and kicks ■ Steers and pedals tricycle ■ Balances briefly on one foot *Small muscles* ■ Buttons and zips with help; uses tools ■ Catches and tosses balls	■ Provide swings, slides, and climbing gyms ■ Plan balancing activities (rim of tire, edge of sidewalk, etc.) ■ Throw beanbags at large target ■ Kick a still or slow-moving ball ■ Bounce large/small balls	■ Allow time for large and small block play ■ Use woodworking, cooking, and art materials ■ String beads ■ Provides puzzles and other manipulatives ■ Let children practice self-dressing	■ Finger painting with scents or textures added ■ Compare sound containers for those that match ■ Shaking activities (shake like a wet dog, a salt shaker, a sheet) ■ Step in tubs of different textures (feathers, styrofoam, pea gravel) ■ Spin around (to feel dizzy sensation)	■ Have children create/move through obstacle course ■ Move in response to music; vary tempo ■ Jump on mattress to music; march	■ Shake arms and legs loosely like limp puppet ■ Provide quiet corner or child-sized bed in housekeeping corner ■ Flop down when music stops
4 to 5 Years	*Large muscles* ■ Can hop but not skip ■ May pump self on swing ■ Catches both large and small balls ■ Balances self on beams *Small muscles* ■ Can copy a few letters ■ Hammers nails in wood ■ Can cut with scissors	■ Allow for free, joyful running and leaping ■ Provide trikes and scooters ■ Offers intricate obstacle courses ■ Encourage cooperative large-muscle play (giving rides in wagon, pretend games on climbing gym)	■ Provide puzzles with more pieces and large unframed jigsaw puzzles ■ Block play (building elaborate structures) ■ Hit balloons with paddles ■ Provide practice cutting with scissors on curved lines	■ Use senses to sort materials by touch, taste, sound, etc. ■ Match flowers or scents ■ Have children guess who they're touching (with eyes closed) ■ Substitute snow in water table; play as it melts ■ Identify sounds on tape	■ Have children propose ways to use parachute ■ Inspire movement with questions: "How would you walk in deep snow? On ice? In honey? How could you cross the room if you couldn't use your feet?" ■ Provide props to enhance movements	■ Have children "tense up" and "let go" ■ Have children pretend to be frozen—then melted—ice cream, or a plate of cooked spaghetti ■ Have children imagine peaceful scenes, such as floating on a cloud, to relax

Source: From *PRE–K TODAY*, Issues from 1987 and 1988. Copyright © 1987, 1988 by Scholastic Inc. Reprinted by permission of Scholastic Inc. All rights reserved.

Play and Special Needs

Play can build confidence and self-esteem in children with special needs. The therapeutic and self-affirming aspects of play provide unique learners a secure environment that is self-paced and reinforcing. Children with an emotional, social, or physical impairment require individualized attention before they can be mainstreamed into a normal day-care environment, and they will need special consideration thereafter. Teachers must be sensitive to developmental differences through nurturing exchanges. They must become sensitive to materials and activities from the perspective of a child with special needs. It is the teacher who sets the tone and models the behavior for a successful and happy experience for each child.

A reinforcing, play-oriented environment will benefit *all* children. Nothing is more soothing than a sandbox, a water table, or an easel set up with fresh, inviting paints. Nothing is more reinforcing than children feeling accepted and loved as they are. In a child-friendly atmosphere, children cease to look on one another as different. If anything, children will extend themselves to protect playmates whom they perceive as vulnerable and less able to perform age-level tasks.

How Teachers Cultivate Play

Through play, children become active protagonists in acquiring skills, competencies and knowledge. Virtually every important concept can be demonstrated and reinforced through play. A simple project such as making a birdhouse can become a focus for dialogue and discovery learning.

Children can design, build and position a birdhouse in a place where they can monitor its activity. A child as young as three can distinguish birds by color and size. A four-year-old can identify sounds, patterns of behavior and food preferences. She can figure out how birds fly and why they migrate before winter. She's not certain how a parrot learns to talk, but this knowledge stimulates her curiosity about bird life.

Her interests may be further reinforced through literature, drama, drawing, and a trip to a pet store or to a zoo. In a discovery environment, a simple thought, idea, or project can become a trigger for extended learning.

Facilitating Play

Adults play a key role in influencing and reinforcing children's play patterns. Teachers should employ a guided-discovery approach that introduces children to challenging and creative ideas. In play, teachers find many opportunities to partner and interact with children.

With two- and three-year-olds, the teacher should be a careful observer and facilitator of children's development. She influences children's play through her interactional style and support. At times she will be assertive and at other times she will follow the lead of the child. When children ascertain that a teacher is a primary, important and reliable adult model, they will accept her guidance.

With four- and five-year-olds, a teacher's role in facilitating play is determined by several variables: the quality of play children are experiencing, the curriculum or objectives she has developed, and the disposition of her children at a given moment in the day. Despite the rich potential for learning through play, a teacher must avoid the temptation to "teach" children at play by joining them as a playmate. Unless there is a need to intervene such as to comfort or assist a child, a teacher's involvement is not beneficial. Similarly, teachers must not allow play to degenerate into an unproductive, chaotic free-for-all. Adults must be sensitive to the rhythm of play and the patterns of play within a given group. They must become sensitive partners in children's play by not participating unless children request their assistance. Children at play should not fulfill preconceived notions of what they should be taught.[35]

Teacher's Checklist for Facilitating Play

- Be open minded and flexible in working with the young child; do not impose standards and expectations that are developmentally unsound.
- Help the child cope with anxieties or negative feelings.
- Encourage children to bond through friendship and cooperation.
- Help the young child to develop patience and confidence as he interacts with his surrounding world.
- Help children to identify and build on individual strengths and interests.
- Discourage competition and favoritism by acknowledging the special talents of each child.
- Avoid discouraging children by overreacting or invoking fear.
- Maintain order and harmony in the environment to lessen children's stress and frustration.
- Encourage children to help and support one another; to become supportive and compassionate friends.

Observing and Recording Children's Play

Teachers can learn about children's play by observing and documenting significant events. Children reveal much about themselves as they interact in an environment. Through play, patterns form, personalities develop, and interests emerge. Teachers should observe a child's progress without being obtrusive. She must notice little things that distinguish one child from another: gestures, mannerisms, humor, habits, or modes of expression. She must also notice a child's approach to a task, level of interest, and attitude. The teacher should document children's projects, progress and productions. By taking the time to observe and assess children, a teacher can better determine a child's needs.

Assessing Children's Play

When teachers observe a child over a period of time, they will note the following behavioral and attitudinal patterns:

- At which type of play does the child spend most of his time?
- Does the child prefer playing alone to playing with friends?
- Are there reasons why a child is not secure in play experiences?
- Does the child prefer construction to dramatic play?
- Is the child developing patterns and logical thinking?
- Does the child make appropriate choices?
- Does the child anticipate consequences?
- Is the child able to solve problems that occur in play?
- Is the child able to exercise autonomy and independence during play periods?
- Does the child's play get out of control? What are the circumstances? How is this handled?
- Is the child developing social skills?
- What kinds of cooperative play does the child engage in?
- How is the child showing empathy and good will?
- Can the child share and take turns most of the time?
- Does the child appear to be happy and in control most of the time?
- Does the child approach play tasks with self-confidence?
- Can the child communicate effectively?
- Can the child play with minimal supervision?
- Do you feel the child would profit from more teacher intervention or assistance?
- Is the child expressing pretense? Examples?
- Does the child show interest in completing play tasks?
- Does the child take pride in her work?
- Is the child demonstrating thinking and reasoning skills?
- Is the child developing small-motor skills?
- What kinds of small-motor play does the child enjoy (e.g., manipulatives, creative assemblages, building, puzzles, games, or patterning)?
- Is the child developing large-motor skills?
- What kinds of physical play does the child enjoy (e.g., rough and tumble, chasing, climbing, or blocks)?
- Is the child demonstrating conceptual development (e.g., can he classify, sort, order, and organize his play materials)?
- Does the child listen and respond to suggestions?
- Can the child sustain interest in a play project?
- Is the child assuming responsibility for managing and cleaning up a play space?
- What toys does the child prefer?
- Is the child developing age-appropriate cognitive skills?

- Is the child developing age-appropriate language skills?
- Is the child developing age-appropriate social skills?
- Is this program meeting the needs of the child?

Assessing an Environment

Knowledge of the child facilitates an appraisal of an environment. It is helpful to ask the following questions:

- What might be added or deleted from the program?
- Are the toys and activities age-level appropriate?
- What environmental alterations am I anticipating? Why?
- If I could introduce new toys or props, what would they be?
- Is there a balance between realistic and imaginative materials that is appropriate to my students' age level?
- How do I plan to improve my construction center?
- How do I plan to improve my dramatic play center?
- Which projects are conducive to play?
- How do I plan to document children's work (e.g., photographs, a personal portfolio, writings, drawings, videos, or samples of crafts)?
- Is there space for displays and documentations?
- Have I explored how a project may be integrated into all components of my curriculum?
- Have I allocated enough space for activity centers, for personal time, and for spontaneous play?

Integrating Play into a Curriculum

A play curriculum should promote an atmosphere of enjoyment, enrichment, expression, and imagination. Teachers can integrate play into a curriculum by:

- Visualizing how basic skills and concepts can be taught through play.
- Selecting themes and units that promote creative play and imagination: a unit on families can be integrated into a drama center through toys and props that show families at work and at play; a unit on community helpers can be integrated into a drama center by setting up themes that interest children (a post office, a firehouse, a library, a hospital, a school); a unit on farm animals can be integrated in a drama center by adding a farm, miniature animals, and other accessories; a unit on Woodland Indians can be integrated into a drama center by making a "long house" out of cardboard boxes, by creating an authentic Indian village, by providing props that depict a farming and hunting community, or by setting up an arts and crafts center that includes stitchery, rugmaking, stringing beads, making jewelry, and making authentic Indian food.

- Changing play toys and areas of interest in activity centers to highlight seasons, holidays, and special themes and events.
- Having a specialized teacher in movement or drama visit a class on a weekly basis.
- Developing techniques for simple classroom presentations that encourage children to select parts, to interpret characters, and to speak spontaneously—creating a production that is something like a familiar story or fable.
- Planning fieldtrips to reinforce children's interests: a trip to a zoo, a nature center, or a firehouse.
- Creating novel play spaces that correspond with classroom themes: a log cabin, an igloo, a cave, a tree house.
- Approaching all learning projects from a play/work perspective that encourages:
  - imagination and creativity
  - self-awareness
  - self-expression
  - self-appreciation
  - decision making and risk taking
  - autonomy and initiative in making choices
  - expressive language
  - social sensitivity
  - divergent, flexible thinking
  - autonomy and independent thinking
  - a sense of self-mastery and self-worth
  - a creative disposition

Activities

Because play is primarily self-directed and self-motivated, teacher-initiated activities should be purposeful educational and creatively presented. When teachers work with children in groups, the focus of play should be primarily on large-motor development (creative movement, gymnastics, and skill-building games), on small-motor development (making a mural, assembling a collage for a hallway, gardening or cooking, playing musical instruments), or expressive language experiences through group activities and drama. (See Chapter 5, The Arts.)

Examples of Fine-Motor Activities for Young Children

1. Acting out finger plays—finger plays are rhyming nonsense verses that coordinate language and sensory development, *I'm a Little Teapot, The Wheels on the Bus, This Little Frog Broke His Toe, Two Little Blackbirds, Open Shut Them, Johnny Hammers with One Hammer, Two Little Eyes that Open and Close.*

2. Playing follow-me games—wiggle fingers, wiggle toes, wiggle nose, wiggle ears, open and clasp hands, open mouths wide, make funny faces, blink eyes,

wink, curl up tight, stand on tiptoes, be raindrops, be rainbows stretching across the sky, be a buzzing bee, be a fly on your nose. Now pretend you're a bean bag—put it on your knee, on your tummy, on your foot, on your head; now pass it to a friend—careful don't let it fall!

3. Using musical instruments—children may tap to music or to rhythms initiated by a teacher; drums, sticks, tambourines, triangles, and bells are favorite instruments of young children.

4. Making group murals or seasonal art projects—children can gather leaves and paste them on a large piece of colored paper; children make a collage using scissors, glue, paste-on objects; children finger paint a mural.

5. Assembling a miniature construct—children can build a gas station, an airport, a farm, a pond in a cardboard box setting; or they can make a birdhouse using a hammer and nails.

6. Cleaning up day—children can sponge tables, clean windows, sort toys, wash doll clothes and hang them to dry, wash trikes.

7. Cooking—children can wash and cut vegetables, knead and roll dough.

8. Doing-a-good-job day—children practice hanging up or putting on their coats, buttoning and snapping, brushing their teeth, setting a table.

9. Writing a note to a friend—children write and mail a "happy note" to a friend.

10. Using-your-five-senses each day—children are given one item, such as an orange, to experience: they feel it, peel it, smell it, squeeze it and listen as it drops into a glass, and, if there is anything left, eat it.

Examples of Large-Motor Activities for Young Children
1. Acting out nursery rhymes—for example, *Jack and Jill, Little Miss Muffet, Jack Be Nimble, Hey Diddle, Diddle.*

2. Playing group games—for example, *Dog, Dog; Duck, Duck, Goose; London Bridge; The Farmer in the Dell; Freeze Tag; Red Rover; A Tisket, A Tasket; Go In and Out the Circle; Giant Steps; Musical Chairs* (or *Carpet Squares*).

3. Creative play on a mat—for example, "Guess What I Am," "Be . . . a slithering snake, a kangaroo with a heavy pocket, a fat frog, a slow turtle, a swinging monkey, a grinning crocodile, a jack-in-the-box, a ballerina, a tight-rope walker, a magician, an old man with a cane, a frightened rabbit, a storm, a swan, a kitchen appliance."

4. Creative play on a parallel bar, a balance beam, wooden steps, or a stage. Be a circus performer, a gymnast, or an amphibian.

5. Creative movement activities using records, musical instruments, or songs (libraries are good resources for children's records).

6. Acting out favorite stories that require gross-motor actions—for example, *Three Billy Goats Gruff.*

7. Using hoops or tires for spatial awareness—children go around, over, through, in and out using one foot, using both hands and feet, going forward, going backward.

8. Cleaning-up-our-backyard day—children gather and rake leaves, wash windows, and clean out a storage shed.

9. Doing gymnastics—children do log rolls and forward rolls (supervised by a teacher), crawl, move in different directions, jump, hop, skip, gallop in place, play Simon Says.

10. Beginning skill-building activities—for example, ring toss, basketball, softball, tennis, roller skating, ice skating, bowling.

Summary

When educators accept children as active, natural learners, they will recognize the power and the potential of play as a primary conduit for development. Since play is so essential to childhood, an early childhood program must be designed from the perspective of the child. Through imaginative and creative play experiences, the child develops self awareness, social competence, and a disposition for learning. In the process of playing, the child is learning. He is forming ideas, applying principles, and testing himself. He is gradually shaping his personality and identifying his interests. Secure in himself and nurtured by his environment, the young child at play is establishing a lifelong foundation for learning.

NOTES

1. J. Levy, *Play Behavior* (New York: Wiley, 1978).
2. Catherine Garvey, *Play* (Cambridge, MA: Harvard University Press, 1990), p. 4.
3. Carlina Rinaldi, "The Emergent Curriculum and Social Constructivism," in *The Hundred Languages of Children*, eds., Carolyn Edwards, Lella Gandini, and George Forman (Norwood, NJ: Ablex, 1995), p. 108.
4. Teresita E. Aguilar, "Social and Environmental Barriers to Playfulness," in *When Children Play*, eds., Joe L. Frost and Sylvia Sunderlin (Wheaton, MD: ACEI, 1985), p. 76.
5. Greta G. Fein, "Play with Actions and Objects," in *Play and Learning*, ed., Brian Sutton-Smith (New York: Gardner, 1979), pp. 69–82.
6. S. Rogers Cosby and Janet K. Sawyers, *Play in the Lives of Children* (Washington, DC: NAEYC, 1988), p. 73.
7. Brian Sutton-Smith, "Play Research: State of the Art," in *When Children Play*, eds., Joe L. Frost and Sylvia Sunderlin (Wheaton, MD: ACEI, 1988), p. 13.
8. Jean Piaget, *Play, Dreams, and Imitation in Childhood* (New York: Norton, 1962).
9. Patricia Monighan-Nourot, Barbara Scales, Judith Van Hoorn with Millie Almy, *Looking at Children's Play: A Bridge Between Theory and Practice* (New York: Teachers College Press, Columbia University, 1987), p. 83.
10. Eric H. Erikson, *Childhood and Society* (New York: Norton, 1950).

11. R. Gould, *Child Studies Through Fantasy: Cognitive–Affective Patterns in Development* (New York: Quadrangle Books, 1972).
12. As cited in Laura E. Berk, in *Child Development* (Boston, MA: Allyn and Bacon, 1989), p. 222.
13. As cited in P. Monighan-Nourot et al., *Looking at Children's Play*, p. 22.
14. Ibid., p. 23.
15. Berk, "Cognitive Development," p. 235.
16. As cited in Dorothy G. Singer and Jerome L. Singer, *The House of Make-Believe* (Cambridge, MA: Harvard University Press, 1990), p. 40.
17. Monighan-Nourot et al., *Looking at Children's Play*, p. 24.
18. Singer and Singer, *The House of Make-Believe*, p. 65.
19. Greta G. Fein, "Pretend Play in Childhood: An Integrative Review," *Child Development*, 52 (1981): 1095–1118.
20. A. D. Pellegrini, "The Relationships Between Kindergartners' Play and Achievement in Prereading, Language, and Writing." *Psychology in the Schools*, 17 (1989): 530–35.
21. As cited in Rosalyn Saltz and Eli Saltz, "Pretend Play Training and Its Outcomes," in *The Young Child at Play*, eds., Greta Fein and Mary Rivkin (Washington, DC: NAEYC, 1986), p. 157.
22. Greta G. Fein and Shirley S. Schwartz, "The Social Coordination of Pretense in Preschool Children," in *The Young Child at Play*, eds., Greta Fein and Mary Rivkin (Washington, DC: NAEYC, 1986), p. 95.
23. Singer and Singer, *The House of Make-Believe*, p. 138.
24. As cited in Saltz and Saltz, "Pretend Play Training and Its Outcome," pp. 157–58.
25. Russell Firlik, "Can We Adapt the Philosophies and Practices of Reggio Emilia, Italy, for Use in American Schools?" *Early Childhood Education Journal* 23(4) (1996): 217.
26. Evelyn Weber, *Ideas Influencing Early Childhood Education* (New York: Teachers College Press, 1984), p. 208.
27. Singer and Singer, *The House of Make-Believe*, pp. 151–52.
28. Lella Gandini, "Not Just Anywhere: Making Child Care Centers into Particular Places," *Child Care Information Exchange* (March 1994): 48.
29. Christine Chaille and Steven B. Silvern, "Understanding Through Play," *Childhood Education* (Annual Theme, 1996): 277.
30. As cited in Berk, "Cognitive Development," p. 256.
31. Anthony D. Pellegrini, "Communicating in and about Play: The Effect of Play Centers on Preschoolers' Explicit Language," in *The Young Child at Play*, eds., Greta Fein and Mary Rivkin (Washington, DC: NAEYC, 1986), pp. 79–82.
32. As cited in Dr. Richard Sinatra, "The Arts as a Vehicle for Thinking," *Early Years* 16(7) (March 1986): 56.
33. Clare Cherry, *Creative Play for the Developing Child* (Belmont, CA: David S. Lake Publishers, 1976), pp. 14–15.
34. Ibid., p. 52.
35. As cited in Carol Vukelich, "Where's the Paper, Literacy during Dramatic Play," *Childhood Education* 66(4) (Summer 1990): 209.

CHAPTER

4 Learning

*Contemporary research confirms the view that young children learn most
effectively when they are engaged in interaction rather than in merely
receptive or passive activities. Young children should be interacting with
adults, materials, and their surroundings in ways which help them make sense
of their own experience and environment. They should be investigating and
observing aspects of their environment worth learning about, and recording
their findings and observations through talk, paintings, and drawings.
Interaction that arises in the course of such activities provides a context for
much social and cognitive learning.*

—Lilian G. Katz

Section I: Creating a Learning Environment

Learning is the cumulative process through which children gradually acquire skills and knowledge and apply them to gain understanding about themselves and their environment. It is during the journey from skill and knowledge acquisition to understanding about themselves and their world that children's personalities and dispositions are shaped.

Children acquire knowledge *incidentally* and *directly* as they interact with an environment. Most learning takes place incidentally as the child makes contact with and responds to the people and the objects that are constant and important to his world. The understandings that children develop through sustained interactions with an environment become the baseline for constructing knowledge.

Developing a Foundation for Learning

As children continue to gain knowledge through experience, they become increasingly interested in and motivated toward their surrounding world. The faces, the attitudes, and the consistent presence of nurturing adults in their lives provides a baseline for a child's development, identity, and social maturation. Teachers nurture a child's readiness for learning by providing for her meaningful interactions that challenge thinking while satisfying a continuing need for support and love.

Children's potential for learning is elevated when they are interacting with adults, materials, and their surroundings in meaningful and satisfying ways. A child who feels good about herself and her accomplishments or near accomplishments will gradually view learning as a lifelong process. The time to cultivate a foundation for learning is in the early years of development when children are receptive and responsive to their relationships and experiences.

The Developing Child

An environment that stimulates the natural learner in every child reveals children who can apply themselves to tasks requiring persistence and concentration. An environment conducive to learning is a challenging one with abundant opportunities for open-ended experiences. Children who test, construct, and are willing to extend themselves are practicing readiness. Animated by their own resourcefulness and creative energy, children become disposed toward learning and motivated to its pursuit.

In a challenging environment that offers open-ended, minimally structured experiences, children naturally *invest in* and *shape* their own learning. They assume the role of young explorers, seeking and finding new challenges. In the process, they are creating a disposition for learning that extends far beyond an activity center or a single experience. In the process of learning about an environment, a child is learning about himself.

As children become immersed in their environment, they experience the excitement of mastering skills and crafting solutions to the problems they experience and confront. Some of the simplest childhood play, like riding a tricycle, becomes an important learning experience when viewed in this way. The child's learning does not cease when he masters riding a tricycle. It continues as he learns to maneuver it through backyard play traffic, reading the signs that cause him to stop, go, and slow down. In so doing, he sets goals, recognizes barriers, plots alternatives, overcomes obstacles, and feels achievement. He has absorbed a range of sensory information and applied it to make the simple motor and complex symbolic decisions necessary to learning. The more a child works out problems, the more adept he becomes at innovative thinking and self-management—for instance, he reroutes traffic or organizes a tricycle wash.

A Community of Learning

A theory of childhood that exalts the image and potential of young children encourages a community of learning. In a community of learning such as the Reggio Emilia system, children are connected to their environment through a philosophy and love of learning. A dynamic of social interaction reinforces collegiality and bonds a group. When people are connected, they are less likely to feel intimidated by challenge or competition. In an open community, teachers seek dialogue and welcome debate. The system is organized around the *centrality* of children that is commonly shared by teachers and families.[1] It is difficult to conceive of working with the whole child without giving equal attention to the wholeness or *oneness* of an environment.

How Teachers Cultivate Learning

The more we learn about intelligence through brain research, the more crucial the role of today's early childhood teacher is. We know that early education and nurturing have a decisive impact on how children develop and on their ability to learn. By age three, the brains of children are two and a half times more active than the brains of adults—and they remain that way throughout the first decade of life. We know that quality care and security of attachment affect children's later capacity for empathy, for emotional regulation, and behavioral control.[2] Teaching to the whole child requires a thoughtful, carefully constructed curriculum that fully engages and challenges the fertile mind of the young child as well as the creative energies of a teacher. For new insights into early childhood development, see Rima Shore, *Rethinking the Brain,* Families and Work Institute, 1997.

Extending Freedom

In *Freedom to Learn*, Carl Rogers suggests that the goal of education is not teaching but the facilitation of learning.[3] Teachers who facilitate learning concentrate on providing resources and opportunities that provoke learning *within* the child. They encourage children to develop understandings through active investigation and exploration. When a mind is alert and engaged, children begin to develop intuitive understandings about their world. Children can be motivated to actively construct learning through their own resources. In the process, they begin to think in terms of wholes rather than parts. When a child perceives relationships between objects and processes, he intuitively begins to apply reasoning and to grow toward wider immediate explanations and solutions to a wider level of comprehension and knowledge.

Instilling a Sense of Wonder

Young children who experience a sense of wonder in their everyday environments are eager knowledge seekers and learners. Loris Malaguzzi suggests that creativity accompanies knowledge in the world of the young child. "It is permissible to think that creativity, or rather knowledge and the wonder of knowledge (our most important right, which so often goes unrecognized) can serve as the strong point of our work. It is thus our continuing hope that creativity will become a normal traveling companion in our children's growth and development."[4] Malaguzzi does not believe that creativity is a separate mental faculty, but a characteristic of our knowledge and the choices we make as we interact with our world.

Teaching the Whole Child

An open learning environment challenges children to think creatively, to make observations, to identify and solve problems, and to test out their own theories. Young children are surprisingly adept in decision making and problem solving. They arrive at solutions by experimenting with objects and by observing one another at play. An open learning environment provides opportunities for children to practice independent thinking through cooperative interactions.

In a whole-child environment a teacher creates a context for learning by:

- Promoting an environment that encourages communication as a natural and important facilitator for learning
- Encouraging children to focus on a task and complete it
- Encouraging children to feel satisfied with their effort
- Encouraging children to develop learning dispositions amenable to trial and error and reflection
- Helping children accept challenge and even criticism as an inevitable part of growing up

- Encouraging children to challenge themselves by experimenting with new ideas and by trying new experiences
- Encouraging children to perceive knowledge not as a contest or a goal but as an integral aspect of growing up
- Encouraging children to be open minded and flexible in their attitude, in their relationships, and in their thinking

Training Children in Life Skills

A primary goal of teachers in child care environments is to nurture and train children to become responsive and responsible adults—the kinds of people who can use their resources to fulfill their aspirations and to benefit others. These qualities are planted in the early years. What are the attributes we would like to see transmitted into adulthood and how do they relate to learning? Early childhood educators and authors, Susan D. Shilcock and Peter A. Bergson, define the skills that create an ideal adult as:

1. The ability to make reasoned choices and decisions to enhance individual goals as well as society's interests.
2. The ability to look at problems from different perspectives, to make new connections, and to develop fresh solutions to old problems.
3. The ability to think clearly and to speak without fear of criticism.
4. The motivation to observe the world as it is, to question and to challenge, to explore, to speculate, and to invent.
5. A positive sense of self that is able to nurture others.
6. The ability to use resources at hand to solve daily problems and create new opportunities.
7. The willingness to use natural resources prudently to build toward our collective survival.[5]

As children continue to gain knowledge, they are increasingly interested in their surrounding world. As their interests expand, their thinking expands. As they begin to see themselves in relation to others, they want to do more and learn more. Specific skills (increments of learning) are developed through training, practice, and motivation. Children learn to read and write, to play a piano, and to master a handstand. They also continue to gain information on a higher level by developing concepts (organizing and categorizing information) and by expanding their knowledge (exercising reflection, reasoning, problem solving). The degree of success a child experiences as she progresses through levels of learning will affect her attitude and motivation. A person who feels good about herself and her accomplishments will view learning as a *lifelong* process—a pursuit that reaffirms and gives meaning to experiences. The time to cultivate and nurture learning is in early childhood.

Establishing Relationships

If we accept learning as primarily an interactional, cumulative process between a child and an environment, then we must assume that a child's experiences will significantly influence the quality and rate of his learning. If a child experiences early success in most aspects of his development, he will continue to build his base of knowledge. A child experiences success through active and positive contact with his physical and human environment. A parent and a teacher play primary roles in a child's development. Without adults to help him interpret, organize, and order his world, a child has less opportunity to develop his potential. It is the adult who designs an environment so that it is conducive to learning, and it is the adult who encourages a child toward competency. In order to accomplish and master tasks, the child must take risks and on occasion, experience failure. He needs to understand that not everything is easy and that not everything is hard; that slowly, with patience, he will arrive at a healthy balance between the two. A caring adult will help a child deal with obstacles, frustrations, and disappointments. She will praise his progress and his near-progress. She will encourage him to try again, to go further, to break through self-imposed boundaries. It is through *interpersonal* relationships with adults that a child discovers more about himself.

The qualities described by Shilcock and Bergson are rooted in an open, *idea-centered* environment: one that encourages children to think and apply reason to their play/work. To test their environment (and themselves), children must feel inwardly confident and trusting. Children's development requires, above all, continuity and stability. A change in an environment can cause a decline in momentum, create confusion, and alter a child's perception of learning.

The importance of security as an element in early childhood education cannot be overestimated. A toddler or two-year-old is still at a dependent stage of seeking and needing continued nurturing and constancy in an environment. Child care centers should provide consistency in an environment for the first two years of development in order for the young child to develop attachments and relationships with primary adults.

Valuing Play

A quality environment promotes learning by providing children with a carefully designed environment consistent with its philosophy of learning through constructive play. In a whole-child environment, children's attitudinal and cognitive development is directly related to the quality of an environment. Self-initiated and cooperative play opportunities are available to children in activity centers. Activity centers promote learning by enabling children to make choices and experiment with their environment in an atmosphere of freedom. Children are free to choose from a range of activities that are organized by content, identified by their surrounding space, and developed according to appropriate age-level themes and interests.

Self-Initiated Learning through Play

Children learn skills through spontaneous play that promotes curiosity, exploration, and active learning. When children play, they learn incidentally as they interact with objects, materials, and playmates. They experiment with ideas and objects in imaginative and thoughtful ways. As they process information, they make discoveries and predictions.

In a block center, a child observes the effect of varying heights of an inclined plane on the speed and distance of objects (small vehicles). He has constructed a ramp by stacking square blocks and elevating a block to facilitate movement. By raising the ramp (adding one more block), he discovers he can change the velocity. Another child may use flannel shapes to create an imaginary story. She experiments with the arrangement of shapes until she creates a pattern that pleases her. Still another child may ask a teacher to assist her in making a balance scale. Together they discuss the idea and the materials needed to construct the project. The child decides to use a string and a piece of wood as the fulcrum and two small plastic containers glued together as weights. The teacher continues to support the child's initiative by suggesting that they find items to test out the scale: acorns, plastic spoons, block cubes, buttons. Lawrence Frank describes the process at work within the child as:

> A conception of play that recognizes the significance of autonomous, self-directed learning and active exploration and manipulation of the actual world gives a promising approach to the wholesome development of children.... It is a way to translate into the education of children our long-cherished, enduring goal values, a belief in the worth of the individual personalities, and a genuine respect for the dignity and integrity of the children.[6]

A child who can function effectively on his own is developing competency through internal controls. He understands that freedom connotes responsibility and self-management. Because he is self-motivated, the child can play for a long period of time and is not easily distracted by surrounding activities; he has his own play agenda. As he plays, he is processing and assimilating ideas to add to his growing repertoire of knowledge.

Cooperative Learning through Play

Children also learn through cooperative play. When children interact with peers at play or in group activities, they extend their interest, curiosity, and ideas. They develop greater levels of awareness and sensitivity to the interplay and importance of human interaction and resourcefulness. They become more tolerant and patient in order to sustain and deepen friendships. Best friendships do not just happen—they progress through mutual accommodation and support. As children develop social skills, they broaden their cultural base and cognitive awareness. As they listen, observe, and identify with peers, they become sensitive to a wider, more complex world—a world far beyond a block center or a language center.

They extend their base of knowledge to incorporate new information and attitudes. Developing positive social skills and relationships is invaluable to the learning process, especially when children are exposed to a diverse, multicultural environment. As children begin to identify with others, they make adjustments in their patterns of thinking and behavior. They begin to see value in discussing and supporting the ideas of others. An autonomous child will adjust what she sees or hears to what she knows. The child understands that she still has the capacity to make choices and to exercise her autonomy. Influenced by peers, however, in a pro-social, value-conscious environment, she can now make decisions from a broader level of understanding.

The Importance of Early Training

Training is an essential responsibility in nurturing and educating the young child. Without firm guidelines and mutual understandings there can be little harmony and order. Early behavioral training provides the emotional foundation to ensure a child's well-being, disposition for learning, and love of people.

Early cognitive training provides the foundation for life skills and competencies. It is the adult who sets the stage for learning and who *guides* the child through the learning process. Guidance is not instructing; it is a *process* that generates self-directed learning and higher levels of awareness. In the process, a teacher extends learning by providing opportunities and an environment that promotes thinking and problem solving. In an atmosphere that values self-initiated learning, children are given time to complete tasks. Children develop thinking skills when they are able to extend and apply their knowledge in both *practical* and *inventive* ways. A child needs to understand the consequences of not buttoning a coat on a cold day and she needs to learn the classroom routines that encourage self-management. A teacher encourages early learning by doing the following:

- Providing many opportunities for children to work with materials and equipment in innovative ways
- Encouraging novelty and improvisation in thinking and problem-solving strategies
- Providing open-ended materials for children to contemplate, manipulate, and interact with
- Engaging children in verbal exchanges that generate thinking by soliciting ideas, asking questions, and affirming children's ideas and interests
- Encouraging children to evaluate their own work
- Encouraging children to connect ideas, analyze, and resolve discrepancies
- Surprising children with the unexpected; with unplanned experiences that trigger excitement and inquiry
- Instilling in children a sense of wonder and curiosity

Promoting Thinking

In a learning environment, children are challenged to question and to make predictions. Do you think it will rain today? I wonder what will happen if we mix these colors together? Something has been changed in this room; can anyone guess what is different? What story would you like to listen to? As children learn to become competent and capable thinkers, they learn to respect the opinions of others, to question and evaluate information, and to discover new ways of thinking.

"Thinking," according to John Barrell of New Jersey's Montclair State College, "is a process of searching for and creating meaning involving the mind's creations—symbols, metaphors, analogies—in an attempt to establish relationships between the world of particulars and the ideas and concepts that give them structure."[7] At the early stages of development, a prelude to thinking is *awareness*. When children develop awareness, they begin to discriminate and reason. Teaching for awareness is more important than teaching for basic skill development. Most children learn skills naturally, but they may not develop thinking and reasoning without external stimuli and training. To teach for awareness is to challenge children to think and to communicate their thoughts.

Barbara Z. Presseisen's model of essential thinking skills identifies "levels of thinking as: *qualification* (finding unique characteristics), *classification* (determining common qualities), *relationships* (detecting regular operations), *transformation* (relating known to unknown, creating new meanings), and *causation* (establishing cause and effect, interpretation, prediction; forecasting)."[8]

Examples of the first level (qualification) might include identifying parts of a body, shapes, or familiar objects. Games such as "What Is Missing?" that require children to identify missing parts (a squirrel's tail or whiskers on a mouse) will stimulate thinking. Examples of the second level (classification) might include sorting, sets, or comparisons. Children might sort blocks by color and size; they may classify food, musical instruments, or play objects by sorting and placement. They would need to understand the common characteristics and use of objects before they can classify them. Examples of the third level (relationships) might include activities that promote sequencing, patterning (part to whole), and discrimination. A child might put sequence cards in order (the apple, making a pie, oven, eating), order beads by their color pattern (what comes next), or identify objects that don't go together.

The fourth level (transformation) involves recognizing analogies and developing concepts. Examples of this level might include children playing word games that show relationships between objects that are physically different but are identified with one another (root is to tree as bottle is to baby as hat is to head); or developing generalizations by categorizing objects found in the water, on land, and in the air. Examples of the fifth level (causation) may include predicting the aftermath of a hurricane or discussing the effects of ocean currents and tides on shorelines and sea life.

Children enjoy brainstorming. Children who express themselves openly are responsive to the thoughts of others. They can discuss the pros and cons of changing a room, of implementing a behavior policy, or of selecting one field trip instead of another. The object of brainstorming is to reach consensus through open dialogue. It is a healthy way for children to express their ideas and feelings without being intimidated or criticized. This should begin at the earliest stages of development: How should we dress our weather girl today? Who can remember what she wore yesterday?

Promoting Problem Solving

Finding out how to do things and solving problems are the tasks of childhood. A classroom must be organized and arranged to maximize problem solving through hands-on experiences. In a prepared, child-centered environment, children develop organizational skills that help them channel and direct their thinking. They apply themselves to a task, making decisions as they work; they set goals and self-evaluate. They take responsibility for outcomes when they are in charge of and committed to a task. What could I have done differently? How do I feel about this grade? What are the consequences? How important is it to organize materials, to set goals, and to self-evaluate—to accept responsibility?

Problem solving is *central* to the thinking processes. In order to solve a problem, children need time to formulate and test ideas. Materials to stimulate thinking include items like a magnifying glass, containers, a sieve, a water table, charts, notebooks, markers, a thermometer, terrariums, growing things, simple machines, a balance scale, discrimination cards, sensory materials, a hammer and nails, string, and blocks of wood.

Children are natural problem solvers while they play. They define a problem by trial and error—moving and changing things until there is an acceptable fit. If a car is too large to go through a block tunnel, a child must find a smaller car or make a wider tunnel. If a baby doll is too big for a carriage, a child will have to find another vehicle (a wheelbarrow, a wagon, a shopping cart). When children realize there is a problem, they evaluate options and think about solutions. They develop a plan and carry it out. In the process, they become resourceful and capable learners.

As children mature, they begin to experiment with problem solving from a social perspective. Time is spent developing and affirming relationships. Interpersonal relationships require different and, in many ways, more demanding levels of communication. Children must learn to accommodate others by adjusting their attitudes and patterns of behavior. Relationships require active listening and *decentering* (taking the perspective of others). Some children lack the maturity required for meaningful sustained interaction. Their perceptions are influenced or distorted by what they have experienced. Reciprocity in social relationships comes slowly for children who are not trained and reinforced in cooperative play at an early age.

Children solve problems by making choices. They think through alternatives and give up something when they make a choice. Children can begin making choices at an early age. They can choose whether they want to swing forward or backward, and whether they want to slide sitting up, lying down, or on their tummies. They can choose a swing mate or a see-saw mate; they can select digging objects for a sandbox, and the songs they choose to sing as they play. Children can choose a snack (I would like raisins, I'd rather not have juice), select their clothes (choices should be limited), their books, their outings, their lunch, and many of their activities.

By giving children choices on a basic operational level, teachers are preparing them for problem solving on a more complex level. A child who must decide whether to play indoors with one friend or outdoors with another friend has a difficult choice to make. What she would like to do is to persuade both friends to play indoors. Because this is not an option, the child must make a difficult decision. John Dewey viewed thinking and problem solving as interconnected aspects of a child's total development. He defined the process as:

1. Becoming aware of a problem (Someone else is using the hammer that I want!)
2. Clarifying and defining the problem (What must I do to solve the problem? I can't connect the wings to the body without that hammer.)
3. Searching for facts and formulating a hypothesis (If I use something equally strong like a block or a pan, I can complete the task.)
4. Evaluating proposed solutions (The block is stronger than the pan but is it as strong as the hammer?)
5. Experimental verification (It works! I got the nail in!)[9]

Promoting Decision Making

When a child makes a decision, she determines the best response among alternatives that are available to her. Before making a decision, a child must think about consequences. An overweight child must think about choosing ice cream with or without sprinkles. Another child must think about the consequences of not inviting a friend to a birthday party. Decision making can create conflict and stress in children, especially when they are not clear about alternatives or are uncertain about their ability to make appropriate decisions. Often children make decisions adults are not comfortable with. Consequently, a decision may become so diluted by parental influence that children feel confused ("You can do it if you want to, but I think you're making a mistake").

Children need to be given fewer options until they are better able to make appropriate choices (choose between two garments rather than selecting from a closet full of clothes). Decision making also can be taught by giving children the opportunity to exercise judgment. Would you wear a sweater on a cold day? Why or why not? Would you pick shiny shoes if you were playing on bars? What might happen? Do you think Janie should have crossed the street by herself? Why or why not? What information do we have about Janie before we make a judgment—for example, how old is Janie, is she allowed to cross streets, did she cross at a corner, how busy is the street, was she cautious? Children soon understand that some choices are easy and fun (like choosing a flavor of ice cream) and others are not so easy (like solving a problem). If parents and teachers *guide* children in decision-making strategies, children will feel autonomous without feeling frustrated or confused. Gradually children will solve their own problems because they have the resources and the confidence to make decisions. Educator Barry K. Beyer has identified the skills involved in decision making as:

- Defining the goal
- Identifying obstacles to achieving the goal
- Identifying alternatives
- Analyzing alternatives
- Ranking alternatives
- Choosing the best alternative[10]

Becoming Flexible and Creative Thinkers

A creative person is an imaginative, inventive person. *Creativity* is identified with fluency (producing many ideas), flexibility (producing unusual ideas), originality (producing unique ideas), and elaboration (adding detail to the ideas).[11] Creative thinking is generated in a process-oriented environment that encourages self-expression. A child who is not hurried through an activity is able to connect ideas and to think about the various choices and combinations that may be used in its development. He is practicing divergent thinking when he can look at his project from several perspectives and points of view. As he progresses in a task, he will naturally make changes and evaluate his work. A child will be enterprising and imaginative in the way he applies himself to a task at hand. Susan D. Shilcock and Peter A. Bergson identify flexible, creative thinking as the:

- Ability to change
- Ability to look at ideas and situations from different perspectives
- Ability to make connections among apparently unrelated ideas
- Ability to think about an idea, take a piece of it, and shape it into a novel solution
- Willingness to experiment and take risks without being preoccupied with other people's opinions
- Ability to create new combinations of objects and ideas
- Willingness to question assumptions and to reach past their apparent boundaries[12]

Developing Concepts

Concepts are a collection of experiences or ideas that contain common attributes. They naturally evolve in an integrated, idea-centered curriculum. As children play, they gather, analyze, and process information. They identify attributes as they organize, sort, and store familiar items. Children label items by the words that describe and identify their characteristics. Gradually they sift through and organize data in terms of meaning and association. Children develop concepts through direct experiences that encourage them to connect ideas. An integrated environment extends the ideas that eventually become concepts. For example, a child develops a concept of water by direct experience (playing in water), by experimenting (with evaporation, water vapor, condensation, and precipitation), and by integrating knowledge (playing in a stream). She will soon learn to distinguish a pond from a river, a river from an ocean, and the kinds of life that inhabit each environment.

A good way to develop concepts is to organize a learning activity around a theme such as food. Under the broad category of food, children can begin to develop an understanding of the basic food groups: meat and meat alternatives, vegetables and fruits, breads and cereals, and dairy products. They can talk about healthy eating habits, the nutritional value of food, and how food arrives at a supermarket and can culminate the activity by making a concept web (see Figure 4.1).

Promoting Organization

A carefully designed learning environment will offer a child sufficient choices to stimulate curiosity and imaginative play through individual and group experiences. It will define spaces and activities so that children can play independently.

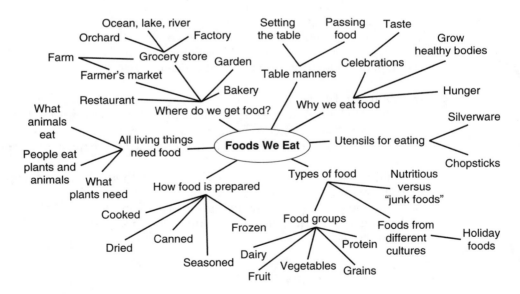

FIGURE 4.1   Concept Web for "Foods We Eat"

Source: From *Educationally Appropriate Kindergarten Practices,* copyright 1991, National Education Association. Reprinted with permission.

Children react to how a center looks and feels. The more personalized and interesting a center looks to a child, the more she will want to explore it. As children play independently, they learn to identify objects by their placement and attributes: A magnifying glass is located in a science center, a record is in a listening center, and a book is in a media center. When children perceive order, they connect objects with a specific environment that complements their function. They understand that objects have properties and purpose. A creative child will move objects and use them innovatively at play, but will continue to perceive them as members of a unit commonly called *activity centers*, for example, a block center, a manipulative play center, an arts center.

Developing Perception

Perception is a sense of awareness that causes children to react or respond to an environment in a personal way. Children derive meaning from experiences that stimulate their senses. They develop impressions or understandings from their total surroundings—smells, textures, appearance, and activities. Children's awareness can be increased by providing a large variety of experiences inside and outside of the classroom. Children develop insight through daily hands-on experiences that capture and hold their attention. They begin to distinguish between indoor and outdoor play, and they begin to identify certain activities with moods and feelings: play time, rest time, and snack time.

Awareness is centered in sensory experiences; the more children can touch, taste, smell, listen to, and ingest, the more sensitive they will become to the nuances that create and define an environment. Awareness leads to discovery, self-understanding, and creative thinking. Teachers should point out or suggest ideas to children at appropriate times, but they should encourage children to extract their own meaning from each experience. Young children need ongoing exposure to visual, auditory, and tactile stimuli. They need to look, to listen, and to touch as much as possible. Children benefit from sensory experiences that inspire curiosity and generate imagination. They need to try new ways of doing things, to open their minds to creative thinking and attitudes.

Encouraging Critical Thinking

Children use higher levels of thinking when they begin to connect ideas, analyze, and resolve discrepancies. Higher levels of thinking in early childhood include the following: reflection, asking questions, making generalizations (a child belongs to a human family; a cat belongs to an animal family), expanding ideas (making a chart of probable members in each category), and extending learning (comparing how families live to how animals live). As children begin to challenge assumptions, they no longer accept simple explanations as truisms. They sift through information, applying their own logic and insight to their base of knowledge. If children are able to exercise their thinking in a social context, their ideas become more fluent and less predictable or conventional.

As children challenge each other in open dialogue, they learn strategies that activate thinking capabilities: "It doesn't go that way, I can show you how it goes." They enjoy analyzing a problem from several perspectives: "Why don't we make one go this way and one go that way?" To persuade others, a child must have an idea, be able to express the idea, and motivate his listener.

Making Discoveries

Children need both spontaneous and directed experiences in order to stretch their imaginations and develop competencies. Education is more than the acquisition of knowledge; it is learning how knowledge can be used. As much as possible, children should use their intuitive reflective resources through self-initiated activities. For example, a child may save a pumpkin seed to plant outdoors; he may bury it in a dry, shallow hole and remember to put a little stone nearby so he can find it again. He'll water the plant for a few days but after a while, the child will forget about it until one day he happens to see a green sprout in the vicinity of the pumpkin seed. The sprout may be a summer weed, but to the child, it will trigger a memory of the pumpkin seed planted a long time ago. The child has made a discovery. When he later reads a story about a pumpkin vine, he will identify with the experience with the slimy seed in a moist hand, the feeling of dirt, and the excitement of a fall day.

Stretching Minds

Children also need exposure to ideas and materials that will engage thinking processes and communication skills. At times, a teacher will assume the role of initiator. On these occasions, she will introduce ideas and stimulate the learner to reason and make observations. Children might plant seeds (and experiment with placement), make shadows (and observe what happens to a shadow as it moves away from the light), examine a puddle (and chart its gradual disappearance), experience the wind (by blowing on a milkweed pod), or study the social patterns of ants (by observing and recording the activities of an ant colony). Or, a teacher may initiate conversation with a child who is sailing a paper boat in a basin of water: "I see your paper boat is floating in the water. I wonder what would happen if you put three marbles in your boat. What about six marbles?" If the child demonstrates interest in the teacher's inquiry, she would test the marbles and observe for herself what happens. The teacher may gather other materials to experiment with, pointing out that some things float and some things sink: "I wonder why?" In the process of discovering, the child may expand a concept by making a larger boat. By providing incentives for children to act on, they will become motivated to learn.

Section II: An Educational Program for Early Childhood

Children learn most effectively when they interact with people and materials in an environment that is carefully organized to facilitate learning. Children develop foundational skills and concepts through play, learning, creative development, and relationships within their environment. A knowledge of child development enables a teacher to integrate learning across a curriculum. A whole-child environment stresses the importance of the integration of knowledge through the continuity of experiences during a child's early years. Teachers nurture readiness when they guide discovery by providing many pathways for children to explore in their own way and in their own time. Teachers must insure that children are given foundational experiences in basic content areas: science, math, language, as well as knowledge of their greater world (social studies).

Teaching Science Readiness

Children do not have to be taught to become young explorers but they do need encouragement and guidance. A two-year-old can find the right place for a shell (in a science center), a five-year-old can sort multiple objects (shells, pinecones, pebbles) by common attributes. Through incidental play and interactions with materials, children discover and test their physical space. They identify a science center with sensory experiences because there is much to touch, ponder, and enjoy. In a place of wonder and imagination, children develop a "let's find out" mentality.

Science blends into and reinforces math, creative thinking, the arts, and literature. There are numerous opportunities for developing process skills and basic content in a discovery environment. Children can learn through direct experience by visiting nature centers and parks, and by becoming aware of their own back yard. They can exchange language by identifying animals, wildlife, and the many features of their natural world. They can go exploring marking trails and making maps to facilitate a safe return. They can chart growth cycles, study motion, and predict the weather. Young children "get into" an exploration mode by becoming young explorers.

The Scientific Method

There are many commonalities between science and math that suggest the wisdom of a combined approach, particularly at the early childhood level. Both disciplines require basic process and thinking skills that are developed through the scientific method. Both are enhanced by a discovery method of teaching and learning. An early childhood program can successfully integrate the two by setting up centers that are integrally connected by materials, methods, and tasks. A child will use science functions when he plants an indoor garden and math functions when he charts its growth.

In a discovery environment, the child is an active explorer, seeking experiences that attract his attention and extend his thinking. A child's laboratory for learning is any space that absorbs and challenges a child; a child's learning field is as wide as his opportunities and interests. Children are born with an instinct to explore and discover why, and how, things work. To develop in-depth understandings about their natural and physical world, they must practice the skills that are basic to the scientific process. To become young scientists, children must have experiences and activities that enlighten and challenge their minds and that test their capabilities.

Observation and Investigation

When children make observations, they are focusing on an activity that holds their interest. They are noticing physical characteristics, texture, shape, function, and prospects for play. Nature's gifts that often go unnoticed by adults are treasures to children. A child observes with acumen. She finds that tiny seeds, shells, and rocks are fascinating items to feel, observe, and play with. She uses them in imaginative ways that challenge her teachers. Ideally, a child should have an opportunity to extend his learning beyond the playground through follow-up activities in a discovery center (observing a snail shell under a magnifying glass).

A teacher can instill a child with the desire to learn by arousing interest in experimentation. He may open a lima bean, talk about the purpose of its embryo, experiment with germination, and discuss its uses. He may bring in seashells for a child to examine, pointing out how ocean tides and currents change shells and shorelines. A teacher may encourage a child to start a personal rock collection; the child may begin by categorizing and labeling rocks. In the process, the child begins to understand at a basic level how some rocks come from volcanic eruptions (igneous rocks such as granite) and some from erosion (sedimentary rocks such as limestone). The teacher encourages the child *to question* and *to extend knowledge beyond* the classroom. He shares the child's interest with parents, suggesting ideas for follow-up activities (visiting a nature center, a quarry, or any water environment), hoping that a child's interest will become a parent's interest.

Sorting and Classifying Information

When children classify items, they collect and organize by attributes and by items that naturally go together. Math and science skills are integrated when children compare and contrast, group, count, solve problems, and as they interact with materials and objects. Children begin to see math and science as a whole integrated discovery process. They arrange objects from nature by making sets (a collection of objects with similar or identical characteristics) arranged in a discovery box.

Children use math and science skills as they compare a set of three acorns to a set of five pinecones using words like *more, less, equal,* and *unequal.* They discuss the concept of quantity and decide how many acorns are needed to make the sets equivalent. A curious child soon learns that a set with the same elements is equal while a set with the same number of members, but not with the same members, is equivalent. They extend their knowledge by matching (making the part equal) and labeling sets of leaves and by creating empty sets (by removing all the objects). They match numbers to objects and they can look for sets in their classroom, such as tools, dishes, musical instruments, markers, coins.

Testing and Predicting

When children experiment with materials and objects, they naturally begin to problem solve. They want to figure out how much water to put on a plant, how to measure temperature, how to be certain all the eggs are turned in an incubator every day, and how to determine what leaves to avoid touching on a nature outing. To solve problems, they must gather information and formulate a hypothesis (if I do this, then this will happen). By observing different kinds of clouds and climatic conditions, a child can predict rain. By mixing colors, a child can predict a new color; by freezing water, a child can predict its change in volume and shape. By experimenting with vibration, a child can produce sounds and predict sound volume (loose strings vibrate at a lower frequency than tight strings).

Documenting and Recording Data

Assisted by a teacher, young children can record and chart discoveries that take place in one day or over a period of time. A simple method of record keeping might include a date, a purpose, a process, findings, and illustrations. The following could be a written example: "Today we learned about fossils. A fossil is something that is dug out of the earth like a leaf print or an animal print that has been preserved in a stone. Fossils tell us about life on earth many, many years ago. Today we made a print of a fern in clay that looked like a fossil. Tomorrow we will dig for fossils in our backyard." Children can record the growth of seeds or plants by measuring and observing changes. Simple picture graphs that compare findings or visual experiences can be displayed in a discovery center (leaves, wildflowers, worms, insects, birds): "Today's Observations: 2 cardinals, 1 robin, and 1 bluejay." "These are the leaves we found today: 6 oak leaves, 4 maple leaves, and 2 magnolia leaves."

Making Generalizations

As children broaden their base of understanding and knowledge, they begin to make generalizations. Concepts develop as children proceed from concrete to abstract thinking. They are able to distinguish between living and nonliving objects and their natural and physical world. They can identify animals, plants, and insects as well as concepts of energy, astronomy, and weather. They are able to perceive life as cyclical and changing and begin to understand the interrelationships between organisms and their environments. They begin to perceive water not just as a drink or a puddle but as a vital life-sustaining element that is all-encompassing. They begin to perceive themselves in relation to their whole environment, identifying themselves as important actors in the continuance and preservation of the environment.

Evaluating One's Progress

By evaluating outcomes, children discover better ways of doing things and become more demanding of themselves. If an experiment doesn't work, a teacher can help a child to understand why. The scientific process is, by its very nature, an open-ended system that challenges children to try things. Trial-and-error learning that promotes critical thinking can begin at a very simple level of making choices and observing and by experiencing consequences. A child who can learn from mistakes is well on her way to being a self-sufficient, able learner.

Thinking in Terms of an Ecosystem

The concept of an endangered ecosystem is no stranger to today's child. Through media coverage, children grasp the significance of an oil spill, especially on wildlife. Through documentaries, they learn about endangered species, acid rain, and the effect of pollutants on the environment. As they learn about the close relationship of all forms of life, they begin to perceive their world as interdependent. In her book, *Science with Young Children*, Bess-Gene Holt describes an ecosystem concept:

> An ecosystem is a community of living things interacting with each other and with their nonliving environment. An ecosystem includes energy, food, living organisms, and such factors as light/darkness, water/dryness, air, temperature, the swell of the land, or currents of water. It may be an ecosystem on or under the land, in the ocean, or in fresh water. You and children share one. You sometimes experience others: the park, the vacant lot, the downtown area, the suburbs, the farmer's fields, the mountains, the deserts, the forests, etc.[13]

An ecosystem approach connects a curriculum and an environment in significant ways. As children mature, they become aware of the environmental factors that influence the space they live in—how the sea alters the land and how land vegetation influences the survival of species. They become more sensitive to seasons, to weather, and to environmental forces that affect life. Children read and respond to issues that describe how communities adjust to falling trees, floods, power outages, dry summers, and cold, snowy winters. They begin to look beyond an event to its consequences; to its impact on a total environment. They begin to perceive science as a natural and necessary way of life. Children see how humans affect environments, and they begin to realize that it takes a community of people working together to preserve and conserve resources.

Through environmental awareness, a child can develop a sensitivity for life in its many and varied forms. For a young child a spider-watching experience may begin with a simple observation—a child watching a spider spinning a web. The child can record an experience with only limited understanding or she can continue to *build on* her experience. A curious child may continue to watch the spider meticulously form its web-house, finding it hard to imagine how something so inexplicably beautiful can come from a tiny creature that is somewhere between insect and animal. The purpose is to entrap, but by understanding the relationship between the web and the spider's survival, the child can deal with the experience in a mature and positive way. A follow-up reading as sensitive as *Charlotte's Web,* by E. B. White, will further a child's understanding and compassion for all living things.

An ecosystem framework that incorporates problem solving and scientific inquiry will challenge children to discover more about their world. A child may find a fern or a cactus plant and attempt to replicate its environment. What conditions are conducive to growth—what kind of soil is needed, how much sunlight, how much water? How many eggs does a queen bee lay? Who takes a queen bee's place in a beehive? What happens to butterflies that don't migrate? How can animals sustain life during periods of hibernation? As children become agile thinkers, they exhibit flexibility and curiosity. They no longer accept simple responses or unsatisfactory answers. They value the interplay of ideas and the challenge of questioning.

Children become original thinkers in a discovery environment. A piece of bark with interesting markings may become a "fossil" for a science table and an unusual, round rock, a "dinosaur egg." Children are profoundly influenced by the quality of their experiences. When experiences permit them "to find out" through the investigatory process and when they begin to apply divergent thinking to their tasks, children use reason in their everyday tasks.

Science Objectives

In a whole-child learning environment, teachers have an obligation to instill in their children the love of nature, a sensitivity to life processes, and a "let's find out" attitude.

- To develop in children a responsibility for their natural environment
- To create an atmosphere of discovery
- To facilitate the development of observational and organizational skills
- To explore scientific concepts, such as change and adaptation
- To design an inviting science/math center that offers opportunities for children to develop a disposition for science, process skills, natural science, physical science, and an understanding of ecology
- To help children develop the tools for independent thinking by encouraging them to think systematically, identify and solve problems, make decisions, make predictions, and record happenings
- To develop understandings about science through active learning such as in project work. For example, a theme on *changes* may incorporate the following ideas for development: Children are given focused objectives in the natural sciences such as, observe and record specific changes in their back yard over a period of time; identify four leaves common to an environment, and illus-

trate findings by making leaf rubbings; create an indoor/outdoor garden, plant seeds and small cuttings from nature and observe and record their progress during winter months, or create a feeding station for small animals and observe and record the patterns and characteristics of its visitors.

The following resources explain ways to teach and nurture the whole child through creative activities that integrate learning throughout a curriculum.

Judith A. Schickendanz, Mary Lynn Pegantis, Jan Kanosky, Annemarie Blaney, and Joan Ottinger, *Curriculum in Early Childhood: A Resource Guide for Preschool and Kindergarten Teachers* (Boston: Allyn and Bacon, 1997).

Jie-Qui Chen (Editor), Emily Isberg and Mara Krechevsky (Contributing Editors), *Project Spectrum: Early Learning Activities* (New York: Teachers College Press, Columbia University, 1998).

Sylvia C. Chard, *The Project Approach: Developing Curriculum with Children*, Practical Guide 1 and 2 (New York: Scholastic Press, 1994).

Sylvia C. Chard, *The Project Approach: A Second Practical Guide for Teachers* (Alberta, Canada: University of Alberta, 1994).

Judy Herr and Yvonne Libby, *Creative Resources for the Early Childhood Classroom,* 2nd ed. (Albany, NY: Delmar, 1995).

Darlene S. Hamilton and Bonnie M. Flemming, *Resources for Creative Teaching in Early Childhood Education,* 2nd ed. (New York: Harcourt Brace Jovanovich, 1990).

Suggestions for Developing Science Themes

Science themes should be age-appropriate and based in the familiar context of a child's own environment. A theme can be a single experience or it can take place over a period of time. Young children especially enjoy thematic topics that they can experience in their classroom or in their surrounding community.

For All Children

Busy Animals Prepare for Fall	A Visit to a Farm
Once There Was a Seed	Caring for Nature
Following Tracks: Winter Is Coming	Animal Homes
Changing Clothes: Butterflies, Frogs	Insects Crawl and Insects Fly
Changing Seasons	Who Lives in This Pond?
Hatching Eggs and Nurturing Babies	Who Makes Tunnels?
Nature Under Logs	Backpack Hiking: What Will We Bring?
A Walk in the Rain	

Four- and Five-Year-Olds Might Enjoy

Living and Nonliving Things	Electricity and Magnets
Motion	Light and Sound
The Weather	The Water Cycle
Ecology	Finding Fossils
Learning about Rocks	Changes
Making a Garden	Planets

Teaching Math Readiness

In early childhood, math skills and concepts are primarily learned through constructive play experiences that activate the child's senses and engage the child's mind. In the process of constructing knowledge, children are continuously organizing and making changes as they play with objects and negotiate their position in space. During the early years of development, object play progresses from functional to more complex levels of engagement as children increase their ability to organize and control their play space. Through experimentation, children learn how objects move, change position, and change in relation to each other. The information children are gaining through constructive play enables them to move from concrete to conceptual levels of thinking. They are beginning to think through a plan, problem solve, execute a design, and visualize its completion.

In the process of experimenting with objects in space—with hoops, pulleys, inclines, marble mazes, mobiles, Legos, pipes and hoses—the child learns to predict cause-and-effect relationships. He is quick to anticipate and solve problems that are encountered in a play experience. He discovers, for example, that bouncing a ball hard will make the ball go higher, while bouncing it with less vigor will enable the child to maintain control of the ball.

Expanding Math Experiences in the Classroom

When young children arrive at a child care center early in the morning, they are particularly responsive to table activities that are set up for quiet, manipulative play. The process of selecting and organizing materials, cutting and pasting, making shapes with clay, or making designs on a peg board absorb children's interests. Children are equally enthralled with sand and water play; with estimating, filling, emptying, and refilling objects of different sizes and shapes. Through concrete, pleasureful experiences such as these, children are learning about and practicing math. They are constructing ideas about relationships (things that go together), measurement (organizing clay creations by size), making sets (putting flowers together and worms together), making patterns (stringing beads), experimenting with volume (filling containers with sand or water), and working with space as productions develop form and shape.

Later in the day, a teacher may transition children to outdoor play by reciting finger play songs, many of which are related to counting:

Two little eyes that open and close,
Two little ears and one little nose,
Two little cheeks and one little chin,
Two little lips with teeth locked in.

or

This little froggie broke his toe,
This little froggie said, oh, oh, oh,
This little froggie laughed and was glad,
This little froggie cried and was sad,
But this little froggie was thoughtful and good,
And she hopped to the doctor as fast as she could.
—Authors unknown

After noticing all the different shapes that are present out-of-doors, a teacher may expand on children's discoveries through art and storytelling. Children may finger paint on paper that is cut into various shapes or they may sponge paint shape pictures (sponges are cut into several interesting shapes). During story time, a teacher may invite her children to listen to a flannel board story about a square. "Poor little square couldn't go anywhere because she was stuck in her chair . . . " as the story unfolds, circle helps, triangle helps—but to no avail. It takes hexagon (with six hands) to get square out of her chair.

Finally near the end of a long day, children may participate in making a nutritious snack: cream cheese on celery topped with raisins. Using plastic knives, children may cut the celery and figure out how much cream cheese to spread on each piece (estimation). They will need to be certain there is one snack for each friend (one-to-one correspondence) and they will need to figure out how many raisins can be given to each child (counting). Children will typically place the raisins in a pattern before eating.

Math Objectives

In a whole-child learning environment, teachers have an obligation to instill in children a knowledge of mathematics, a disposition for solving problems, a sense of logic, and a desire to use their expanding knowledge.

- To acquaint children with the language of math (i.e., equal, less than, more than, patterns, a set, inches, feet, yard, addition, subtraction)
- To identify and use numbers
- To acquaint children with shapes, patterns, classifying and sorting, ordering and comparing
- To acquaint children with sequence and spatial relationships
- To acquaint children with directionality
- To acquaint children with measurement and time, graphs and record keeping

- To introduce children to cause-and-effect relationships
- To develop organizational skills that promote perception, problem solving, and conceptual development

Application: Ages Two and Three Years
- Children are introduced to numbers and counting (1–10).
- Children are introduced to classification skills through informal experiences by pointing out common attributes such as leaves, shells, nuts, and other go togethers; grouping items by color, shape, or patterns; sorting items; organizing activity centers by categories; making simple charts such as a weather chart, a job chart, a pet chart, or a birthday chart.
- Children are introduced to one-to-one correspondence such as giving one napkin to each child.
- Children are introduced to sets and classifying by grouping things by shape, size, color, or function.
- Children are introduced to ordering (longest to shortest, thick to thin, big to little).
- Children are introduced to comparisons such as more/less big/small, fast/slow, near/far, high/low, loud/soft, cold/hot, heavy/light.
- Children are introduced to parts and wholes.
- Children are introduced to four basic shapes: circle, triangle, square, rectangle.
- Children are introduced to space such as over/under, bottom/top, near/far, in front of/behind.
- Children are introduced to problem solving such as what is missing, what comes next.
- Children are introduced to measurement and time such as, breakfast comes before lunch and snack is in between.
- Children play with classroom materials that encourage math skills such as matching objects to numbers, finding pairs, sorting blocks, setting a table in housekeeping, making patterns with beads, making designs with a pegboard, polishing a pair of shoes, placing objects and numbers on a flannel board.
- Children begin to develop beginning concepts by:
  — Working with weights, measurements, and volume
  — Playing estimating games
  — Anticipating time through calenders, birthday charts, and classroom activities (for example, feeding a fish in the morning, listening to a story in the early afternoon, and checking a mailbox before going home)
  — Playing math games and enjoying math activities during table time
  — Graphing information and perceiving outcomes (for example, comparing brown eyes to blue eyes to green eyes)
  — Working with spatial concepts (for example, making snow sculptures, planting a garden, playing physical motor games with designated parameters, arranging cookie dough on a bake sheet)

Application: Ages Four and Five Years
- The early math program is continued and expanded on.
- Children identify and begin to use numbers 1–20 by recognition; matching items to numbers; perceiving simple concepts of adding and taking away number objects (flannel board manipulatives provide an excellent tool for teaching math skills); and working in teacher-made beginning math books.
- Children understand the concept of set and can group equal and equivalent member sets.
- Children are exposed to the language of mathematics through games and activities that reinforce relationships such as between/around, over/under, far/near, and so on.
- Children use shapes creatively in artwork and in play, forming structures, designing play spaces, and so on.
- Children become more aware of time (I go home at 3:00; the month is . . . , the day is . . . , my birthday is . . . , when it's winter I will . . .).
- Children engage in problem-solving activities that include making choices, predicting outcomes, discussion, testing and validating, cooperative learning and decision making, record keeping, development of open-ended thinking (what if, let's find out, etc.).
- Children expand knowledge of measurement, time, positional concepts, graphing.
- Children may be ready for a real math book.

A Math and Science Discovery Center

A math and science discovery center should be carefully organized so that children can perceive the relationship between the two components as well as their integral relationship to language and the arts. A small table with two chairs will encourage children not only to investigate objects on a shelf but to actively use the materials in their own way. A science theme such as *Finding Out about Invertebrates* can be set up on the surface of a wide shelf. Invertebrates include little animals without backbones such as worms, insects (anthropods), spiders, snails, and starfish.

The display may include a worm or an ant farm, replicas of homes such as a log, ferns, and moist dirt set up in a large foil pan. Tiny plastic animals and insects will add character and interest to the display. Charts, children's drawings, a magnifying glass, a ruler, art supplies, and other unique items from an outdoor environment may be added. A spider web may be gracefully arranged on a nearby window, and a real hive may be hung on an indoor plant or tree. Math and language activities such as puzzles, books, magazines such as *Your Big Back Yard* and *Ranger Rick,* manipulatives, and games will enhance and extend the exhibit. A teacher will need to have additional containers to accommodate children's findings—and there will be many.

Teaching Language Readiness

A whole-child program views language development as a natural extension of the child's need and desire to communicate with his environment. A child's ability to use and understand language contributes to his social and emotional confidence. A child who can express himself through words commands attention from peers. In a supportive environment, the young child is better able to communicate his needs and feelings. A teacher plays a significant role in promoting and encouraging language development. She is the role model for children to imitate and learn from. In a whole-child environment, the communication skills defined as *listening, speaking, writing,* and *reading* are interactive and interdependent.

There is no specific order for introducing language in a language-rich early environment that offers the young child a variety of experiences. Teachers should expose children to all facets of the language arts in a natural atmosphere of learning that follows the lead of the learner. As with any developing skill, children do not all acquire language at the same time or at the same rate. Some children may become quite verbal at an early age while others may show a disposition for reflective language activities such as listening to tapes, observing playmates or experimenting with early writing. Children acquire communication skills through play, through social exchanges and through organized activities that activate and extend language, such as project work. An early childhood program must provide many opportunities for children to communicate with one another (oral language), to listen to language, to develop comprehension, and to recall previously learned information. As young children become increasingly aware of their surrounding environment, they develop their own unique style of conversing: a style that reveals their background, emerging personalities, and special qualities.

It is important for teachers to remember that many children come to centers with limited language backgrounds. These children may have little or no familiarity with standard English. Children who use language patterns modeled from home environments do not have the advantage of building on a known experience. They may feel embarrassed because they perceive themselves as different from many of their peers. A reinforcing approach is to accept children's language as it is without imposing corrective suggestions (even though they may be well intentioned). Gradually, as children are exposed to a primary language, they will adjust their own patterns to accommodate to an environment that they want to feel successful in. These children will have the advantage of becoming bilingual at an early age.

In addition to cultural constraints, there may be social/emotional constraints that impact on a child's language development. Some little children hold back speaking for reasons that are not known to a teacher or to a parent. For whatever the reason, these children are particularly vulnerable in social situations. A teacher will need to spend extra time talking with and for the child until the child is ready to communicate on his own. Often a nonverbal child's receptive language is sharpened by the absence of speech. A teacher may discover extraordinary paintings or constructs that can be used to reinforce a child's esteem and position in a class.

Oral Language and Listening

Children develop vocabulary at a prodigious rate. There is a difference, however, between using (mimicking) language and understanding language. Comprehension develops gradually through exposure to language and through opportunities to practice language, for example, dramatic play, finger plays, or dictating stories to a teacher. Children should not learn language in isolation. Rather, they should experience language in its entirety through selective activities that stimulate speech. A whole-language approach widens a child's cognitive field. As children listen to language they become aware of semantics (word meanings), syntax (the arrangement and interrelationships of words) and phonemes (the sounds and patterns of language). As children begin to comprehend language, they become empathetic listeners and communicators. They can derive meaning from the messages that they are receiving in books, on the playground, and in their relationships with special friends.

A teacher plays a significant role in fostering language by providing many opportunities for children to experience and develop language. When children are given time and space to play with peers, they become sensitive to the language of peers. Spoken words are sound symbols that can be recognized and endowed with meaning.[14] The common words and expressions that a child is hearing are transferred into later reading and writing experiences. A language pattern that emerges from and is cultivated by a child's known environment promotes socialization and language production (see Table 4.1).

Teachers of young children understand the crucial relationship between language and literature. Story-reading experiences are an important part of a child's continuing success in learning to communicate. Children need constant exposure to books, particularly at the earliest stages of development when their intelligence and disposition for learning are forming. At early childhood levels, a book is judged primarily by its pictures. Illustrations stimulate a child's sense of awareness, curiosity and intimacy with characters. As children become familiar with picture books, they want to read them over and over again. Children's books can be humorous and compelling as well as sensorially stimulating: A little worm is hiding in the crack of an apple, the wind is creeping around a corner looking for things to get into. Books can be subtly suggestive and imaginative: A little cat is peaking out from behind a garbage can. Books can also be instructional, introducing children to colors, shapes, numbers, letters, and most importantly, to concepts. Books can be predictable (children delight in knowing the ending) and unpredictable (full of surprises and unanswered questions).

A teacher stimulates a child's interest in books not only by the stories she reads but by her voice tone. A teacher's voice should reflect the mood and the content of a book. By inviting children into a story through pauses (nonverbal language), a teacher provides openings for children to fill in the words, to make

TABLE 4.1   How Language Develops

Age	General Development	Ways to Encourage Language
Infants to 18 months	■ Cries and uses body movements to communicate ■ Vocalizes with cooing (three months) ■ Babbles (6 months) ■ Gestures to express needs ■ Acquires pacing and rhythm of adult language ■ Responds to spoken cues—waves bye-bye ■ Uses one-word sentences having different meanings ■ Vocalizes less while learning to walk	■ Use nonverbal communication: expressive sounds, gestures, smiles, clapping, tone of voice, facial expressions ■ Converse during caretaking routines of feeding, bathing, and dressing, as well as during playtime ■ Talk purposely, slowly, clearly. Use short, simple sentences, naming objects that interest the child ■ Parallel talk: Describe what the child is seeing, hearing, thinking, and doing as the action is happening ■ Self-talk: Describe to the child what you are doing, hearing, seeing, as you are doing it
18 to 24 months	■ Uses two-word sentences—"go car," "up play" ■ Depends on intonation and gesture ■ Points and/or names objects in pictures ■ Responds to many words (receptive language), though he can not speak them (expressive language)	■ Share stories about concrete objects, people, and situations in his life ■ Stop and listen to child's verbalizations, even if unintelligible ■ Ask questions requiring a choice (e.g., "Do you want a bath with the rubber duck or the horsie?") ■ Provide outings and shared experiences to the store, zoo, park, and library ■ Play folk tunes, nursery rhymes, and marches
2 to 3 years	■ Generalizes—apple is a ball; all four-legged animals are dogs ■ Uses pronouns *me* and *mine* ■ Uses *no* ■ Enjoys imitating and mimicking nursery rhymes ■ Acquires past, possessive, plurals, prepositions ■ Obvious increase in communication behavior and interest in language ■ Large jump in vocabulary growth ■ Fifty percent correct in articulation	■ Discuss daily events before, during, and after they occur ■ Even if not coherent, stop and listen to child's verbalizations ■ Read stories that involve the children in finishing a rhyme or giving a different ending to a story ■ *Tell* stories, freeing child from looking at pictures and bringing him closer to the power of words ■ Give labels to children's expressed emotions (e.g., "You're feeling sad that the paper tore") ■ Collect pictures from magazines showing action to encourage use of verbs

(continued)

TABLE 4.1   Continued

Age	General Development	Ways to Encourage Language
3 to 4 years	■ Communicates needs and questions: who, what, where, why ■ Dysfluency (hesitates and/or repeats whole words or phrases) ■ Three- to four-word sentences; 400–900 word vocabulary ■ Responds to directional commands, *beside* and *under* ■ Responds to two active commands: "give me your plate and sit down" ■ Knows parts of songs; retells familiar stories ■ Rapidly acquiring the rules of grammar, using adjectives, verbs, and pronouns	■ For dysfluency: Be patient, wait, do not interrupt; slow down your speech; be matter-of-fact; do not pressure child to speak before strangers. (Most children outgrow this stage without professional help) ■ Use open-ended sentences requiring more than one word for an answer (e.g., "Tell me what your dog looks like") ■ Provide language experiences rich in rhyme, repetition, fantasy, humor, and exaggeration ■ Encourage children to dictate stories about themselves, their families, friends, pets, and the things they do
4 to 5 years	■ Uses irregular noun and verb forms ■ Talks with adults on adult level in four- to eight-word sentences ■ A great talker, asks many questions ■ Uses silly and profane language to experiment and shock ■ Giggles over nonsense words ■ Makes similar speech adjustments as adults when speaking to a younger child ■ Tells longer stories ■ Asks what words mean ■ Recounts in sequence the events of the day	■ Provide opportunities for children to act out favorite stories ■ Create group discussions about a class problem to solve, a decision to make, activities to plan ■ Set aside a listening center with records of children's poetry and stories ■ Plan weekly themes and have children bring in objects that relate to the theme. Display and discuss objects ■ Drum patterns: Children can repeat the sound pattern by clapping hands or stamping feet

Source: From *PRE–K TODAY,* Issues from 1987 and 1988. Copyright © 1987, 1988 by Scholastic Inc. Reprinted by permission of Scholastic Inc. All rights reserved.

comments, or to participate in the narrative. She lets children know that the book she is reading is as important to her as it is to her children.

Listening is fundamental to child development and to the development of life skills. Children must be given time to hear and respond to the many sounds in their environment: harsh sounds, soft sounds, familiar sounds, and unfamiliar sounds. Children must also become sensitive to the sounds and messages of the people who influence their lives. Listening is not only a developmental skill that facilitates literacy, but a social skill that facilitates friendships, reciprocity, and genuine caring for one another's point of view. To listen is not just to hear; it is the active construction of meaning from all the signals (verbal and nonverbal) a speaker is sending.[15]

Listening may perhaps be the most underestimated component of language development. In traditional early childhood settings, listening has often been isolated from the language arts and rarely written into a curriculum. Often, it has negative connotations such as "you are not listening to me," or "you will need to go to the listening center until you are ready to join your friends."

Through listening, children acquire not only language skills but beliefs, values, and knowledge about their society. Through listening, children develop a disposition for learning and the fundamental tools for mental growth and development. Listening develops in an environment that values and nurtures language as both an *active* and *reflective* contemplative form of communication.

Young children can be trained to become discriminating and attentive listeners. A puppet friend may become a teacher in circle time, reminding children to sit quietly, close their eyes and listen, open their eyes and clap very loud, then softly—so softly that we can hear the quietest sounds.

A young child develops insight when he listens for comprehension. Through the messages he is receiving, the child constructs knowledge, skills, and attitudes. There are many ways that a teacher can focus children's attention on listening skills. A walk through the woods, a trip to a hatchery, a trip to a nature center, or playing listening games can heighten sound awareness and discrimination. As children listen, they make associations, ask questions, and reflect on ideas. They appreciate and value an experience that they can identify with, participate in, and remember.

Emerging Literacy

Educators today use the term *emerging literacy* to describe how early reading and writing behaviors and experiences precede and develop into conventional literacy.[16] Most preschool classrooms offer many opportunities for children to engage in early writing and reading activities, for example, helper charts, calendars, weather wheels, and common words (often referred to as key words). Through everyday experiences, children are forming images of word patterns, meanings, and relationships. With repeated exposure to "written down talk," children become sensitive to the sounds of language matching what they hear to what they see. They are implicitly perceiving (at a very basic level) that written words are visual symbols, which, when associated with known sound symbols, arouse meaning in the mind of the reader. As children become familiar with the meaning of words, they begin to create words inventively by using sound clues (phonemes), memory, and their own perceptions of how a word should look. They typically select words that are familiar and important. For many children reading begins not through instruction, but through their own invented writing efforts. An early childhood program that cultivates and values communication as a natural unfolding process, is providing a foundation for reading and writing.

Early Reading

Children who are exposed to a variety of language experiences in an enriching environment will develop a strong foundation for reading. A child-centered program doesn't promise that children will learn to read. It encourages reading by providing children a variety of books at different skill levels and by individualizing a reading program. In this context, children read at their own paces and in their own time. Language specialist Dolores Durkin points out the importance of early exposure and training:

> A set of common features that characterizes young children who are early readers has emerged from the literature. Early readers enjoyed learning to read so much that they persisted in seeking answers to their questions about written language—questions about the sounds of letters, spelling, writing, etc. They tended to come from literate homes in which books abounded, adults read, and someone was available to read to them and to answer their questions about reading.[17]

An early reading program begins with simple word recognition. Children learn words that have meaning, that relate to a familiar or desirable experience. A teacher might, for example, label items in activity centers. Children will soon imitate by making another set of word cards or eventually by replacing their teacher's words with their own version. A teacher may also introduce key words by reading charts (and emphasizing familiar words) that relate to classroom themes and activities and by rereading familiar books that encourage children to participate.

At a five-year level of development, some teachers might want to introduce children to high-frequency words (words that often appear in early reading experiences) through creative language experiences. Unlike key words—familiar words that children can identify with an object—high-frequency words are not easy to recognize or recall, for example, *have, the, in, is, yes, no, they, what, when, go, on, come, here, to, and, he, she,* and *you.*

A "kangaroo word game" is an example of a creative way to introduce high-frequency words. A large kangaroo carries words in her pocket for children to take home in their pockets. They must return them (and read them) the next day so kangaroo's pocket is always full of words. At the end of the year, the children make their own kangaroo filled with pocket words to practice over the summer.

Nurturing Reading through Literature

Repeated experiences with quality books during the early childhood years nurtures a love of literature and a desire to read. Story books trigger a desire in children to draw and to write. At an early childhood level of development, a favorite story does not end with the last page of a book. Children tend to recreate their images and impressions on paper or through dramatic play. They may select and print key words from a story such as *Little Red Riding Hood* to include in their dramatic play center or they may begin their own picture book about the story using inventive spelling to identify the characters and key events that are important to them.

By exposing children to familiar words in natural ways, teachers are promoting the reading process. As teachers introduce children to simple books and as children develop language competency, they will discover:

- A book is read from left to right, from the top to the bottom of a page, and from beginning to end.
- A book contains a story with characters, with whom the reader may identify.
- A story generates feelings and attitudes in a reader.
- Authors and illustrators express ideas in many different genres such as folktales, fairy tales, rhyming verse, narratives, and wordless books.
- Setting, characters, and plot are important to understanding stories.
- There are many ways to develop characters and many ways to develop themes.
- Authors and illustrators have personalities and distinctive ways of writing and drawing.
- Reading is fun and books are companions—forever!

A teacher who loves literature fosters in young children a curiosity about language through story telling techniques and follow-up activities. (For a wealth of activities to expand children's favorite books, see Shirley C. Raines and Robert J. Canady, *Story Stretchers* and *More Story Stretchers,* books 1 and 2, Gryphon House, 1989, 1991.) An experienced teacher knows which books trigger imagination, identification, and a sense of wonder in a young listener. She knows that children adore hearing a favorite story over and over. They have memorized the words and the pictures. They can tell a reader that she has missed (or skipped) a page, or even a word. They can also probably identify many of the words that hold meaning for them. Teachers promote whole language by:

- Using puppets and role-playing as catalysts for language
- Reciting nursery rhymes, doing finger plays, and singing
- Encouraging language production during group circles
- Promoting language awareness through literary and personal experiences
- Providing an atmosphere that stimulates oral language
- Respecting children's natural language
- Reading stories that evoke curiosity, imagination, identification, and sensitivity
- Encouraging original writing

- Providing opportunities for language experiences
- Emphasizing a *total* language approach
- Reinforcing word recognition through labeling, visual clues, games and activities, and art projects
- Helping children make connections between speaking, writing, and reading
- Helping children realize that a library is a "friend"

Nurturing Reading through Language Experience

The language experience, whole-language approach to teaching reading incorporates the highest standards for teaching reading at early childhood levels. A curriculum that views early education as an *emerging process,* values teaching methods that encourage child-centered, independent learning. In the language experience approach (LEA), children develop confidence in their ability to produce a picture story that holds meaning for them. The fact that a teacher is available to assist in a language production makes the experience even more meaningful to the child. He may assist a child in getting started, in organizing her thoughts, and in processing the experience from beginning to end.

Since children are primarily visual learners, a language experience generally starts with a picture (although teachers may use this method to develop a group story after a field trip or special event, in which case illustrations follow children's dictation). As children write down and read back familiar words, they become inspired to continue what is becoming an enjoyable experience. They begin to perceive that reading is woven into the language arts—it is perceived as a part of a larger experience that is, as yet, untapped. They recognize that their words are recorded in print and that their story is something like a real book. They may ask a teacher to write down their words (dictation) or to help them read back their words (partnering). Children at the beginning stages of reading (four-year-olds) will enjoy hearing their stories read by a teacher (who will encourage them to underline word friends that they think they know). Teachers may select a small number of children's favorite words, write them on a chart and play word games during a follow-up circle. They may, for example, have children match a picture (or a word) with a word on the chart.

Teachers may extend the approach by assisting children in making a group book, or by using the method for project work. A whole-language experience is generated by:

- A child's natural desire to write
- A teacher's enthusiasm and support
- A stimulating project or activity
- A writing center that offers a variety of materials that capture children's interest
- Feelings of success and mastery that accompany a picture story
- The pleasure of sharing the experience with classmates

For a young child, a language experience meets cognitive, affective, and social needs. Feeling comfortable and uninhibited, children are capable of creating amazing pictures and stories. Sometimes, children enjoy collaborating with a friend in developing a project. Since each child/author has a personal investment of pride in her work, she will begin to bridge the distance between oral and written communication without the stress that frequently accompanies more formal early reading programs. As a child expands in language facility, he is developing the confidence and skills for reading. A whole-language approach enables children to:

- Connect reading and writing.
- Become personally involved in a reading experience.
- Use art as a catalyst for original writing and reading.
- Gain immediate satisfaction by seeing their words written down and read back.
- Experience the stages involved in developing a book.
- Extend leanings through word banks and journals.
- Contribute their books to a classroom library for everyone to enjoy.

Philosopher and educator Bruno Bettelheim reminds us to teach reading as a joyful experience because it is a joyful experience:

> If the child did not know it before, it will soon be impressed on him that of all school learning, nothing compares in importance with reading; it is of unparalleled significance. This is why how it is taught is so important; the way in which learning to read is experienced by the child will determine how he will view learning in general, how he will conceive of himself as a learner and even as a person.[18]

As young children progress in language awareness and acquisition, they begin to experience the power and potential of language. Surrounded by print, they begin to use more complex sentence structures and more elaborate forms of communication. They understand the importance of language to expression, feelings, needs, and friendships. In a wholistic environment, children's success in early reading is closely associated with positive feelings that allow a learner to explore and develop literacy through natural channels of communication.

Writing

Children are taught to write by exposing them to print and by providing opportunities for them to practice writing the natural way such as the LEA method described previously. Learning to write can be an exciting adventure, filled with experimentation, or it can become a tedious process if children are uncomfortable and unmotivated by a writing experience because it is improperly presented.

In the eyes of a child, making letters or words is no different than making scribbles on paper, in the dirt, or on window panes. As a child plays with letter or word configurations, he experiments with shapes until he is satisfied with an out-come. The letter *A* may begin on its side and shift to an upside-down position until it eventually stands on its feet.

When a child becomes aware of how lines and shapes can be transformed into letters, a new dimension of communication and self-confidence emerges. Children readily make the transition from early scribbling to writing. Mock letters (imitative letters that resemble conventional letters) appear over and over in various forms and shapes. It is not always easy for teachers to distinguish between early writing efforts and artwork. Patterns can be discerned, however, suggesting the importance of keeping children's graphic representations over a period of time. As children mature, tracing and copying letters or words from print facilitate perceptual motor development. At four and five years of age, children may well prefer copying words (copy work) to inventing words. A language experience story may take on new and extended meaning when children do not have to struggle to figure out how to spell a word or write a short sentence. Through copy work children are not only experiencing correct English, but they are feeling the pride associated with writing real sentences.

When key words and short sentences related to a project or activity are carefully printed on a small easel positioned in a writing center, children are quick to help one another. If they are not expected to write in lines or to make perfect letters, they totally enjoy the sense of freedom and "grown-upness" that accompanies the task.

Nurturing Writing and Reading through Phonics

Both whole language (seeing and reading words as units) and phonemes (identifying the sounds of words) are equally important components of language acquisition. Children typically print letters (graphemes) before they print whole words. In the process of developing literacy, they are exposed to a myriad of language enriching experiences: rhyming verses, finger plays, songs, and literature that often repeat initial sounds (alliteration). Children are also exposed to circle activities that encourage the identification of beginning sounds through games and activities. As children develop language proficiency, they recognize that sounds combine to make words, and words combine to make sentences. A program that exposes children to the *whole* process of language acquisition, *by not excluding phonics,* is recognizing the natural evolution of language. A critical dimension of early childhood training is to maintain a natural rhythm, method, and sense of joyfulness when teaching and training young children in all facets of language development. At early childhood levels, teaching is training through awareness, consistency, and exposure; it is not rote or superficial teaching that is structured for a specific outcome. Children learn in different ways at different rates, and at different times, but eventually, through competent and creative teaching, they do learn.

Children love to play with letters just as they love to play with words. They enjoy magnetic letters, sandpaper letters, tracing letters, organizing flannel letters with matching objects, and letter printing or stamping. They especially love all kinds of markers (both fat and skinny), colored pencils, fat pencils, and lots of hand-me-down computer paper to practice their emerging skills. Exposing children to phonics will:

- Facilitate reading and language competency.
- Sharpen sensory perceptions and discrimination skills.
- Reinforce children's natural progress and proficiency in acquiring language.
- Enhance appreciation for music, poetry, and literature.
- Encourage good listening habits.
- Enable children to feel positive about themselves.

Ways Teachers Can Encourage Phonological Awareness

Teachers can encourage early reading by cultivating foundational skills in whole language and in phonetic development by practicing sounds in classroom activities. They especially enjoy hearing phonics through rhyming verse: "A hunting we will go, a hunting we will go, we'll catch a fish and put it in a (dish), a hunting we will go." Words such as *bug* and *mug, cat* and *hat, star* and *jar* will add humor and challenge to the activity. Children also enjoy vowel strips created in innovative ways, such as *in* (i.e., *fin, win, tin, bin,* and *pin*) positioned on a pinwheel or *ug* (i.e., *bug, rug, tug, snug,* and *hug*) positioned on a flower, a kite tale, or a spring bug bonnet. Vowel sentences such as *The cat is on the mat* (letter *a*), *The hen is in the pen* (letter *e*), *The mit is in the pit* (letter *i*), *Spot is not hot* (letter *o*), and *Pug will not tug on the rug* (letter *u*) are appropriate for five-year-olds to copy, read back, and keep in a personal word bank.

Physical motor games that require quick responses, such as passing a ball around a circle and requiring children to think of a word that begins with the letter *r*, are challenging thinking as well as developing sound awareness. During outdoor play, children enjoy jumping rope, bouncing a ball, or crossing monkey bars to rhyming words. The more exposure children receive, the better equipped they will be to enter the world of formal books—early readers.

Vowel Family Words for Ages Four and Five Years

A good way to practice sound discrimination is through vowel family activities. Teachers should select familiar rhyming words that can be introduced through creative activities, nonsense verse, and sound games.

Short Vowel Sounds

ad:	bad, dad, lad, mad, pad, sad
ag:	bag, lag, rag, nag, tag, brag, wag
am:	am, bam, ham, jam, Pam, Sam
an:	an, can, Dan, fan, man, Nan, pan, ran, tan, van
ap:	cap, lap, map, nap, sap, tap
at:	at, bat, cat, fat, hat, mat, pat, rat, sat
ed:	bed, fed, led, red, Ted, wed

en: Ben, den, hen, men, pen, ten
et: bet, get, jet, let, met, net, pet, set, vet, wet
ig: big, dig, fig, jig, pig, wig
in: in, bin, fin, pin, sin, tin, win
ip: dip, hip, lip, rip, sip, tip
it: it, bit, fit, hit, kit, lit, pit, sit
ob: Bob, cob, job, lob, mob, rob, sob
op: bop, cop, hop, mop, pop
ot: cot, dot, got, hot, jot, lot, not, pot, rot, tot
ug: bug, dug, hug, jug, rug, tug
un: bun, fun, gun, run, sun
ut: but, cut, hut, nut, rut

Long Vowel Sounds

Teachers may want to extend this activity to include long vowel sounds such as: ay, ake, ate, eed, eat, eep, ile, ine, oke, old, ook, ool, orn, and unk (Example: Bake the cake before it is too late.)

Familiar Digraph Sounds

ch: chair, chase, check, chin, chat, chick, choice, choose, chop
qu: quack, quarrel, queen, question, quick, quiet, quit
sh: shall, shake, shave, shed, shell, shelf, sheep, sheet, shine, ship, shoe, shop, short, shut
th: thank, that, than, the, then, there, they, thin, this, throw, thick, throat
wh: whale, what, wheat, wheel, when, where, while, white, whine, why (Example: Charles does choose to sit in a chair.)

Nurturing Writing and Reading through Play

Young children especially enjoy integrating their emerging language facility with dramatic play. Around four years of age, children spend more and more time in a writing center making pictures and words that describe and illustrate a play theme. Masking tape, markers, and paper are the favorite tools for creating and displaying their work.

In order to cultivate children's natural learning, teachers are seeing the value in changing dramatic play themes and in providing language props to facilitate interest (see Figure 4.2).

Nurturing Writing and Reading in a Child's Whole Environment

Children's early writings are influenced by momentary moods and interests and by the careful preparation of an environment. A table arrangement of interesting materials, textures, and shapes may invite attention and spark interest. A project center, enriched by children's productions, is a natural catalyst for children's writ-

FIGURE 4.2   **Print Props to Add to Children's Dramatic Play**

House Play
Books to read to dolls or stuffed animals
Empty food, toiletry, and cleaning containers
Telephone books (Make them with children's names, addresses, and telephone numbers.
    Cover pages with clear plastic adhesive.)
Emergency numbers decal to attach to the play phone (Write in numbers for doctor,
    ambulance, fire station, and police.)
Cookbook (Can be made with children's favorite recipes.)
Small notepads and a container with pencils
Wall plaques with appropriate verses
Stationery and envelopes
Magazines and newspapers
Food coupons
Grocery store food ads
Play money

Doctor's Office Play
Eye chart posted on the wall (Make one with rows of different size letters.)
Telephone book
Message pad and pencils
Signs such as *Doctor is in/Doctor is out, Thank you for not smoking, Open/Closed*
Magazines and books for the waiting room
Pamphlets for children about health care (brushing teeth, eating good foods, wearing
    safety belts)
File folders and ditto sheets for health charts
Index cards cut in quarters for appointment cards

Grocery Store Play
Empty food containers
Labels for store departments (dairy, produce, etc.)
Food posters (Ask a supermarket for old ones.)
Brown grocery bags with the name of the store written on them
Signs for store hours
Numeral stamps and stamp pads to price foods
Play money, cash register
Grocery store ads

Restaurant Play
Menus
Magnetic letters and board to post specials
Placemats (Cover construction paper with the name of the restaurant written on it in clear
    plastic adhesive.)
Note pads and pencils for taking orders and writing checks
Play money, cash register
Open and closed signs

(continued)

FIGURE 4.2   Continued

Transportation Play
Recipe cards cut in half for tickets
Maps or an atlas
Suitcases with luggage tags
Travel brochures
Little notebooks for record keeping

Post Office Play
Envelopes of various sizes
Stationery supplies, pencils
Stickers or gummed stamps
Stamp pad and stamp to cancel

Office Play
Typewriter or computer terminal and paper
Telephone book
Ledger sheets
Dictation pads, other note pads
Three-ring binders filled with information
Sales brochures
Business cards made from file cards
Filing supplies
Date and other stamps and stamp pad

Source: From Judith A. Schickendanz, *More Than ABCs: The Early Stages of Reading and Writing,* (1988) pp. 112, 113. Reprinted with permission from the National Association for the Education of Young Children.

ing. Similarly, a science center documenting the birth of baby chickens, provides an incentive for sustained participation.

A Writing Center

A writing center is a special place for children to work independently and cooperatively. The availability of writing tools, listening activities, and books provides an atmosphere for language development. A comfortable chair or small sofa, a work area, and displays of children's productions will complete the setting.

Language Objectives

In a whole-child learning environment, teachers have an obligation to instill in children a love of literature, a strong foundation in listening and literacy skills, and many opportunities to experience original writing.

- To help children acquire knowledge through emerging literacy skills
- To provide a language-rich environment that is age appropriate, integrated into a curriculum, and creatively conceived
- To provide opportunities for children to listen for meaning, appreciation, and understanding
- To develop an awareness of common vocabulary that is used in many language experiences
- To learn to write independently by integrating the arts and language
- To identify and promote literature as a powerful force for language development
- To provide language enriching experiences that encourage original writing through freedom of expression, creative thinking, and immediate satisfaction
- To experience language through cooperative learning (themes, projects, field studies, field trips)
- To become sensitive to the sounds and playful expressions of language through phonics and word games
- To organize activity centers that build on language skills through creative play and the inventive use of language

Application: Ages Two and Three Years
- Children learn language informally as they play and communicate with peers. An early literacy environment provides ample time for young children to develop language usage and comprehension through cooperative experiences with playmates.
- Children are introduced to initial sounds through verse, music, and group activities.
- Children participate in language experience activities that include repeated exposure to nursery rhymes, fairy tales, visually appealing stories, imaginative picture books, puppetry, finger plays, familiar songs, beginning drama, storytelling, and poetic verse.
- Children are introduced to words and sounds in creative, playlike ways that promote movement, recall, and good listening.
- Children learn to read words that are familiar and present in their environment.
- Children integrate language experiences in a writing center, in play centers, and through the project approach.

Application: Ages Four and Five Years
- The preschool program is continued and expanded on with a greater emphasis on specific areas of language development (i.e., identifying common words, making books, playing rhyming games, playing word games, printing and reading back short sentences, increasing language experiences, and keeping journals and word banks).
- Children learn phonics as they learn whole words. Letters are selected in accordance with a theme or project that is being studied (e.g., the letter *E* may

be introduced during an Eskimo unit, the letter *F* during the Fall season, or the letter *B* during a Bug or a Bear unit). Children may have a sharing session for toys that begin with the letter *B*, a *bear* day that includes a banana bread snack, a trip to the zoo, or play time in a bear cave.

- Children practice printing letters and words in a writing center.
- Children dictate or write language experience stories.
- Children keep a word bank of project words and other key words that hold importance to the child.
- Children check out books from a center's library.
- Children learn language through cooperative play/work, such as writing thank you notes or making a mural that identifies objects by name.
- Children are provided a personalized reading program that is tailored to their developmental level and to their interests. The best books are those that are written by teachers and illustrated by children. Original books should contain a key word list (children select, print, illustrate, and read back the important words in a story).

For a helpful guide on the early stages of literacy, see Judith A. Schickedanz, *More than ABCs*, NAEYC, 1998.

Themes and Projects

In the past decade, there has been a resurgence of interest in a thematic approach to early learning that engages children in ongoing, in-depth projects of interest. At preschool levels, teachers have traditionally developed and planned a curriculum around themes (or units) that they believe to be appropriate and challenging mediums for learning. Themes provide a framework for organizing and presenting content in ways that facilitate growth and development at early childhood levels. Content-rich programs integrate the world of the child in meaningful ways that incite curiosity and build on a child's emerging skills and competencies. In a whole-child program, themes enable children to make connections between creative and cognitive activities.

Themes provide the study content for projects.[19] A project provides an in-depth learning experience that holds the potential for further exploration and investigation. Project work is an emerging process that evolves through active engagement between a child and his environment. A project differs from a theme in that it is developed *with* the child and therefore more responsive to a child's *impressions, ideas,* and *strengths.* A child will invest in an activity that he can actively experience, identify with, and control. Projects that pique a child's interest encourage him to commit time and creative energy. An important purpose of the project approach is to instill in the child a disposition for *process learning* and a positive attitude toward cooperative learning.

The project approach is rooted in John Dewey's theory of progressive education. Dewey envisioned learning as a dynamic process of cooperative interaction between students and teachers. The atmosphere was one of inquiry, investigation and active learning. The classroom was perceived as a laboratory for active learning; a place where students became experts in a field or area of study that incited interest, investigation, and a quest for knowledge. The method has regained prominence through the writings and contributions of Dr. Lilian G. Katz, and Dr. Sylvia C. Chard, and through the Reggio Emilia approach to early learning (see *Engaging Children's Minds: The Project Approach,* Ablex, 1991).

Developing Themes

A theme may be presented in one day (a Discovery Theme) or it may be presented over several weeks. The age, developmental level, and background of a group of children will determine the parameters and content for a study theme.

Learning through Experience

For two- and three-year-olds, themes should be limited in duration and content. Young children tend to be responsive to ideas that they can relate to and experience first-hand. The young child interprets and constructs knowledge through active, concrete experiences that offer immediate satisfaction and stimulation. A stimulating experience is one that engages a child's senses, curiosity, and desire to learn. A young child learns about water by catching raindrops and discovering a puddle. He can experience the difference between ice and water by touch and taste, and he can even predict rain by observing a darkening landscape. A curriculum that integrates knowledge through age-appropriate activities and direct hands-on experiences is establishing a foundation for learning.

Challenging Children

As children begin the transition from three to four years of age, they are ready to operate at a somewhat higher level of thinking. They are willing to extend themselves for a theme that is challenging and stimulating; one that takes them comfortably beyond their immediate environment. A child in the city is excited to learn about a farm with orchards and haystacks, and cats in barns. The challenge for teachers is to figure out how to *authenticate* an experience so that children can experience their expanding world in meaningful and educational ways through a variety of carefully selected themes and projects.

At four- and five-year levels of development, children are less limited by the here and now, and better able to conceptualize their reasoning and thinking skills, that is, to perform at higher levels of operation.

Partners in Learning

In order to build on emerging knowledge, themes must challenge and inspire children's understandings and capabilities. When children share in the development of a theme, their participation is ensured. They can, for example, accompany a teacher to a library to obtain books, bring in special items from home and participate in designing and equipping play centers to correspond with the topics they are studying. Play props are wonderful ways to extend participation in classroom activities.

As children become partners in learning, they are increasingly entrusted with responsibility. They are given the freedom to experiment with ideas and materials because they have proven that they can be trusted to work responsibly and independently.

Preparation Time

Teaching for content requires research and organization. A teacher plans, prepares, and presents a theme. She organizes special activities and events that reinforce a theme. She researches her ideas for extended knowledge and creative ideas, soliciting ideas from other professionals in the field.

In developing content, preparation becomes a springboard for the success (or failure) of a theme. A teacher will need to select a theme that incorporates play and the arts with emerging literacy. He will need to solicit assistance from parents, colleagues, librarians, and other community resources in developing projects. Sensitive to the need for children to participate in their own learning, he will invite their ideas and suggestions in selecting projects that they might like to learn about. Some themes like *Changing Seasons,* can be developed within a child's surrounding environment, while other less-immediate themes may challenge a teacher to find secondary "near authentic" resources. For example, a theme on the *Arctic Region* may culminate in a visit to a museum that offers exhibits of Eskimo life as well as a hands-on experience with walrus tusks, masks, carvings, and even a stuffed bear standing on hind legs, which appear very much alive to an enthralled young child.

Selecting Topics

The following list of themes represents a sample of topics that are appropriate for preschool levels:

My Five Senses	My Family
I Am Growing Up	Getting to Know You
My Community	A Post Office
Once Upon a Time	Signs of Seasons
Baby Animals	My Shaping World
Measuring, Counting, and Cooking	My Back Yard
Making Pottery	The Story of a Basket
If I Owned a Bakery	What's Inside This Egg?
The Circus	Motion Is Movement
Building and Construction	Watching Weather
Let's Pretend	Water, Raindrops, and Puddles
Nursery Rhymes	

Four- and five-year-olds may also enjoy:

Changes	Designing a Park
Life on a Barge	Famous Painters
Photography	Early Settlers
Literature and Folk Tales	Caring about My Environment
A Harbor	Discovering Space
Learning about Other Countries	What I Want to Be When I Grow Up
A Community Project	The Eskimos
Making a Garden	Making Prop Boxes for Pretend Play
Funday: The Eighth Day	Making Games
Famous Athletes: The Olympics	All About a Swamp
Insects Are Interesting	Designing a Newspaper
Adopting a New Friend	Grandparents Are Great

A Format for Developing a Theme

A theme requires a great deal of research, preparation, and reflection before it can be presented to children (see Figure 4.3). A helpful way to structure a theme is as follows:

1. A brief description of the theme
2. Main objectives
3. Procedures and materials
4. New words
5. Integrated activities
6. Complementary literature
7. Special events and culminating experiences

Evaluation

At each level and stage of production, a teacher will record information and keep samples that provide insight into the value and importance of a theme to:

- A child's personal development
- A child's cognitive development
- A child's social development
- A child's attitudinal development
- A child's creative development
- A child's emerging literacy

Discovery Themes

An important dimension of early learning is to offer children experiences that are spontaneous and joyful without predictable outcomes and extensive planning. Creative ideas tend to sprout quite unexpectedly for early childhood teachers just

FIGURE 4.3   A Theme

1. *A Brief Description of the Unit.* A teacher plans to present a science unit that will integrate learning and the arts through hand-on activities. She wants children to learn to identify and appreciate nature from first-hand experience in their own backyard, and she wants children to become aware of how seasons and nature interact.

2. *Main Objectives.* To identify, compare, and contrast items in nature; to develop sensitivity toward living things; to develop understandings about changes—falling leaves, migration, and preparation for winter.

3. *Procedures and Materials.* Teacher will have children collect leaves, materials for nests, feathers, and nutmeats. As they gather items, children are encouraged to use their senses, to discriminate, and to make observations. Children's findings are sorted, labeled, and stored for placement in a discovery center. During the following days, the teacher plans to extend children's learning about leaves and related subjects such as a life cycle, self-preservation, and ways that children can help nature during the winter months. To develop her three themes she will use objects from nature, literature, films, projects, and language experience activities. She also will plan field trips and special events.

4. *New Words.* The teacher makes a chart of the words that children have selected, e.g., leaf, tree, fall, winter, migration, hibernation, nest, food, snow, sleep. Next to each word, a child is asked to draw a corresponding picture.

5. *Integrated Activities*

For leaves—Children will identify and sort leaves by shapes and names. They discover that some leaves are smooth, some have prickly points, others are lobed. Some leaves are green, some turning colors, and some are brown. The teacher points out that some trees hold onto their leaves (evergreens) while others drop their leaves (deciduous). The latter are leaves that can no longer make food for plants; they are tired leaves that can no longer give off oxygen (photosynthesis). The teacher will read A. R. Tresselt's *Johnny Mapleleaf*, a sensitive story about a leaf that finally decides it's time to let go. Additional activities include leaf rubbings (place a leaf between two pieces of paper and rub the surface with the flat side of a crayon); stained glass leaves to hang in a window (shave pieces of multicolored crayons, put shaving on a real leaf placed between two pieces of wax paper, press lightly with a warm iron until the wax has melted and blended); and leaf people that will become the focus of an original language experience story (paste a leaf on paper, add personality with markers and create an illusion of dancing or falling leaves). Children also may enjoy leaf imprints (painting a leaf and pressing it onto plain paper), leaf play (raking and jumping in leaves), and making their own fall tree. The children may enjoy being falling leaves:

> *The red leaves are falling, are falling, are falling,*
> *The red leaves are falling, all over the town,*
> *And winter is coming, is coming, is coming,*
> *And winter is coming, when the leaves are all down.*
> *The squirrel is sleeping, is sleeping, is sleeping,*
> *The squirrel is sleeping, curled up in a tree,*
> *And snow falls so gently, so gently, so gently,*
> *And snow falls so gently, on you and on me.*

FIGURE 4.3   Continued

For migration—A teacher may introduce the concept by reading Eric Carle's *Very Hungry Caterpillar* and Charlotte Zolotow's *Something Is Going to Happen* to stimulate children's senses about forthcoming changes. She may direct attention to birds by pointing out the concept of migration for some animals, hibernation for others, and winter survival for those that neither migrate nor hibernate. She may expand understandings by asking about ways that grown-ups and children prepare for winter. Activities will include: finger-print drawings that depict birds in flight, making bird stations, recording bird sounds, identifying birds that stay behind, making birdfeeders and reading *The First Snowfall*, by Anne and Harlow Rockwell. Depending on children's interest, the unit can be expanded to how animals adapt to winter, the squirrel gathering and storing acorns, the rabbit nesting, the bear seeking a quiet place to sleep.

For people—This unit provides an opportunity for teachers to discuss seasonal changes and their impact on people, animals, and plant life. Children might discuss seasonal activities such as raking, cleaning, furnaces, and canning. Discussions might include how people interact with nature in positive ways such as feeding animals, mulching plants, and protecting vulnerable plants from winter's cold. Discussion also might include how people can help one another through seasonal changes by focusing on people who have special needs or who are deprived of necessities.

   6. *Complementary Literature.* In addition to the above activities, teachers may plan to read favorite stories that depict seasonal changes and a need for adaptation—for instance, *The Sleepy Bear* by Lydia Dabcovich, *The Snow Day* by Ezra Keats, *Frederick* by Leo Lionni, *Sylvester and the Magic Pebble* by WIlliam Steig, *The Ugly Duckling* by Hans Christian Andersen, *Annie and the Old One* by Miska Miles, *Katie and the Big Snow* by Virginia Lee Burton, *Goodnight Moon* by Margaret Wise Brown, *The Caterpillar and the Polliwog* by Jack Kent, *Animals Sleeping* by Masayauki Yabuchi.

   7. *Special Events and Culminating Experiences.* Teachers may take children to visit nature centers, invite park rangers and scouts to speak to children, show educational films such as *Winter Comes to the Forest,* and plant bulbs for spring blooming. Children may enjoy raking leaves, making jam, making feeding stations, and planning winter projects for people in their environment with special needs (visitations, letter writing, and ongoing group projects). They may shop for favorite consumables like hot chocolate, pancake mix, and lots of peanut butter for long winter days in child care.

as they do for children. An immediate bonding takes place between a teacher and her students when something is about to happen—when ideas are fermenting. Children love the sense of anticipation that precedes or introduces an experience. A discovery theme is a "mini" theme that is presented experientially in a group circle or in an outdoor setting and opportunities for follow-up activities in play and project centers are provided. A discovery theme:

- Engages the imagination and curiosity of a child
- Creates an atmosphere of anticipation

- Builds on an initial idea
- Connects an idea with an experience
- Bonds teachers and children

Selecting Topics

A discovery theme should begin with an experience that activates imagination such as watching a spider spinning a web. Children will enjoy making webs, naming spiders, learning about spiders, playing with patterns, making spider hats and writing a story about their experience. Older children may enjoy making webs on geoboards using rubber bands or they may enjoy interpreting Eric Carle's *The Very Busy Spider* in their own words. Examples of topics for discovery themes are:

Under a Rainbow	A Cloud Goes By
A Balloon Dances	A Falling Leaf
A Worm Wanders By	A Pet Rock
A Feather Is Found	The Story of an Acorn
Under a Log	A Seedling
A Dandelion	A Sunflower
A Spider Spins	A Bee Makes Honey
A Camel's Hump	What Can We Do with String?
Shadows and Groundhogs	What Is in This Shell?

A Format for a Discovery Theme

Both children and teachers will delight in the unpredictable unfolding of a discovery theme. Even spontaneous experiences, however, require preparation (see Figure 4.4).

1. An idea: Why did you select this theme?
2. Focus: How will the theme be developed?
3. Main objectives: What do you hope to accomplish?
4. Procedure and materials: How will the theme be presented?
5. Follow-up: How will you extend this presentation?
6. Outcome: How did the children benefit? What would you do differently? What can be added?

Selecting and Developing Projects

Projects are usually selected and developed from a larger theme. They are specific areas of study within a theme that hold promise for deeper investigation and extended learning. Because project work is a focused in-depth experience, preparation is vital to its success. At the preschool level, both the teacher and the child are active participants throughout the process. Autonomy is encouraged, how-

FIGURE 4.4   A Discovery Theme

1. *An Idea:* The teacher would like children to understand the practical uses for beans as well as their creative potential. In the course of a day, she will provide many opportunities for children to discover beans.

2. *Focus:* Teacher intends to use this method to introduce letters.

3. *Main Objectives:* The teacher would like children to understand the food value of beans, how they grow, different ways they can be eaten, and their creative potential. She would like children to take a concrete object and expand their thinking toward conceptual awareness.

4. *Procedures and Materials:* The teacher shares various kinds of beans with children during a group circle, identifying them by name, comparing them, and discussing how they are eaten or used. The children get to open up beans and to examine the interior. Children may compare moistened beans to packaged beans to demonstrate expansion or growth (the wet beans swell). Each child then gets to plant a bean in a styrofoam cup filled with dirt. The teacher talks about how beans grow and their environmental needs. She points out that bean plants, if taken care of, can grow very, very tall—like Jack's beanstalk. The teacher will complete her circle by reading, *Jack and the Beanstalk.*

5. *Follow-Up:* Children may make a bean collage on a paper plate (arts and crafts), play beanbag games (movement and listening skills), make baked beans for lunch, and sort and count beans (science and math). At the end of the day children can play a bean game. A child sits in a chair, hides her eyes, and a classmate takes a bean that had been placed under her chair. All children put their hands behind their backs. The child says, "Bean, bean, who took my bean, someone who is VERY mean." The player gets three turns to pick the mean friend who has taken her bean.

6. *Outcome:* Teachers will want to evaluate each experience in terms of objectives and student participation.

ever, as in most activities, the young child needs direction and encouragement from a teacher. The project approach has been traditionally identified with early elementary education because it is a time when children can presumably work independently, conduct research, set their own goals, and generate their own learning.

In recent years, project-based models for child development have attracted the attention of early childhood educators who endorse a child-centered, wholistic approach to learning. This method of working with children is premised on the belief that children learn by doing if they are actively engaged in something that holds significance for them. This requires an open-ended, hands-on environment that allows children to experiment with ideas and materials. For greater insight and understanding of the project approach and how it works from a theoretical and contemporary perspective, see Sylvia C. Chard, *The Project Approach: A Practical Guide for Teachers*, University of Alberta, 1991.

The Value of Project Work to Children

The real value of in-depth, experiential learning is what it engenders in children. Rather than focusing on fragments of information, the project approach invites children to connect and use information within a larger and more meaningful context. When children commit to projects they:

- Perceive learning as an integrated process.
- Develop patience as they share and work with peers.
- Become conversational.
- Become active and autonomous learners.
- Work closely with their teacher.
- Make discoveries and build on knowledge.
- Challenge ideas and voice opinions.
- Develop important cognitive and affective skills.
- Develop inquiring minds.
- Value the ideas of others.
- Are able to make changes in their own work.
- Are able to see the progression of a project from conception to completion.
- Experiment with many mediums and materials.
- Experience feelings of success, pride and accomplishment.

The closer a child gets to interpreting and constructing a project, the more he is able to shape and direct its process. Through direct experience, children figure out their own answers. In a science-related project, for example, a child observes that a bug has three parts to its body, six legs, and sometimes wings. Through observation, a deeper awareness is planted in the mind of the child. Children appreciate the profound beauty of nature in the color and patterns of its inhabitants: the delicate, transparency of a green praying mantis, the bold orange and black spots on a ladybug, and the intricate symmetry of a butterfly's wings. Children are eager to recreate the many images of nature in a setting and an atmosphere that engages their creativity.

As children work independently or cooperatively in small groups over a period of time, they experience the full potential of whole learning. They perceive themselves and their work as an integral part of a learning process that is shared and valued by peers. They also sense that their environment is not competitive or judgmental. The value of a project approach is that it engages children in serious work without requiring more of children than they want to or are able to give. Furthermore, project work often awakens and stimulates specific areas of talent or emerging strengths in young children that were not heretofore recognized.

In the process of examining and exploring topics, children are given an opportunity to acquire and apply their findings on their own, or with teachers and peers. The child also benefits from the social and interpersonal relationships that accompany a project as much as he enjoys all of the choices and decisions that are made unilaterally throughout the span of a project. He must decide who he will sit near; he must negotiate table space, and select the tools that will enable him to begin a project. As a project grows, the child decides what should be added, or seeks advice from a friend. At times, advice comes without solicitation, but that too is part of interaction.

The Value of Project Work to Teachers

In project work, the role of the teacher dramatically shifts from one of initiator and mentor to one of partner and learner. One of the most exciting outcomes of a project is that it happens *without* a teacher's direct influence, input, and expectations. To witness the unfolding of a project in the hands of the child is to discover the special magic that is within the child.

Teachers are inspired by the project approach because it generates a positive and enthusiastic disposition for learning that becomes ingrained and natural to the learner. In project work, there are fewer expectations and more time to experiment with ideas than in teacher-dominated learning environments. Because time is not an imperative in a project-centered environment, children are able to experience an activity from multiple perspectives and moods. They are free to converse, debate, move things around, and rework their images. They challenge themselves and one another. A project literally grows in the hands of a child, particularly if the child is given freedom to make changes in a nonhurried atmosphere.

Another important dimension of this approach is that projects provide teachers with an opportunity to get to know children's interests, talents, and shortcomings in nonjudgmental, productive ways. Teachers observe the following in children:

- Level of interest and ability
- Approach to a task at hand
- Thinking and problem solving patterns
- Perseverance and commitment to a project
- Emerging skills
- Developing concepts
- Disposition for learning
- Ability to self-manage and follow directions
- Language and thinking patterns
- Social maturation

Criteria for Selecting Projects

Teachers should select themes and projects that are age appropriate and within a child's level of experience and understanding. They may elect to develop one or two long-term projects over the course of a year in addition to monthly themes and projects. Examples of long-term projects are the following: Making a Garden, Designing an Aquarium, The Wonders of Nature, We Are Growing Up, From Seed to Plant, and From Baby to Mother (caring for and observing the growth of rabbits, gerbils, mice, or hamsters).

It is important to remember that the young child's orientation is closely tied to observable events and specific information. Each community will have its own unique features and opportunities for a project study. During field trip activities, children will see and experience a project in its natural environs—at its source. They will gather information for classroom projects based on first-hand information, samples, photographs, and artwork.

It is not always possible, however, to provide children with a direct experience. At times, a teacher will be required to develop a project with less authentic representations, such as photographs, realistic looking models, books, videos, and so on. They can add authenticity by inviting visitors to share their knowledge and talents with children (e.g., a park ranger, a policewoman, a botanist, or an artist who designed a fountain or a sculpture garden near a child care center). When planning long-term projects, teachers should:

- Select and develop a theme that can be represented through play, learning, the arts, and nurturing (see Figure 4.5).
- Consider possibilities and resources for projects.
- Identify areas of knowledge and interest; ask children to assist in selecting two or three projects that they would like to learn about.
- Evaluate ways that the projects can be brought into a child's field of understanding and identification.
- Find ways to extend projects into play centers and community activities.
- Plan a culminating activity that holds meaning for each child, for example, children can share their project word banks or portfolios and then can choose a special treat that is identified with a project.
- Document and evaluate children's work at appropriate times.

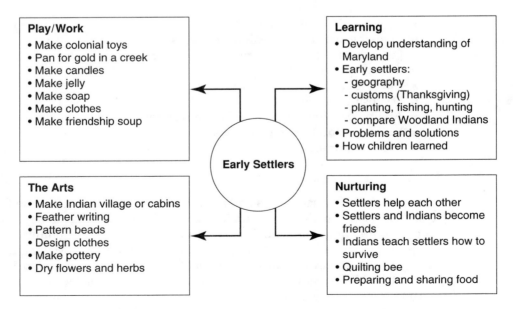

FIGURE 4.5   Integrating Themes

Stages of Project Work

As a teacher conceptualizes a theme, she considers projects as integral parts to its development. She should learn what children know about a theme and what topics they are particularly interested in exploring. Ideas may be written down on a chart. After some discussion, two or three favorite projects should be selected for investigation and study (see Figures 4.6 and 4.7). A project is generally completed within a month. As project work progresses, and children's interests increase,

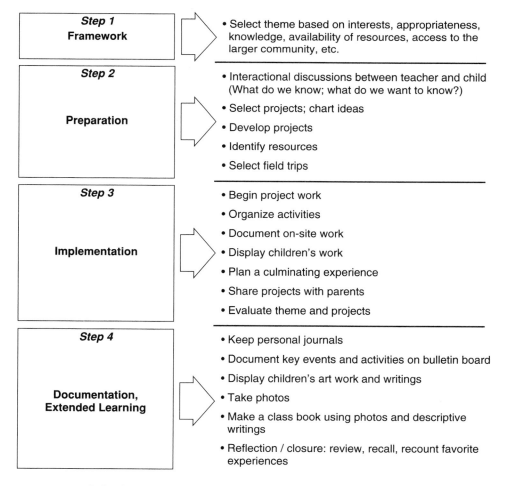

FIGURE 4.6   Selecting and Developing Projects

Source: Inspired by Sylvia C. Chard, *The Project Approach* (New York: Scholastic, 1994).

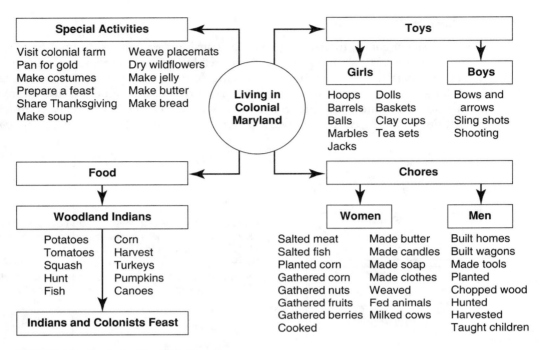

FIGURE 4.7   Projects: Early Settlers

teachers extend activities. Children's work is documented, displayed, and shared with parents.

Documentation

It is important to continually assess and document children's work in a project center. Displaying project work is extremely reinforcing for the child and enlightening to parents. Since displays are generally kept for the duration of a project, parents have no way of knowing what is going on in their child's life unless they are in frequent communication with teachers. Children especially take pride in sharing their ongoing work and their projects center with parents. Keeping up with names, with who has done what, and with missing pictures is definitely a challenge for teachers.

Examples of ways that a teacher can document children's work in a project center include but are not limited to the following:

- A selection of children's drawings and writings carefully framed and displayed
- Samples from children's field trip activities
- Photographs of children engaged in project work, and related events
- Language experience stories and other original writings

- Graphs and time lines that illustrate facets of the project from inception through completion
- Evidence of planning such as a chart of a word list, library books, models, and special items for display
- Evidence of the development of a project
- Models that represent a project
- Personal journals for children's writings and drawings
- A portfolio for pictures, writings, and special memories

A Project Center

A project center may become the most important activity center in a classroom. Ideally, a project center should be located in a section of a room that has windows and interesting possibilities for creative development, such as places for hanging objects and plants, with areas of light and shadow. Primary furnishings include a work table and chairs, shelves, bulletin boards, and charts. Shelves will be needed to organize art material, resources, and related books, as well as to display models and constructs that children have created.

Because the primary function of a project center is to engage children in constructive/cooperative interaction, there are numerous possibilities for its extended use. A project center can be combined with an art center. When a center is not being used for project work, it can be available for artwork. A project center may also share space with a science/math shelf. An aesthetically pleasing science center with items for exploration such as a real bird's nest, feathers, wind chimes, colored water shakers, a piece of sheep's wool, crabs, or gerbils, will enhance children's imagination and prolong interest in a center.

As important as a project center is to a classroom, it should not become merely a showplace for children's productions. As a place of cooperative interaction and serious engagement, a project center should be understated and authentically illustrative of the child at work. There are times when it will be cluttered and messy. Also, too much emphasis should not be placed on documentation. A teacher who is consumed with displaying and recording children's work, may not get to enjoy the magic of the moment—like observing a child's conversation with another child.

Extending Learning through Social Studies

Social studies is the study of human beings; how they live, where they live, their relationship to one another through cultural needs and common concerns. A child's universe begins with self, extends to family, and then to the concept of meaningful communities. If the community is a child care center, the child may have a unique opportunity to interact with other races and cultures. A child caring environment cultivates common values, a widening base of knowledge, and positive attitudes that continue to influence and shape a child's lifelong development. It is the responsibility of teachers to do the following:

- Promote an understanding and respect for all people.
- Extend the concept of community into the larger world.
- Make children aware of global issues and responsibilities in appropriate and caring ways.
- Help children become knowledgeable about leadership and governments in appropriate and caring ways.
- Foster concern for people in need in appropriate and caring ways.
- Engage children in projects and activities that extend their sense of identity and civic responsibility into their surrounding environment.
- Sponsor activities that promote a multicultural environment such as an international dinner.
- Develop themes and projects that extend children's knowledge of people and places, such as An Eskimo Village in Alaska, A Cotton Plant in Georgia, A Bakery in France, A Paper Mill in Maine, The Rain Forest in the Amazon, and The Nile River in Egypt.

Assessing Children's Learning

Teachers should make informal observations as children play in activity centers, share in teacher-initiated activities, and engage in group experiences. Teachers should ask the following questions:

- Am I encouraging children to think divergently?
- Do I encourage them to seek alternative solutions and to solve problems?
- Are my objectives broad enough to include creative thinking as an approach to learning?
- Are children exercising initiative, independence, and self-management in their attitude toward learning?
- Is my language program meeting the developmental level of my students?
- Am I encouraging children to develop foundational skills in math and science?
- Have I integrated my curriculum in ways that are meaningful and exciting to young learners?
- What resources can be added to my curriculum and to my classroom?
- How can I make better use of parent's interests and talents in forwarding my program?
- Am I achieving a healthy balance between teacher-initiated activities and child-initiated activities?

See Appendix, Developmental Checklist.

Group Activities for Early Childhood
1. *A reading tree.* Children bring in a tree branch from out-of-doors and decorate it with key words or with words that relate to a theme (fall: leaves, rake, red,

yellow, squirrel, nuts), the words may be printed on color paper shaped in patterns such as leaves, flowers, hearts, snowmen, apples, or pumpkins.

2. *A class word bank.* Children (or teacher) print key words on 3" x 5" index cards, provide a picture clue on the reverse side; cards can be categorized by subject and put in a file box or in large envelopes.

3. *Original books.* A classroom book should relate to a special event or theme—when each child has contributed a page, the teacher can bind the book, have children make/create a cover design, and a title (books should be laminated for wear and tear).

4. *Original teacher books.* Children can illustrate and learn to read original teacher books.

5. *Flannel board stories.* Children can create stories themselves—they can think of a theme, make the characters (from cardboard), add a velcro backing, make a flannel board (using heavy cardboard), and enjoy their own creations.

6. *Mail a letter.* Children can compose a letter each week to someone special—each child can contribute a comment and make a picture. After the teacher addresses the letter, the children can add stamps and mail it. (These can be thank you letters, which are important to value training.)

7. *Friend of the week.* Each week a child can select and honor one classroom friend. They can make a book about the child and her playmates, write special comments on a star (I like the way Barbara plays ball, and so on), help a teacher organize a "Barbara bulletin board" with family pictures and children's drawings; and they can plan a special event for Barbara—put on a puppet show, read a book, or make her favorite cookies.

8. *Circle games.*

   Telephone. A message is passed quietly around the circle and the last child in the circle repeats the message out loud.

   Matching Items. Teacher distributes picture card sets of animals and their homes. Children need to find a match before the drum beats.

   Sharing. Children bring something special from home, put it in a bag, give clues, and classmates guess what the object is.

   Planning. Plan a special day each month—color day, pick-your-own clothes day, pet day, senior citizen, or grandparent day. Children get to make choices and love the anticipation that precedes a special day.

   Learning Letters. A four-year-old can practice letters by sound. A teacher introduces children to one letter per week. On letter day a child brings a novelty item from home that begins with the letter sound and classmates have to guess what the item is. The children make a letter snack (banana bread), a letter project (a bear puppet), and enjoy a related story *(Goldilocks and the Three Bears).*

   Making Changes. The teacher may change the sequence of a story, the characters, or the ending and observe reactions. (The children also can be asked to change the ending of a familiar story, e.g., Goldilocks broke papa bear's chair, Red Riding Hood met a bear on her way to grandpa's house).

Tall Tales. A story is begun in circle and grows bigger and bigger as it is passed around.

Finishing Sentences. The teacher provides a message and the child provides the ending—A zebra lives... A monkey eats... A bee makes... A mailman... A forest ranger...

Rhyme in Time. A teacher sings or tells a rhyming sentence or verse and the children continue—I met a man, his name was... That big fish, lived in a little....

Polly or Pete Parrot. The teacher whispers a message to a child (touch something hard, something cold, something yellow). The child (Polly) must fly to items whispered, touch them and fly back home without forgetting the message.

Seeing Patterns. The teacher makes a pattern on a flannel board with objects (e.g., a square and a triangle). Following the pattern, the child must add the next shape. (The task can become more challenging by making more difficult patterns, e.g., three squares, two triangles, and one circle.)

Sequencing. The teacher asks the children "What comes first, picking apples, baking a pie, or planting an apple tree?"

Discrimination. The teacher draws a picture on chart paper. The children must guess what is missing on the objects drawn by adding the missing object (e.g., a house without shutters, a bus without a door, a face without a nose).

What's Wrong? The teacher shows children picture cards of objects that belong to a set and adds something that does not belong (e.g., a hammer, a nail, a banana, or a bird, a nest, a bee, an egg). The child responds appropriately.

Take Away. The teacher lines up colored blocks. The children look, hide their eyes, and the teacher takes away one or two blocks. The children must guess which blocks were taken away.

Observing. The teacher makes changes on a child's garments outside the classroom. When teacher and child return, a classmate must guess what has been changed (sleeve rolled up, shoes reversed, glasses removed, hairclip removed).

Who Am I? A child hides behind a screen and sings *Do You Know the Muffin Man?* One friend comes up and knocks on the door, which prompts the child to sing. The friend must guess who is behind the screen.

Guess What's Inside? The teacher fills a bag with a familiar item (clothespin, a brush, a toothpick, a fork), and each child gets a turn to feel and name the object.

What Could This Be? The teacher brings an object to circle (a scarf, a tennis racket, a clothespin, a rolling pin, or a bar of soap) and children must think of all the ways the object could be used. (The teacher can write down the responses to show children how imaginative they are.)

We're Going on a... The teacher tells children where they are going and children have to think about what they will bring on their trip (on a bear hunt, a rock climb, a trip to the moon).

What Am I? Children act out being an animal or an object and their class-mates must guess what they are. Children may give a clue—I have wings or I like milkweed pods, or I hum and live in a meadow in a tiny nest.

Hide and Seek. The teacher hides something, gives clues, and makes an approximate map of the location. Children must find the item or items.

Books That Promote Learning at Early Childhood Levels

Anno's Counting House by M. Anno (number concepts)

Airplanes, Boats, Trains, Trucks, Machines That Work by Byron Barton (concepts)

Seven Little Rabbits by J. Becker (counting)

The Snowman by R. Briggs (prediction)

Mr. Grumpy's Outing by John Burningham (sequence, counting)

Your Five Senses by R. Broekel (perception)

The Grouchy Ladybug by E. Carle (time and size)

The Very Busy Spider by E. Carle (concentration, design)

The Very Hungry Caterpillar by E. Carle (sequence)

We Read A to Z by D. Crews (letter names, recognition)

The Most Amazing Hide-and-Seek Counting Book by R. Crother (pop-up counting)

Strega Nona by Tomie de Paola (prediction)

The Story about Ping by Marjorie Flack (cause, effect)

Chicken Little by S. Kellog (sequence, prediction)

The Biggest Pumpkin Ever by S. Kroll (size relationships, divergent thinking)

First Book of Human Senses by G. Liberty (perception)

Inch by Inch by L. Lionni (thinking, problem solving)

Alphabet Word by B. Miller (letters and sounds)

Sesame Street Book of Opposites by Z. Mostel and G. Mendoza (demonstrates meanings of antonyms)

Colors by J. Reiss (the many shades of colors)

The Seeing Eye by V. Scheffer (perception: texture, color, form)

How Much Is a Million? by D. Schwartz (speculation)

Sylvester and the Magic Pebble by W. Steig (time changes)

Have You Seen My Duckling? by N. Tafuri (observation)

Deep in the Forest by B. Turkle (counting, groupings)

Bears in Pairs by N. Yektai (rhyming number concepts)

Where's the Guinea Pig? by H. Ziefer and A. Lobel (curiosity, problem solving)

Summary

Young children are most receptive when they are actively engaged in something that challenges and pleases them. Nearly every important learning concept can be demonstrated and reinforced through play, creative movement, interactions with the natural world, language experiences, and the arts. In a play/work learning environment, teachers and children work together and learn together. They experience learning as a multidimensional experience that goes beyond the walls and the fences of a child care center. When early education is valued as a cumulative process that incorporates many venues for learning, teachers will become curriculum experts.

N O T E S

1. Loris Malaguzzi, Catalog of the Exhibit, *The Hundred Languages of Children* (Reggio Emilia, Italia: Reggio Children, 1996), p. 29.

2. Rima Shore, *Rethinking the Brain: New Insights into Early Development* (Washington, DC: NAEYC, 1997), pp. 18, 41.

3. Carl Rogers, *Freedom to Learn* (Columbus, OH: Charles E. Merrill, 1969), p. 106.

4. As cited in Carolyn Edwards, L. Gandini, and G. Forman, eds., *The Hundred Languages of Children* (Norwood, NJ: Ablex), p. 31.

5. Susan D. Shilcock and Peter A. Bergson, *Open Connections: The Other Basics* (Bryn Mawr, PA: Open Connections, 1980), p. 5.

6. As cited in Joan Moyer et al., "The Child-Centered Kindergarten," *Childhood Education* 63 (4) (Wheaton, MD: ACEI, April 1987): 238.

7. As cited in Ruth Duskin Feldman, "What Are Thinking Skills?" *Instructor* XCV(8) (April 1985): 35.

8. Barbara Z. Presseisen, *Thinking Skills through the Curriculum* (Bloomington, IN: Pi Lambda Theta, 1987), p. 14.

9. John Dewey, *How We Think* (Boston: Heath, 1910).

10. Barry K. Beyer, "What's in a Skill?: Defining the Skills We Teach," *Social Science Record* 21 (1984): 19.

11. Anne Schreiber, "Fire Up Those Brain Cells," *Instructor* 98(3) (October 1988): 63.

12. Shilcock and Bergson, *Open Connections*, p. 11.

13. Bess-Gene Holt, *Science with Young Children* (Washington, DC: NAEYC, 1977), p. 110.

14. Doris M. Lee and R. V. Allen, *Learning to Read through Experience* (Englewood Cliffs, NJ: Prentice Hall, 1963), p. 2.

15. Mary Renck Jalongo, "Promoting Active Listening in the Classroom," in *Childhood Education* 72(1) (Wheaton, MD: ACEI, Fall 1995), p. 13.

16. W. Teale, "Emergent Literacy," in *The Literacy Dictionary: The Vocabulary of Reading and Writing,* eds., T. L. Harris and R. E. Hodges (Newark, DE: International Reading Association, 1995).

17. As cited in Ida Santos Stewart, "Kindergarten Reading Curriculum," *Childhood Education* 61(5) (Wheaton, MD: ACEI, May/June 1985): 357.

18. Bruno Bettelheim and Karen Zelan, *On Learning to Read* (New York: Vintage Books, 1982), p. 5.

19. Sylvia C. Chard, *The Project Approach: A Practical Guide for Teachers,* (Alberta, Canada: The University of Alberta, 1992), p. 5.

5 The Arts

I am convinced that the quality of our individual lives and the quality of our society are directly related to the quality of our artistic life. We need the arts as the key to the higher order of things—our cultural heritage, our gift of expression, our creative faculty, our sense of beauty.

—John D. Rockefeller

A child care program that cultivates the arts in early childhood is cultivating the creative process. The creative process is vital to early childhood because it nurtures all facets of human development—play, learning, physical, social, moral, and emotional. Self-expression is an *integral* part of children's daily experiences. A child who is encouraged to invent and experiment with ideas and materials in activity centers or at an art easel is expressing himself creatively. What teachers sometimes fail to realize is that a child who is role-playing is not just pretending, and a child who is painting is not just dabbling. Each child is expressing in a different way something about himself: his perception, his experiences, his personality, his interests, or his needs. The creating child is making important connections between his internal and external worlds. He can make puppets talk using his own words. He can paint and produce language to express his artwork. He can use his body to become something or someone that stirs his imagination.

Art should never be limited to an art center or to a dramatic play center. Art is inside and outside a center and implicit in every learning experience. It is whatever a child decides to play with or think about or imagine; something that is an extension of one's self. A child needs to experience many forms of art to satisfy his curiosity and his need for self-expression. When a child tires of building castles in the sand, he will look for another way to express himself. He might carry little cups of water back and forth from a water fountain to a dirt pile, excited by the texture, look, and feel of wet dirt. He doesn't perceive that dirt is dirty. A child doesn't understand why he can't play in mud; he views it as a natural part of his world. Nor does he understand that rocks or sticks can be dangerous to his playmates.

When a child engages in the arts, he is a creator. He is producing an authentic art form that has intrinsic meaning for him. As such, the child becomes a meaning-maker absorbed in a pleasing experience that he can control. He will find ways to prolong something that he likes. He will add sticks and rocks to a mud construct and paint over a painting. He will make a mess and be oblivious to its consequences. *Art is integral to play and play is integral to art. Both are integral to the child.*

A child engaged in the creative arts demonstrates awareness, imagination, and autonomy. Awareness comes from experiences that *stimulate* the senses. Multisensory experiences are excellent catalysts for the creative arts. The more a child can observe, interact with and respond to her total environment, the freer she will become to express herself through the arts. *Imagination is generated by the act of creating.* It can be cultivated by teachers and it can be promoted in an environment that has aesthetic appeal and creative tools to draw on. Autonomy is the child at play/work. The arts, like play, is child-initiated and a relatively free form of expression.

In an environment that cultivates originality, children's original productions are respected and valued. Children vary in their interests and are therefore selective in the way they express themselves. Some children may be adept at constructing with blocks, but disinterested, and therefore less developed, in artwork. If the meaning of art can be expanded to include anything a child creates, it will include all of the arts—the visual arts and the expressive arts. *And, all children will become creative artists.*

In a child-centered environment, children are free to experiment with many expressive media. Through cumulative experiences, a child develops a creative attitude. With each personal experience, she becomes more confident and more expressive. A child who carefully studies and selects flowers for a bouquet is expressing an art form; a child who is loving toward a doll is expressing an art form; a child involved in dramatic play is expressing an art form; a child playing and singing with musical instruments is expressing an art form. Creativity is any experience that satisfies and holds a child's attention. It is the child at play/work.

Through creative expression, imagination abounds. Children can become tiny insects and huge birds on a musical fantasy trip. They can feel and experience their environment in new and exciting ways. Children communicate with their bodies, their minds, and their spirits. Through creative experiences, a child *expresses* what he already knows, *experiences* what he needs to find out, and *experiments* with the unknown. He is able to find extraordinary meaning in ordinary everyday objects and experiences.

Defining the Arts

The expressive arts are basic and necessary to child development. A few children may have innate ability that is identified early as gifted, but all children hold the potential for becoming artistically creative human beings. A child care program that cultivates the arts in early childhood is cultivating the creative process. The arts serves not only as a primary medium for learning and self-expression but as a conduit for understanding and appreciating human development. A child's development and early training in all of the arts is an important feature of the PLAN curriculum.

In child care environments, a definition of the arts should be extended to include all creative constructs or experiences that occur as a child interacts with his environment. Art must be seen as a *bridge* that connects all areas of a curriculum in meaningful and relevant ways. No longer confined to an arts and crafts table, art is perceived as *integral* to all play centers and to all learning experiences.

An arts-oriented curriculum will incorporate learning from a different, somewhat less conventional frame of reference than traditional programs. It will be less time bound and less structured. It will redefine the arts from a child-directed perspective, taking into account children's creative instincts. It will develop program objectives that acknowledge the importance of originality, resourcefulness, inventiveness, and independence to a child's development.

In a position paper, "The Child's Right to the Expressive Arts," the ACEI (1990) has defined the arts as music, art, drama, dance, and writing, stating that:

- Every child has a right to opportunities for imaginative expression.
- Educating the child's imagination is education for the future.
- The educated imagination is the key to equity and intercultural understanding.
- Children's creative productivity is qualitatively different from adults'.

- Creative expression should permeate the entire curriculum.
- Imagination is the key to artistry in teaching and excellence in our schools.
- We must refashion our schools for the twenty-first century.[1]

Integrating the Arts into a Total Curriculum

Like play, the arts are fundamental to early childhood education. In an integrated arts program, opportunities to connect children's creative development with basic areas of skill development are boundless.

Children's art reflects the development of their thinking. As children become more cognizant and competent, they become better taskmasters and performers. Through exposure to ideas and materials, they are capable of elaborating and refining their productions. Art is an important dimension of learning, not only because it nurtures and validates the inner world of the child, but because it enables children to develop skills and knowledge that may not otherwise be available to them until much later in life. For example, children learn music by listening, practicing favorite songs, and by imitating what they hear. Over time, as children hear nursery rhymes, folk songs, and contemporary songs, they begin to coordinate music with inventive words, sometimes combining melody, rhythm, and pitch. Each new experience, such as attending a concert of *Peter and the Wolf*, or a ballet of *Hansel and Gretel*, nurtures their need and desire for experiences with music. With each new layer of discovery, children acquire a disposition for music and, perhaps, a desire to play an instrument.

The importance of the arts in defining and structuring the creative process challenges traditional ways of thinking about early education. Readiness, as a time of preparation for higher levels of learning, is now far more inclusive than traditionally was the case. An art-centered curriculum values the arts as a crucial dimension of communication and self-development in all content areas.

The Arts and Learning

Art is identified with creative thinking. Creative thinking may be described as a way of using one's mental processes to find unusual or divergent solutions for problems. A creative thinker uses reflection, reasoning, fluency, and flexibility in developing and expressing ideas. He is a child who can think about alternative solutions to a problem without feeling overshadowed by less flexible and less tolerant playmates. Paul Torrance describes the qualities and characteristics of a creative thinker as:

> [The child] is becoming sensitive to or aware of problems, deficiencies, gaps in knowledge, missing elements, disharmonies, and so on; bringing together in new relationships available information; defining the difficulty or identifying the missing elements, searching for solutions, making guesses or formulating hypotheses about the problem or deficiencies, testing and retesting them; perfecting them and finally communicating the results.[2]

When children are free to create, there is no *right* way. There is only the child's way. Early childhood is a time for opening doors to self-expression and creative thinking. It is not a time for molding or modeling children according to adult expectations, theories, or concepts of beauty. When children (and adults) explore materials, it is the *process* that shapes and determines the outcome.

Personalities are shaped and influenced by the quality of experience. Children who are confident in their ability to express themselves through the integrated arts are empowered by their own energy as they:

- Explore multiple uses of a medium.
- Use their imaginations and take intellectual risks.
- Develop visual/spatial intelligence.
- Engage in a self-directed project.
- Work at their own paces and levels.
- Explore the symbolic function of the arts.
- Engage in dialogue with others about their creative processes and works.
- Build skills in self-evaluation.[3]

Integrating the Arts into Activity Centers

A science center may integrate the arts and learning. If children are studying Woodland Indians, for example, there might be a large wooden bowl filled with real vegetables and nuts for children to smell, feel, and sort on a science table. The teacher and children might add a long house (made from a milk carton) and a wigwam (made from clay and covered with bark) to the science display. Leaf prints and pressings may be hung on a wall nearby. Each week a new artifact is added: moccasins, a totem pole, jewelry, dolls, tools, an animal print mold, bark, baskets, an Indian alphabet, Native American music, and musical instruments.

Through ongoing, multisensory experiences in a discovery center, children get to experiment with different textures (smooth, soft, rough), with smells (vinegar, vanilla, pepper, garlic, lemon, cinnamon), with environmental stimulants (charts, plants, growing things, animals, soft cushions), and with eye-appealing activities that encourage creative thinking and exploration (geoboards, tangrams, cubes, terrariums, sorting trays, water experiments).

Virtually all science and math skills can be presented artistically in a child's natural play setting. Similarly, a social studies unit can be presented through arts and crafts, visuals, literature, and hands-on experiences that are a natural and pleasurable function of play. A language-experience story often begins with a child's artwork. Cooking experiences become aesthetic and sensory delights when presented creatively.

A play center can be transformed into a bear's cave, an igloo, a bee's hive, or the witch's cottage in the fairytale *Hansel and Gretel*. A play house covered in brown or white cardboard and decorated for particular themes will elicit a mood for pretend play. Bear tracks can be taped on the floor leading into a cave that has become a home for hibernating bears. A tunnel can be made at the entrance of an igloo; a honey comb may contain costumes for a queen bee and worker bees; and, with a little imagination, a cottage in the woods can become the setting for dramatizing a favorite classic for children of all ages.

A project center can display pictures of famous artists and their work. A class of four- and five-year-olds might enjoy focusing on one artist each month. As children get to know artists, they become familiar with their work. They can identify a technique or style that is unique to an artist such as pointilism with Seurat, cubism with Picasso, portraits and windmills with Rembrandt, flowers with Van Gogh, a still life with Cézanne, and dancers with Degas. As a follow-up experience, children may collect postcards of famous works of art, arrange them in an album, and write words to describe their feelings about the artist and his work. They may become so intrigued with windmills that they design their own classroom model. As children develop perspective, they begin to experiment with space. They discover that outdoor paintings are generally three dimensional while indoor paintings are two dimensional. Taking their sketch books out-of-doors, children can study subjects from the perspective of size, shape, space and light. They will begin to experiment with hues as they blend colors into original artworks.

In a creative classroom, the arts are natural to the environment. Children make observations and record their impressions by drawing, writing, and modeling. It is through art that a child is able to activate his senses, construct knowledge, and communicate ideas.

Every community holds potential for children to make new discoveries about their surrounding world. Knowing in advance what children are studying enables a naturalist, an architect, or a librarian to design a program that will reinforce and authenticate children's learning.

Young children become sensitive to the arts by working out-of-doors. Children may paint their playground (with water and brushes), they may finger paint on plastic, press leaf or flower prints on windows, paint rocks for a rock garden, paint to music, or make a mural large enough to hang on a building. An awareness of one's environment develops slowly through experiences that create a sense of wonder and anticipation in the young child.

Setting Up an Arts Studio

In Reggio Emilia schools, an art teacher (attelierista) works with children in an art studio (an atelier).[4] He encourages students to make observations and to reflect on a subject before beginning a project. He encourages them to experiment, evaluate and make changes throughout the life of a project. In the process of creating artwork, young children become keenly aware of design, organization, and detail. A small object is often the source of creativity for a young child, such as a flower that is just beginning to open, a spider spinning a web, a falling leaf, an icicle, or a snowflake. In a discovery atmosphere, children are noticeably self-directed and committed to their project/work, continually tapping their own resourcefulness, creativity, and interests in new and distinctive ways.

As children become familiar with an art center, they quickly develop independence and discipline. They figure out how to apply glue sparingly and how to control paint on brushes. They soon learn that tools and materials are not used in the same way. For example, working with water colors, charcoal, tissue paper, small paint brushes, painting at an easel, or finger painting on paper are all quite different experiences. As materials become more challenging, the child becomes more absorbed in the process of making discoveries—something that cannot be obtained in an immediate experience with paint and a paintbrush.

A teacher may assist a child by anticipating needs, asking questions, and supporting her work. When children are working cooperatively, as in painting a mural or constructing a model, a teacher will need to assist children in solving problems related to sharing materials, sharing space, and developing a theme. She may need to identify working areas to prevent disagreements, at least at the initial stages of a project. Once children begin a project, they are more receptive to dialogue and may even surrender their space to a friend who has an interesting idea or needs more room.

Experiencing Materials

An art center provides many materials for children to experiment with, such as crayons, markers, pencils, charcoal, clay, play dough, stencils, watercolors, glue, and scissors. An assortment of collage materials such as glitter, doilies, flannel shapes, pieces of ribbon, tissue paper, and gift wrappings provide endless opportunities for designing pictures. Scissors, paper, and various kinds of drawing materials and modeling materials should also be available for children's use.

An art center may also offer woodworking materials such as various sizes of wood, assorted nails and screws, pliers, small hammers, a small saw, clamps, a vise, sandpaper, string, a ruler, and a tape measure. All materials should be selected for age appropriateness and safety.

When the arts are presented and valued as integral components of a whole-child curriculum, young children feel comfortable in a cultural milieu that extends beyond their immediate community such as visiting an art gallery, a theatre, a sculpture garden, a botanical garden, or a museum. They continue to experience art as a natural and meaningful extension of themselves and of all the experiences that they have shared with others.

Objectives for an Integrated Arts Program at Early Childhood Levels

A creative teacher who values self-expression is able to do the following:

- Cultivate in children a disposition for pretending, imagination and curiosity.
- Provide opportunities for young children to engage in dramatic play through literature and the arts.
- Provide a literary foundation that extends language by enhancing creativity.

- Appreciate music and movement as pleasureful and developmentally challenging experiences for young children.
- Encourage children to learn about and appreciate their artistic heritage.
- Provide many tools and opportunities for expression to stimulate children's creative resources and energy.
- Encourage children to develop good work habits that instill a sense of pride in accomplishments.
- Help children experience the beauty of their surroundings from a tiny wildflower, to a pumpkin ripening on a vine, to a spider's web still moist with dew.

How Teachers Cultivate the Arts

Observation

A teacher can serve an important role in cultivating visual, sensual, and kinesthetic awareness by drawing children's attention to the aesthetic and physical world that surrounds them. A teacher may take children on daily *seeing walks,* encouraging them to listen, touch, and notice things. She can point out little things like a centipede, and big things like a helicopter twirling around interrupting the tranquility of a sky-scape.

A teacher can take children on a *shape walk,* pointing out various shapes in a natural environment, having children sketch what they see, compare what they find, and identify common characteristics. She can take children on a *feeling walk,* pointing out the textures (and smells) of nature and collecting interesting things for observation, like worms, mollusks, anthropods, and other tiny creatures. (Live creatures should be returned to their natural environments in relatively good health after visiting with children.) She can take children on a *space walk,* observing how distance changes one's perspective, noticing how space moves around and through freestanding objects, asking children to sketch a one-dimensional and perhaps, a two- or three-dimensional picture. She can take children on a *body awareness* experience that encourages freedom of movement—playing with balls and balloons; swinging; running up hills; rolling down hills; dancing with scarves; moving in, out, and around hoops; crossing pretend streams (on a balance beam) and pretend oceans (on a nesting bridge); blowing and chasing bubbles; flying kites and following birds in flight. She can take children on a *surprise walk,* a walk that is done so quietly that not even the birds hear; a walk that is meant for finding special treasures (hidden by a treasured teacher). Firsthand experiences that extend perceptions help a child identify and interpret the physical world.

Through observation, a child becomes more knowledgeable about space and his own place in space. He notices large, imposing buildings and small clusters of houses. He notices big things and little things. A child notices things that often go unnoticed to the casual, uninterested observer.

Personalizing Experiences

A teacher who values the arts as a primary developmental process recognizes the importance of working closely with a young child without appearing intrusive or instructional in demeanor. Even though children need independence in making choices and carrying out a task, they enjoy a teacher's attention. A teacher can make suggestions and assist a child in selecting materials that reinforce an idea. Whether children are working in a project center or making interesting creations out of doors, they are responsive to a teacher's presence and to the special relationship that is shared throughout the day.

In a whole-child environment, a teacher looks at each child as an individual capable of *a hundred languages* (and more) expressed so eloquently by educator Loris Malaguzzi. By personalizing and praising each child's projects, a teacher is recognizing and reinforcing the inordinate potential within each child. In this atmosphere, a teacher's innate capacity for creativity and love may be expressed in unexpected and reinforcing ways.

By observing a child's creative process, a sensitized teacher begins to notice things such as:

- A child's understanding of spatial concepts
- A child's ability to concentrate
- A child's disposition for creative thinking and learning
- A child's perceptual and artistic ability
- A child's willingness to experiment with ideas
- A child's large- and small-motor development
- A child's expressive and receptive language skills
- A child's ability to think abstractly
- A child's uniqueness

Valuing Originality

Creative expression can be a never-ending source of satisfaction for a young child. She delights in the process and in her natural, unedited productions. She creates when she plays with blocks, when she arranges a play center, and when she assembles a collage of dried flowers and lace doilies. She creates when she makes pictures, when she arranges clothes on a doll, and when she arranges a tea set on a table.

Creativity must be understood and reinforced by teachers if it is to flourish in children. A teacher who interferes with the artistic process or who identifies a ditto as artwork may, unknowingly, destroy it. She is replacing children's original artwork with a reproduction (something that is produced by adults).

Teachers must appreciate that originality is the hallmark of the child's creative process. Their productions may not conform to our notions of form or beauty, but teachers must avoid the temptation to substitute their own efforts for those of the child, even if that means the project is not "completed" from an adult's perspective.

A child who exhibits originality through freedom of choice is a creative child. Her symbolic representations reflect the way she perceives and experiences the things in her world.

The characteristics of a creative person are defined by Leon Burton and Kathy Kuroda as:

Interest in ideas and meanings	Persistence in examining
Eagerness to explore the environment because of a need to know	Sensitivity to problems
	Spontaneity
Willingness to risk the unknown	Curiosity
Openness to new experiences, ideas	Playfulness
High tolerance of ambiguity	Flexibility
Interest in personal expression	Independence
Preference for complexity	Intuitiveness[5]

Praising and Encouraging Children's Artwork

Adults can cultivate the arts by affirming children's self-expression. Children receive messages by the way a teacher communicates and responds to authentic artwork. A teacher who throws artwork away because it is too messy or is reluctant to hang artwork on a wall because it does not fit into his visual scheme is not supporting creative expression. Similarly, a teacher who touches up artwork or who directs projects is giving a child a message that her work is not acceptable.

Teachers should take time to sincerely recognize children's artwork but need not lavish them with praise (children already feel good about their work). They should notice special things about children's artwork: "I like the pink flowers so much. I wish I could pick them, put them in a vase, and keep them forever!" She encourages children to be inventive: "Would you like to see what happens when we mix red and white, green and yellow, black and white?" "What can we call this color . . . it's not red, it's not black, it's not green." She encourages children to try ideas—to design and create using many textures, mediums, and materials. In self-challenging activities that enable a child to feel in control, the child and the process are one. The child creates as the child experiments with materials. Unlike the school-age child, the young child tends not to be concerned about finished products. He is absorbed in using materials in inventive ways. In the untrained eyes of the child, everything is beautiful—especially his own work. It is an adult who introduces self-doubt: "Why don't you add a little yellow to your picture? I think it would make it prettier, don't you?"

Selecting Appropriate Art Experiences

Appropriate art experiences should reflect children's levels of development and interests. In *Early Childhood Art,* Barbara Herberholz describes the categories of experiences that may prove useful in developing an arts curriculum as visual and tactile perceptual encounters, production of art, aesthetic judgment and valuing of art, and heritage of art.[6]

Visual and Tactile Experiences

At early levels of development, these experiences are natural, ongoing activities that invite exploration such as painting at an easel, finger painting, experimenting with colors, cutting and pasting paper, sand and water play, coloring with large crayons, drawing on a blackboard with chalk, playing with play dough, playing with textured fabrics that are in a feel box, reading picture books, planting seeds, caring for baby animals, taking seeing walks, and exploring one's play environment. They are important stimulants for children's creative instincts.

Production of Art

As children become more interested in the art process, they move from simple to more complex levels of production. They know what they need and they know how and where to obtain materials. They can design and complete a multistep art project without adult intervention. A child involved in an art project can work for extended periods of time without distraction. As he works, he is developing an awareness of tactile and shape variations, of design and composition, of figure-ground orientation, of parts to a whole, of spatial awareness, and of balance. Encouragement always factors into children's continued interest in an activity. An art center must have a place to display artwork and a teacher who appreciates and understands children enough to display it, as is.

Aesthetic Judgment

It is very difficult to assess the artwork of children other than on its own terms. Although children should not judge one another's work, they can develop aesthetic appreciation that will prepare them for aesthetic judgment as they near adulthood. In his book, *Art and the Creative Development of Young Children,* Robert Schirrmacher defines aesthetics:

> Beauty can be found in nature, in one's surroundings, and in everyday objects. Children can use their senses and their bodies in their pursuit of beauty. The eyes can visually explore art, the ears can listen to sounds and music. Three-dimensional artworks can be touched, scents can be smelled, foods can be tasted, and the body can respond through movement and dance. Young children can learn to appreciate and have beautiful experiences.[7]

Aesthetic appreciation is a gradual perceptual skill that is linked to experience. When children experience live entertainment, they naturally become art critics. A teacher will promote aesthetic appreciation by challenging children's ability to think and respond from their perceptions. She might ask questions that pertain to plot development, character development, costumes, set designs, lighting, sound effects, the moral or meaning of a story, seating, interactions among the characters and the audience, the length of a production, and feelings generated by the experience.

Creating a Heritage of Art

As children mature, they can appreciate all forms of artistic expression through direct experiences with theatre and cultural activities. Children should become familiar with the various forms, styles, and periods of art. They will pick out a Rembrandt painting by its use of dramatic lighting and a Picasso by the placement of dissimilar shapes on a flat, one-dimensional surface. They will become knowledgeable about periods of art and their characteristics: medieval and classical art, romantic art, neoclassical, impressionism, expressionism, cubism, and modern art. They will become familiar with themes and styles that are identified with certain artists, such as, landscape, seascape, portrait, sculpture, still life, impressionism, geometric abstracts, splash paintings, and pop art.

Stages of Art

Scribble Stage

Young children progress in the arts much as they do in any other skill, from simple to complex levels. Most educators specializing in the arts agree that children's artwork tends to develop sequentially. Although chronological ages may vary, the sequence of stages tend to be fairly predictable.[8] Early artwork that appears between the ages of fifteen months to around three years reflects a child's developmental level. At this basic level, children's art resembles random scribbling. Early scribbles are primarily zig zags, curves, or spontaneously placed splashes that appear to have little meaning. One marking often fills up a whole piece of paper. As primitive as early art is, it represents a child's increasing level of awareness and coordination.

As children develop eye–hand skills, scribbles become more controlled and recognizable—circles, loops, and intricate swirls indicate the beginnings of representational art. Familiar objects begin to appear, often creatures that resemble amoebae (tadpoles). By adding lines for arms or legs, the little creature becomes more humanlike. A child begins to identify his picture as a person when he adds dots for eyes, and if somewhat more perceptually advanced, clawlike fingers and toes. The child, who is very pleased with his accomplishment, identifies the picture as "mommy, daddy," or, never lacking in ego, "me." If the experience is positive, the child will ask to make another picture; this time with a marker (or two), or, with a Q-tip that can be dipped in paint, creating a whole new experience for the child.

Preschematic Stage

Between the ages of four and seven, children progress into a preschematic stage (also referred to as a pictorial stage). Children's pictures take on form and symbolic meaning (simple drawings begin to represent something or someone). The child has control over the direction and size of lines and has advanced in levels of motor control. Objects that are important to a child are the subjects of most early artwork. A circle with four legs is identified as a dog or a cat, a circle with a vertical base is identified as a tree, a dash of color on the ground is a flower. As a child's perception heightens, his pictures begin to fill more space and gradually convey an impression of balanced composition. A person once floating sideways in the air will be firmly placed on a grass line. Clouds and raindrops will be placed above the person and the composition may well be framed by a border.

By centering and reducing the size of primary objects, children discover there is more space to fill with birds, flowers, bugs, and raindrops. A child's paintings often reflect her current interests at a developmental stage, for example dinosaurs and action figures. Familiar subjects such as family members, pets, homes, friends, and seasonal symbols (hearts and pumpkins) are fairly constant themes of the young painter.

Schematic Stage

Between the ages of seven and twelve, a child's artwork enters a schematic stage that reflects children's interest in their ever-expanding world. Despite occasional forays into fantasy, children like to depict a very detailed, precise world in their drawings. They become intrigued with features, parts, and balance. Their artwork requires organization, time, and thoughtfulness.

The way a child approaches artwork reflects his disposition, interests and developmental level (see Figure 5.1). Some children will meticulously arrange shapes according to some preconceived pattern, while others prefer spontaneous bold strokes that may or may not develop into a recognizable form. Most children tend to experiment with both *free form* and *idea-centered* compositions especially if they are in a creative classroom.

Valuing the Arts

Art Is Learning

As children experience themselves in an expressive environment, they clarify and expand meanings; they discover cause-and-effect relationships, the power of nonverbal communication, and the possibilities of using their own ideas. Because art is primarily a subjective, internalized experience, children are not so dependent on external reinforcement for gratification as they are in many social or content-oriented activities that make children feel like they have to perform.

When children are free to create, they apply divergent (flexible) thinking to their tasks. As ideas are generated, children invest in their production and become less concerned with outcomes. They become more fluent in producing and developing ideas. They adapt and modify their combinations until they feel satisfied.

Stage			
Random/disordered scribbling	Controlled scribbling	Basic forms	Pictorial stage (first-drawings stage)
Age Range			
1½ to 3 years (Toddlers)	Young preschoolers	3 to 4 years	4 to 5 years and older
Motor Control			
Lacks good motor control and hand-eye coordination	Improving motor control and hand-eye coordination	Has more developed motor control and hand-eye coordination	Has control over direction and size of line. Has most advanced motor control and hand-eye coordination
Purpose			
Scribbles for pure physical sensation of movement	Scribbles with control	Enjoys mastery over line	Communicates with outside world through drawing. Expresses personality and relationship to symbols drawn
Characteristics of Stage			
Lacks direction or purpose for marks. Does not mentally connect own movement to marks on page	Explores and manipulates materials. Tries to discover what can be done—explores color, texture, tools, and techniques. Often repeats action. Makes marks with intention and not by chance	Masters basic forms: circle, oval, line, rectangle, and square. Discovers connection between own movements and marks on page	Combines basic forms to create first symbols. Names drawings as a form of true communication

FIGURE 5.1   Developmental Levels in Children's Art

Source: From *PRE–K TODAY*, Issues from 1987 and 1988. Copyright © 1987, 1988 by Scholastic Inc. Reprinted by permission of Scholastic Inc. All rights reserved.

The personal satisfaction a child derives from an original production is enormous. They do not require external gratification. Self-directed children trust and follow their own ideas.

Art Promotes Social/Emotional Development

An informal, relaxed atmosphere invites children's participation. A nonthreatening environment puts forth positive signals and feelings. Children naturally respond to activities that stimulate good feelings. All children profit from the freedom to express themselves. Joyful children experience more joy as they create. Troubled children release the tension that is holding them back or interfering with happiness. In either situation, a child who is free to pound, to hammer, to splash, and to create is a happy child.

As the child develops self-confidence, he sifts, identifies, and expresses problems through vicarious experiences. As he expresses his feelings, he is able to let go of some of the fears that restrict his movement and limit his capabilities. He learns to trust his instincts and to experiment with his talents. As a child makes contact with his extended self, he gradually affirms his own potential and enjoys his own productions.

Art Promotes Creative Thinking

Creativity can be enhanced or stifled during the formative years. Creative opportunities often are lost in highly regimented programs: A child doesn't get to make stick drawings in the dirt because sticks are prohibited, or climb a tree because it's too dangerous, or wear a ballet outfit in block play because it is not allowed. When a child's movements are unnecessarily restricted and challenged, she loses her inquisitiveness and imagination. Eager to please, a child becomes a product of the conventional environment that surrounds her.

Early childhood is the time to foster original thinking through the expressive arts. Creative imagination peaks at four to five years old. Through acculturation, however, creative imagination declines at school-age levels. The challenge for early childhood teachers, therefore, is to stimulate—to keep alive children's natural desire to create so that as an intrinsic part of the child, it grows with the child.

Implementing the Arts

The Visual Arts

Arts and Crafts

For the child younger than three years of age, table art should focus on tactile experiences and aesthetic enjoyment. Seated or standing at an art table, children might enjoy such activities as string painting (dipping string in paint and smearing it on a piece of paper); marble painting (rolling marbles dipped in paint on a piece of paper that is contained in a box); printing (dipping vegetables, shapes, or leaves in paint and stamping designs on plain paper); finger painting with paint, shaving cream, or whipped soap flakes; painting cardboard boxes; making hand-prints or footprints; or assembling and pasting (using various shapes and textures). For holidays or special events, teachers may initiate a special art project that can be enjoyed by children and parents: an apple or pinecone turkey, paper bag pumpkins, tissue paper ghosts, a simple puppet, dried flower arrangements, or holiday ornaments. As pleasing as these projects are, they should not be considered original productions unless the child controls the process. They should be labeled *crafts.*

When a child reaches four or five years of age, she has a better concept of form and design and enjoys more extensive experiences at an art table. She is especially attracted by colorful, unusual materials and will delve into construction and assemblage with fervor. Children exercise choice and decision making in the materials they select and the compositions and constructs they design. Arts and crafts give children a chance to experience a multistep art project that requires attentiveness to one task. In addition to cognitive stimulus, a craft project also should provide many opportunities for experimentation and free association. Children should be able to make choices and to orchestrate their production without teacher interference. Some materials like foil, felt, glitter, and doilies are particularly eye-catching and appealing for a collage (an assemblage of materials arranged in random order on a plain piece of paper). Here are some ideas for arts and crafts:

- Holiday gingerbread houses
- Mobiles
- Wildflower arrangements and molding a vase
- Corn meal and sand drawings (add powdered tempera paint to sand)
- String art
- Designs by stitching on fabric
- Wire sculptures
- Baker's dough (1 cup flour, 1/2 cup water, food coloring)
- Oily dough (3 cups flour, 1 cup salt, 3 T oil, 1 cup water)
- Gadget junk art sculptures
- Costumes and shirts by tie-dyeing
- Prints (draw designs with pencil point on interesting surfaces such as styro-foam trays, cover with paint and press onto paper)
- Crayon-resist pictures (draw designs with crayons and paint surface of paper)
- Drawings out-of-doors with charcoal, feathers, or colored chalk
- Objects from toilet paper rolls
- Colorful baby food jars made by layering with different colors of sand
- Placemats made with materials gathered or designed by children (should be laminated for continued use)

- Magnets made with cute eye-catching objects
- Shoe box art themes
- Alphabet or number art
- Puppets (from socks, fruits and vegetables, paper bags, paper plates, peanut shells, tin cans)
- A puppet stage from a large cardboard box
- Interesting variations on collages

The act of gluing, organizing, and assembling artwork is far more important to the child than the finished project. A picture or creation eventually emerges—sometimes incredibly balanced and beautifully orchestrated and sometimes a potpourri of glue, drips, holes, and blending colors that have long since lost their distinctiveness. As the child works with media and materials, he becomes more aware of composition and design. He studies and selects from the various materials that surround him. He balances his composition by repeating designs and by arranging shapes in harmonious and sometimes bold, uneven patterns that add variety and interest to his design. He transforms ordinary shapes into extraordinary assemblages, into unique art forms.

The Teacher's Role.   It is the teacher's responsibility to provide the materials and experiences that promote creative expression. An arts and crafts table/shelf should have a wide variety of materials for children to assemble and interact with. Some materials to include are paper plates; styrofoam trays; paper bags; a scrap box containing material, tissue paper, newspaper cartoons, wrapping paper, flannel shapes, fabric, yarn and other visual delights; an odds and ends box containing gadgets, paste-ons and novel accessories; and, of course, play dough and modeling clay. By adding simple accessories to a paper bag such as buttons, yarn, and pipe cleaners, a child can create a hand puppet. By stuffing a bag with paper, she can make a cute little creature, adding feet, ears, hands, a tail, and a face. She can name the creature and write a story about it.

Some children who lack fine-motor control get frustrated with tedious tasks that are identified with finished products such as, stringing clay beads, sewing, or completing a diorama that has little meaning to a child. These children should not feel compelled to engage in a "creative activity" that is not creative for them. Art projects and experiences should be *choices* and not requirements for children. If a teacher has set up an art experience that requires more than an initial explanation, the project is probably too difficult for a child to understand and manage independently.

Four- and five-year-olds will especially enjoy arts and crafts. They like the challenging projects and interesting materials a good program provides, in large part, because they are able to transform and work with materials in their own way. They can benefit from innovative projects such as making masks, candles, home decorations, marionettes, little creatures made with styrofoam or pom pom balls, collages, murals, mosaics, prints, corn husk dolls, embroidery, and stitchery. Children's artwork soars when they are involved in group projects or dramatic productions. For many children, making scenery or simple costumes is as important as acting in a play.

Painting

At the early stages of artwork, children enjoy the pleasure derived from holding a crayon and scribbling on paper. Early scribble art strengthens children's small muscle development, making them more agile in eye–hand coordination. The same strokes used in scribble art are used later when children begin to write. When young children are introduced to painting, they typically experience a three-step process: holding a paint brush, dipping it in paint, and transferring the paint to a piece of paper. Often one or two strokes will satisfy a child's initial interest in painting. At the early stages of development, children should choose among primary colors: red, blue, or yellow. A large supply of white paint always should be on hand to soften and change color tones and to add excitement to a child's creative experience.

Like children's babbles, early painting experiences do not appear to say very much but they are a necessary part of a child's development. Through early art experiences the child becomes aware that he can make things happen; he can change things; he can create something. Somewhere between three and four years of age, random strokes evolve into lifelike objects. These early expressions of form gradually evolve into more realistic and recognizable objects and people: a house, the sun, an animal, a child, or a parent. A child paints what he sees, what is familiar to him, and what is important to him. Children typically use geometric shapes to symbolize people and objects, and horizontal lines to identify the ground and the sky. There is little linear perspective and symmetry in their early productions. A child will often exaggerate important objects in a painting, such as a life-sized father or mother, a tiny new baby, or an oversized pet.

As children develop coordination and a sense of composition, their paintings and drawings become enchanting expressions of childhood. When children are four or five years of age, their artwork begins to reveal perceptions and emerging personalities. Some children love bold, open strokes, others paint linear drawings that are meticulous in form and design. A girl, sensitive to patterns, may frame a painting with a border of alternating flowers and hearts. A boy, preoccupied with dinosaurs, may paint dinosaurs and huge eggs until the fixation is replaced by something else. As perceptions sharpen, paintings become more and more detailed. Figures are elongated when necks, feet, toes, arms, and fingers are added. Animals get tails and eye lashes; birds get long beaks, long legs, and worms in their mouths.

Four- and five-year-olds enjoy painting with many colors and media and in various settings. They enjoy mixing and blending colors and using a variety of materials: paints, crayons, water colors, acrylics, oil, and chalk. Children enjoy sketching out-of-doors; coloring in a loft; and drawing on blackboards and sidewalks. They love to decorate sets for plays and performances, making props and costumes from boxes, containers, kitchen and attic discards, and whatever else suits their fancy.

Color Principles. An arts program for young children should help children to become cognizant of color and color harmony. They should recognize primary colors (red, blue, and yellow), secondary colors (orange, green, and violet) and experiment with complementary colors (colors that are opposite each other on the color wheel, such as violet and yellow).

Methods of Painting. Young children love to paint and enjoy experiences that create new levels of awareness and enjoyment such as:

Sponge painting	Finger painting
Feather painting	Roller brush painting
Q-tip painting	Bubble painting (blow bubbles in colored water onto paper)
Wet chalk painting	
String painting	Object printing (paint bottle tops, acorns, pinecones, a cork, or vegetables, and transfer onto paper)
Pressings (paint leaves and flowers and press onto paper)	
Crayon reliefs (children color with crayons and lightly watercolor or paint over it)	Scratch and print painting (scratch a design onto a styrofoam tray with a toothpick and press onto paper)
Whipped soap paintings	Straw paintings
Roller brush and print on paper	Sprinkle paintings
Screen (splatter) painting	Glitter paintings
Marble painting	

Children also enjoy working with starch and water to assemble a tissue paper collage, arranging and pasting interesting fabrics and textures on paper, pen and ink sketches, painting on ceramic tiles and on sandpaper, box, wire, and soap sculptures, making mobiles and gadget assemblages.

Stimulating the Senses. Children's artwork is stimulated by objects and materials in their environment. An easel or art table that is positioned near windows and mirrors provides an atmosphere that arouses children's images and imagination. Surrounded by light and shadow created by a natural environment, children's paintings take on new and interesting dimensions. They may, for example, become softer (blending colors) and more intricate in design as children experiment with paints.

Children's artwork is also complemented by aesthetically appealing objects and textures in a science center such as:

A feather	A kaleidoscope
Clear bottles filled with glitter in water	A view master
A prism	Shakers
A magnifying glass	An hour glass
A magnet	A microscope
Origami paper; cellophane	Shells
A tray of dried flowers	Sequins, gemstones, rocks
Cellophane color paddles	Spice and herb samples
Pieces of contrasting fabrics (velvet, burlap)	A book of wallpaper samples
Delicate glass window decorations	Mobiles and chimes
Pottery	A bird house
Samples of clay and dough	A bucket of sand
Bark and moss	Animal parts (snake skin, a horseshoe crab, a turtle's shell)
Fish and small animals	

Displaying Children's Artwork.   There are some simple guidelines to keep in mind when planning a room environment and displaying children's work:

1. Remember that the child's eye level is much lower than an adult's. Displays should therefore be placed fairly low, so that the child can be close to his own work.
2. A child-oriented environment leaves plenty of undecorated wall space to allow the child freedom to use his own imagination.
3. When a child's work is displayed, it must not be improved on by a teacher.
4. When displays are changed, the teacher should always leave some areas unchanged so the child will not feel uncomfortable with new arrangements.
5. From time to time reproductions of famous paintings or original art by professionals should be included for display.[9]

The Teacher's Role.   Teachers should spend considerable time on the aesthetic arrangements of children's artwork, charts and bulletin board displays. Adding a frame to a child's painting, or displaying samples of artwork and photographs of children at play creates a feeling of balance and harmony in a room. A wall does not capture the feeling and activity of children when it is laden with commercial cutouts and skill-building visuals. It does not inspire creativity or authenticity—two very important aspects of a child's development.

In a genuinely creative environment, children should be encouraged to construct with sand, mud, and dirt; arrange leaves, berries, and nutmeats in interesting patterns; finger paint with soap on doors and windows; make chalk pictures on sidewalks; and paint a building with water. By expanding the arts to include all hands-on, creative experiences, children will perceive art as an integral part of their natural world.

In an arts environment, children should be introduced to important artists and their works. A young child will enjoy looking at the primitive, childlike paintings of Grandma Moses, at a soft impressionist painting by Renoir, or at the bold angular lines of a Cézanne landscape.

Four- and five-year-olds may become familiar with periods of art and famous artists: with classical painters such as Michelangelo, DaVinci, Raphael, and Rembrandt; with romantic painters such as Delacroix and Copley; with impressionist painters such as Renoir, Monet, Pissaro, and Manet; with post-impressionist painters such as Cézanne, Van Gogh, Gauguin, Matisse; and with contemporary painters such as Picasso, Léger, Chagall, Klee, and Kandinsky. Children may become familiar with distinguishing techniques used by artists: El Greco's use of elongated figures, Cézanne's unfinished paintings, Vermeer's detailed, meticulous organization of objects, Kandinsky's musical composition themes, and Rembrandt's use of light.

Woodworking

Children in child care environments love the challenge of woodworking. Woodworking provides an important emotional and physical outlet for children. Young children's experiences with woodworking should be limited to large blocks of wood, small light hammers, and large-head nails. A tree stump provides a wonderful base for hammering. In time, children can progress to independent projects with wood.

As children mature, they enjoy organizing, measuring, and coordinating constructs, and using tools that perform specific functions. They soon discover that hammering nails into a block of wood or using a small saw to cut light wood is not easy. Nails bend and frustrate a young builder. Wood splits easily and is not always soft. The task of assembling a construct or a sculpture requires patience and perseverance. Children also enjoy using assorted materials such as hardware accessories, ice cream sticks, parts of games, buttons, packing materials, wire, string, rubber bands, and bottle caps as parts of their design. They like to organize novelty items and make unique arrangements in space. Three-dimensional projects introduce a whole new dimension to children's artwork.

Children may enjoy seeing how space can be used dramatically in both architecture and in sculptures. Frank Lloyd Wright fused buildings into the natural settings; Henry Moore used space to make figures stand out, creating a sense of vitality and permanence in their settings. By studying artworks, children are impressed by a great variety and individuality of the styles that have preoccupied artists. They learn that an artist works to perfect his style and his skills. Some works are impersonal and abstract, some convey explicit expressions of feelings and emotions, while others have a hidden meaning.

The Teacher's Role.   Teachers can encourage woodworking constructs by arranging materials and tools so that they are accessible and inviting. Various sizes of soft wood and tools will challenge children to construct creative objects. Accessories will provide incentive and guidance in developing and shaping constructs. Pictures of buildings, bridges, railroad trestles, welders, and artisans may be displayed in a woodworking center. Certain individuals may be singled out for their contributions to the art of woodworking, such as architect Frank Lloyd Wright or sculptor Henry Moore.

Original Writing

Children write when they have something to communicate or when they are absorbed in a creative experience that requires something more than pictures. In most instances, writing emerges in a social context as children identify and communicate with peers. In every class, there are some children who can make letters and write inventively. Since children are comfortable learning with and from peers, those with special abilities are recognized and followed by others. A child's visual representations usually precede or accompany their early writings. Pictures illuminate meaning by helping children to make the connection between the visual and the literal arts.

Children often begin writing on their own in a project or writing center. They imitate real books by making books. They are especially intrigued with assemblage (putting papers together and using a stapler). For the industrious child gathering materials, a book of six pages may have only one or two markings on a page. Nonetheless, to the child the book represents a serious piece of work. With practice and some assistance, children will gradually begin to write inventively, using their own words to create a story or to communicate a message.

The Teacher's Role

A teacher encourages writing by giving children freedom to write in their own way. Children who are lacking in fine-motor skills should not be required to write in lines or to follow public school standards in the way letters are shaped. Nor should children feel that a picture always needs words or that words always need to be shared with teachers. The best way to inspire creative writing is to give children the freedom to experience writing in their own way.

Children's picture writings reflect their memories and experiences with literature. Four- and five-year-old children love to recreate nursery tales and favorite stories through artwork, original books, puppets and songs. In order to refamiliarize children with early literary experiences, teachers should read and recite old favorites such as *Jack, Be Nimble, Old King Cole,* and *Bah, Bah, Black Sheep.* In the old favorite *Peter Peter Pumpkin Eater* the sound of *p* and the full, round shape of the pumpkin create an image that makes every reader want to crawl in a pumpkin shell and "be kept very well" forever.

As children discover the elements of writing through literature and language activities, they soon notice that writers and illustrators have unique styles and characteristics that distinguish them from other writers and illustrators. This alone can become an enlightening experience for a beginning writer who can identify the literary style of Maurice Sendak, William Steig, Ezra Keats, or Dr. Seuss. It is through literature that children receive powerful and lasting images that surface and reveal themselves at unexpected moments and in unanticipated ways.

As children progress in early writing, they become familiar with the elements of a story (plot, characters, form, and setting), and the particular appeal of a story. An integrated curriculum recognizes that literature is a springboard for language development and artistic expression. It is through literature that children receive powerful images that surface and reveal themselves at unexpected moments in unanticipated ways.

Music

The Value of Music

Music is an important dimension of creative development. It nurtures both cultural literacy and skill development. Most of all, music is a joyful and satisfying form of communication. At early childhood levels, play activities often are accompanied by music. Music is aesthetically calming and pleasing to a young child. A listening experience can stimulate a child and unleash his creative instincts. It can put him in the mood for nonverbal communication and creative pursuits.

All children love to sing and listen to music. Music is a vital part of daily living because it produces joy and relaxation. Research on the social effects of music indicate that it has tremendous potential for associative play. Music has been found to:

- Sustain children's participation in group activity.
- Encourage their positive emotional arousal.
- Promote their readiness to participate in group activities and their acceptance of group recommendations.
- Promote trust and cooperation.
- Reduce anxiety.[10]

Children can enjoy music by playing instruments, singing, playing games, and quiet listening. Music, like art, can be integrated into all activities. It can be used in theme-building (to reinforce language and listening activities), in dramatizations (as an accompaniment to role-playing and plot-building), in language activities (look and listen records), in discovery centers (discriminating and identifying sounds by tone, sound, and timbre, the source of the sound), during group circles (creative movement, counting songs by rhythms or singing phonics, e.g., *B* is for *Baby* . . . B, B, B), and in writing centers (to stimulate ideas). Music can be a specialized activity that focuses on instruments (a guitar, a piano, or an autoharp) and lyrics (folk songs, holiday songs, action songs, theme songs, and favorite songs). It also can be an authentic child-centered experience—putting on a musical talent show or a musical such as *Annie* or *Oliver*.

Music Develops Naturally

At the early stages of development, music and rhyming verses are virtually indistinguishable. A three-year-old hears rhythm when she recites finger plays and nursery rhymes. The songlike, lyrical patterns that are repeated in nursery rhymes are similar to children's first songs. In both instances, motor movement, voice inflection, repetition, and rhyming words are used. By imitating and repeating rhyming words, children are hearing the same melodic sounds and rhythmic beats (cadences) that are used in many songs: "This is my right hand; I raise it up high; This is my left hand; I touch the sky; Right hand left hand round, round, round; Left hand right hand pound, pound, pound" (author unknown).

Children perform as they listen and chant—mimicking characters, memorizing words, and making appropriate movements (and faces). They listen for cues and favorite verses: "And frightened Miss Muffet away! . . . Jack jump over the candle stick! . . . Just tip me over and pour me out!" They listen for discrimination and appreciation and they learn about the nuances and patterns of language. A teacher who can read with intonation, knows when to raise or lower her voice. She knows how to share the beauty and power of language with children.

As children mature they are able to expand their musical abilities through practice and training. In *Music in Our Lives: The Early Years*, Dorothy T. McDonald points out that:

- Musical sounds may be high or low in pitch.
- Melodies may move up or down by steps or skips.
- Many melodies move home to a tonal center that may be felt and identified; a satisfactory sense of completion results.
- Certain melodic phrases may be repeated in a song; such repetitions may be recognized and identified.[11]

At early childhood levels, a music experience should incorporate movement as well. Music and movement are enhanced by descriptive pictures (visuals). A teacher, for example, may present the Froggie finger play visually on a flannel board. The children sing the song while each one gets a turn to move a froggie on a flannel board. Four froggies may jump into a pond and the last one (everyone's favorite) may hop off the board on his way to the doctor. *Row, Row, Row Your Boat* is another example of a song that has potential for multibody movements. Glen T. Dixon and F. Graeme Chalmers write:

> For young children, experience in music and art can compensate for the pervasiveness of verbal interaction and abstract symbolism in the classroom, at an age when words and written symbols may have insufficient relevance to their own expression of ideas. Plastic, visual and aural media provide means for children to realize

ideas that need not rely on verbal or numerical concepts stressed in other areas of the curriculum.[12]

The Teacher's Role

Teachers should provide opportunities that stimulate children's interest in music. A child's early interest in music increases when he is encouraged to use instruments regularly. Instruments provide creative outlets for experimentation with sound and self-expression. Each instrument has a name, a shape, and an individual sound. By combining instruments and listening for directions, children can make an orchestra or a marching band. In a creative approach to making music, Emil and Celeste Richards describe everyday objects such as washboards, thimbles, glasses, funnels, plastic bottles, coffee cans, scraps of wood, coat hangers, and garbage cans that can be used to create musical instruments.[13]

Homemade instruments might include banjos, bells, drums, tambourines, sand blocks, sticks, triangles, and tuning pipes. As children invent and use their own instruments, they become aware of the elements of sound and the rhythmic patterns of music, melodies, and tempo. They choose favorite instruments for favorite songs. Some children develop an interest in playing a real instrument. Child care centers may respond by providing specialized classes in piano or in string instruments.

Movement and Drama

Creative Movement

Creative movement is a wonderful, expressive outlet for children in child care centers. Children can dance on their own or they can enjoy creative movement during group experiences. Initially, teachers may feel apprehensive about organizing a creative movement curriculum, but with the help of records and musical instruments, most teachers can move into a "dance motif" with little difficulty. Through movement, children can learn to follow directions, to develop listening skills and rhythm, to express feelings, to explore locomotion (how a body can move in space), to develop body coordination, and to project themselves into becoming something or someone else.

Children especially enjoy free and spontaneous movement. They love to move like animals or pretend to be bubbles, the wind, or quiet snowflakes. They enjoy parachute games; role-playing on mats; pretending with hoops, scarves, and bean bags; climbing beanstalks and hiding from the giant; circle games; and inventive games that are generated by a teacher (e.g., "Pretend you are a caterpillar looking for a friend. Who will be your friend? Worm? Mouse? Grasshopper? Why?").

Beginning Stages of Drama

At early levels of development, creative dramatics, movement, and literature are inseparable companions. When young children engage in a dramatic experience, they act out familiar stories using movement to express themselves. Literature is a bridge that connects the child to a creative experience. When children act out a favorite story, they become its characters. Young children may not recall words or sequence, but they can interpret a story using their own expressive language. When a teacher attempts to follow a script too closely, children become distracted and lose interest. Simple story lines, minimal props, and an enthusiastic, expressive teacher who is willing to accept many different versions of a story will ensure a successful experience.

Poetic Verse

Children should have early experiences in dramatic arts and creative movement before they are introduced to a real play. At early stages of development, a teacher introduces drama primarily through familiar finger plays, rhyming verse, and stories. The following poems are examples of dramatic experiences that can be presented through drama or on a flannel board (with children assisting the teacher in the placement of objects):

Mr. Tic Toc
My snowman has a cold today,
He's sneezing and freezing and refuses to play,
He wants to go south with the birds on the block,
But he has not wings to follow the flock.
I'll dress him in earmuffs, mittens, and socks,
And give him a name like Mr. Tic Toc,
I'll tell him a story and serve him hot tea,
He'll soon be better to play with me.

A Turtle Tale
I have a little turtle,
He lives in a box,
He swims in a puddle,
And he climbs on a rock,
He snaps at a mosquito,
He snaps at a flea,
He snaps at a minnow,
And he snaps at me,
He catches the mosquito,
He catches the flea,
He catches the minnow,
But he doesn't catch me.

A Spotted Fish
Once there was a spotted fish,
Who made a very special wish,
She wished she was a little pet,
Living in a bowl,
Far away from fishing nets,

And little kids with poles.
Lots of food to eat each day,
Watching children laugh and play.
From her house of glass she'll dream,
Of ponds and lakes and distant streams.

Pantomime

Pantomime facilitates creative expression and it encourages participation. As a quiet activity, pantomime requires children to become good listeners and thinkers. When children use pantomime as a dramatic form of art, they imitate through gesture, movement and postures, a person, an object or a feeling, such as wind going through a tunnel. At early childhood levels, teachers stimulate interest by inviting children to guess the role that a child is performing. Children love to:

- Become circus people.
- Walk or move like animals (a mat may be needed for this activity).
- Pretend to be eating something that is familiar such as a double-scoop ice cream cone, a sour pickle, a hot or cold drink, or an orange.
- Pretend to play tennis, baseball, or volley ball; to skate, ski, mountain climb, or paddle a canoe.
- Pretend to ride an elevator or an escalator.
- Pretend to be playing a game such as checkers or hopscotch.
- Pretend to go exploring. What did you find?
- Pretend to go on a picnic. What did you bring?

Improvisation

Teachers improvise an experience by being spontaneous, by introducing a creative activity that children can identify with and perform, and by providing just enough information and props to generate excitement and participation.

1. *Beanbag Rock.* Children dance to a favorite record. Each child is given a bean bag (or a scarf). As they dance, they follow directions such as place the bean bag on your head, on your shoulder, on your nose, or on your toes. Children will enjoy the rhythm, the movement, and the physical challenge.

2. *The Magic Hat.* The teacher passes a hat around a circle of children. When she claps her hands, the child with the hat must do what the hat tells her to do. (The teacher assumes the role of the hat instructing a child to dance, gallop, fly, waddle, or become a rag doll or a clown).

3. *An Imaginary Trip.* The teacher selects a theme such as a zoo, a circus, an amusement park, a farm, or a city street. After brainstorming ideas, the teacher assigns a role to a child or to a small group of children. They are given a few minutes to figure out how they are going to present their role. The object is to guess what role the child or children are playing. Using simple props and pantomime, children create a character or a scene. Children may work out being a roller coaster, a fire hydrant, a taxi with a flat tire, an organ grinder, or a tired scarecrow surrounded by bothersome, hungry crows.

4. *Build a Story.* The teacher empties story telling objects from a story telling sack. Each child selects one object and identifies it by name in circle. Children then close their eyes, think about the object or character they are creating, and with the teacher assisting, build a story.

5. *A Bear Hunt.* The teacher accompanies children up creeks, down mountains, over bridges, under a waterfall, into a thicket, close to a bee's hive, and through the woods, until they get very close to the bear's cave when quickly, they retell their adventure all the way home, chased by the bear.

6. *Acting Out a Story.* After a story is read, a teacher may extend the story through dramatization. He may improvise a setting with simple props. Children are invited to participate in the reenactment using their own words to express a character. Children who are not in the play can participate in the role of an audience. Stories work nicely when there is rhythmic verse that is repeated, such as "Hunkercha, hunkercha, hunkercha...Where for you go?" in *The Gunniwolf,* or "Who is tripping on my bridge?" in *Billy Goat Gruff,* or "Run, run as fast as you can, you can't catch me, I'm the Gingerbread Man," in *The Gingerbread Man.*

For selecting stories that lend themselves to impromptu dramatization, see Shirley C. Raines and Robert J. Candy, *Story Stretchers,* Gryphon House, 1991.

Group Activities: Improvisational Drama for Young Children

Teachers guide children in acting out a story using their own ideas and words to reenact the plot. Every child gets a turn and chooses a character or object to become. Simple props such as a chair or a basket will hold children's attention during the activity.

Improvisation Examples
Billy Goat Gruff by M. Brown
Props: Wooden steps, a balance beam, or a nesting bridge
Follow-up: Grow fresh, juicy, green grass in a styrofoam cup; when the
                seeds sprout, children can make a Billy Goat face on each cup
                and add cardboard horns.

The Three Little Pigs by The Brothers Grimm
Props: A cardboard house, cut-outs to symbolize straw, sticks, and
                bricks for a chimney
Follow-up: They can make puppets out of felt and make the pigs talk.

Goldilocks and the Three Bears by The Brothers Grimm
Props: A housekeeping table set for three; one little bear in a highchair
Follow-up: Children can make a snack of porridge using instant oatmeal;
                they can invite a favorite stuffed animal to join them.

Hansel and Gretel by The Brothers Grimm

Props: Use masking tape to make a path through the woods; add a plant and a moon to the scene.

Follow-up: Children can make their own gingerbread house using milk cartons, graham crackers, meringue (to hold the parts together), and all kinds of good things to eat.

The Chalk Box Story by D. Freeman

Props: Use a large cardboard box colored in pastels that match the colors in the story; neck scarves that match the colors in the story for each child to wear.

Follow-up: Children can make wet chalk pictures; each child may be given a box of colored chalk and a pad to make their own original stories.

The Little Red Hen by P. Galdone

Props: A bunch of wheat, and a loaf of French bread

Follow-up: Children can make their own bread.

The Little Engine That Could by W. Piper

Props: Painted cardboard boxes in assorted sizes; add wheels

Follow-up: Children can fill the boxes with special items and ride over the mountain.

Little Red Riding Hood by The Brothers Grimm

Props: A red scarf, a basket, a bouquet of flowers

Follow-up: Have children make a mural about the story and have them make cookies for their grandparents or for a special friend.

The Gunniwolf by W. Harper

Props: An orange flower placed in a vase on a small table, a gunniwolf puppet made out of a paper bag

Follow-up: Children can paint orange flowers to bring home to mother. They can retell the story using their gunniwolf puppets.

Additional Books for Dramatizations

Who's in Rabbit's House? by V. Ardema

Mooncake by F. Asch

Snow White and the Seven Dwarfs by The Brothers Grimm

The Very Hungry Caterpillar by E. Carl

Book of Nursery and Mother Goose Rhymes by de Angeli

Corduroy by D. Freeman

The Birthday Wish by C. Iwasaki

The Snowy Day by E. Keats

Chicken Little by S. Kellogg

The Teddy Bears' Picnic by J. Kennedy

Alexander and the Wind-Up Mouse by L. Lionni

Frederick by L. Lionni

Tico and the Golden Wings by L. Lionni

Mousekin's Golden House by E. Miller

The Tale of Peter Rabbit by B. Potter
Caps for Sale by E. Slobodkin
Mr. Rabbit and the Lovely Present by C. Zolotow

For Young Elementary-Age Children. The following circle warm-ups encourage imagination:

Let's Pretend. Children act out being a skater, a wilting flower, a melting snowman, a storm, a pumpkin seed, an elf, an airplane landing, a hot-air balloon, a shooting star, Humpty Dumpty, The Mad Hatter, circus performers, the last leaf on a tree, or a ball that is losing air.

Guess Who I Am? Children pantomime being an animal, an insect, a household gadget, or a color of the rainbow.

Once Upon a Story. One child starts a story and everyone adds to it.

Guess Who Is Coming to Dinner? Teacher whispers a guest's name to a child who must act out the character or object (an umbrella, a monkey, a hippopotamus, a ballerina, a rock star, a space man or woman, a friendly giant, a top, a mosquito, a spider).

A Story in a Box. A teacher fills a box with novelty items that have potential for storytelling (small animals, items for a magic show, a circus, or a birthday party). Children must create stories from the objects.

Imagination. Teachers share novelty objects with children who must think of creative uses for each item, such as an egg beater, a doorknob, a screen, a top hat.

Movement. Children move to a drum beat—stop, freeze, and have three seconds to become something that is called out by a teacher.

Follow the Leader. Children must follow their partners without laughing or making a sound.

Relaxation. Teacher guides children in relaxation techniques that allow them to free their bodies and their minds.

Three Guesses. Children are given an object (or a picture of an object) that is not seen by the group. A child has three chances to describe the item, without using body language to give clues. The group has to guess what the object is from the verbal description.

Storytelling

Children who are acquainted with the early stages of self expression soon become comfortable with storytelling experiences. The simplest way of organizing an activity is to start with a prop such as an interesting object, a wand, or a feather. After sharing an object, children will be encouraged to close their eyes and get in touch with their feelings and imagination. A child who is holding the object will voluntarily begin a story, and probably continue the narrative until another child joins in. Ideas blossom into simple plots that require specific characters and eventually an ongoing theme. Young children connect with an experience through the power of suggestion, reflection, and multisensory stimulation that triggers a sense of inquiry and wonder within a child. When a child is in a state of excitement, they bring objects to life—be it a coconut, a piece of ribbon, or a sequin. Visual and tactile explorations are critical to the creative process.

Because early dramatic experiences require discrimination skills, children should be sensitized to sound as well. Teachers may encourage children to identify familiar sounds that are indigenous to a community, such as a train whistle, a fog horn, the ocean, a dog's bark, running water, a mixer or blender, traffic, carnival sounds, a bell ringing, or a chime chiming.

Teacher's who engage children in pretense through imaginative storytelling are making a valuable contribution to creative development by:

- Stimulating the imagination and promoting creative thinking
- Developing critical thinking skills
- Promoting language development
- Heightening effective listening skills
- Strengthening comprehension by involving the senses as an integral part of the learning process
- Increasing empathy and awareness of others
- Fostering peer respect and group cooperation
- Reinforcing a positive self-concept
- Providing teachers with a fresh perspective on teaching[14]

A Play

From simple dramatizations, four- or five-year-old children may be ready to progress into a more serious and more organized production. Unlike spontaneous dramatizations, a play requires more attention to prepare and execute.

Children who participate in dramatic productions instinctively sense that dramatic play is an empowering form of self-projection. It can also become an extremely nurturing experience. The Lion, the Tin Man, the Scarecrow, and the Oz in the favorite classic *The Wizard of Oz* can be seen from a new, and more sympathetic perspective. Children select characters that hold personal meaning; characters that they choose to identify with. As children role-play, they begin to affirm themselves; they sense that a particular place is a safe place to become someone or something else. The experience may strongly influence their lives, as well as their feelings about themselves. Through drama, children become actively engaged in a pretend world that they want to identify with, a world that demands something different from them, that has new meaning and tremendous possibilities. *The Red Balloon* is an example of a theme with numerous opportunities for creative expression (see Figure 5.2).

FIGURE 5.2   A Discovery Theme: The Arts

1. *Name and Author. The Red Balloon* by Albert Lamorisee.

2. *Focus.* This tender and symbolic story about a lonely little boy's love for a red balloon is a cherished contribution to children's literature. When neighborhood bullies taunt Pascal and throw stones at his beloved balloon, the sky is suddenly filled with balloons rising in freedom, carrying Pascal away from sadness and loneliness. The interpretive focus is on creative movement.

3. *Main Objectives.* The teacher shares the book with her children to prepare them for interpreting the moods and feelings that are generated. The story is extremely symbolic—the balloon is real to Pascal who is a very lonely little boy. The balloon symbolizes to Pascal and to the reader freedom, hope, and companionship. The teacher wants to generate awareness and identification in children so that they can experience empathy. She wants them to express themselves symbolically through creative movement by "becoming" balloons.

4. *Procedure and Materials.* There is one red balloon used as a prop near a circle area that will be used for dramatic improvisation (the children "become" balloons). The teacher creates a mood of sensual identification between a child and a balloon fantasy. She tells a story:

> Oh wouldn't it be fun to be a balloon for just a little while; to pick a favorite color, curl up tight, and slowly move through space? Would you like to be a balloon for just a little while? Just close your eyes and imagine yourself a balloon. Gradually unfold—open your arms and expand your bodies into space. You are swaying back and forth until you feel at one with your world. The gentle wind is your friend, guiding you through your journey into space. Soft raindrops will fall on you. Soft clouds will be there for rest. Balloon friends will pass, nodding and bobbing about, happy to be free and open to whatever comes next. . . . Stop for a moment and pretend you are looking at haystacks, hills and mountains, grazing cattle, rushing streams, and old sleepy houses . . . flashing lights, bustling cities, and the organ-grinder man! Fly high, little friends, until you are at your journey's end. . . . Then, fall gently back to earth and be with your friends—red, yellow, blue, green, and deep purple; and all the colors of the world.

5. *Follow-Up.* The children follow up the experience with an original book about balloons; the children select the key words to print in their book: balloon, boy, fly, clouds, red, yellow, green.

6. *Outcome.* Teachers will want to evaluate each experience in terms of objectives achieved and staff development.

Assessing Children's Productions

Teachers should be attentive to children's development in the arts by observing a child's:

- Eye-hand coordination skills
- Developmental level
- Use of materials and activities that interest her
- Barriers to self-expression
- Attention level
- Ability to communicate verbally
- Ability to communicate nonverbally
- Ability to discriminate and draw inferences
- Ability to work independently and stay on task
- Ability to make choices and organize a project
- Willingness to cooperate and engage in dramatic play
- Interest in completing a dramatic production
- Ability to interact socially with peers
- Ability to be inventive and resourceful
- Interest in being adventurous and innovative
- Ability to think divergently and flexibly
- Attitude toward the creative process

Summary

In child care centers, opportunities for creative expression through the arts are everywhere. They are present when a child examines a milkweed pod, witnesses the unfolding of a butterfly's wings, and experiences the first snowfall of winter. They are present when a child makes discoveries with paint or invents a new toy. The more children experience the wonders that surround them, the more artistic and creative they become. A busy, happy child does not distinguish between art, play, and learning. By extending her imagination, she is extending her thinking. Her environment becomes a never-ending resource for cultivation and enjoyment. A child's artwork is an extension of her unique and special personality—it is the emerging child.

N O T E S

1. As cited in Mary R. Jalongo, "The Child's Right to the Expressive Arts: Nurturing the Imagination as Well as the Intellect," *Childhood Education* 66(4) (Summer 1990): 195–200.
2. E. P. Torrance, *Guiding Creative Talent* (Englewood Cliffs, NJ: Prentice Hall, 1962).
3. Mary Renck Jalongo, "Awakening the Artistry in Young Children," *Dimensions of Early Childhood* (Little Rock, AR: SECA, 1995), p. 11.
4. Vea Verchi, "The Role of the Atelierista," in *The Hundred Languages of Children*, eds., C. Edwards, L. Gandini, and G. Forman (Norwood, NJ: Ablex, 1995), pp. 119–134.

5. Leon Burton and Kathy Kuroda, *Arts Play: Creative Activities in Art, Music, Dance, and Drama for Young Children* (Reading, MA: Addison-Wesley, 1981), Introduction, ix.

6. Barbara Herberholz, *Early Childhood Art* (Dubuque, IA: William C. Brown Company, 1974), p. 2.

7. Robert Schirrmacher, *Art and the Creative Development for Young Children* (Albany, NY: Delmar), p. 115.

8. Lilia Lasky and Rose Mukerji, *Art: Basic for Young Children* (Washington, DC: NAEYC, 1980), Developmental Chart, p. 12.

9. Clare Cherry, *Creative Art for the Developing Child* (Belmont, CA: Fearon, 1972), p. 17.

10. Andrew Gunsberg, "Improvised Musical Play," *Childhood Education* 67(4) (Summer 1991): 223.

11. Dorothy T. McDonald, *Music in Our Lives: The Early Years* (Washington, DC: NAEYC, 1979), p. 25.

12. Glen T. Dixon and F. Graeme Chalmers, "The Expressive Arts in Education," *Childhood Education* 61(1) (Fall 1990): 12.

13. Emil and Celeste Richards, *Making Music around the Home and Yard* (New York: Award Music Co., 1972).

14. Lenore B. Kelner, *The Creative Classroom* (Portsmouth, NH: Heinemann, 1994), pp. 4–6.

CHAPTER

6 Nurturing

No matter what else it does, a good school will seek to build greater enjoyment of people. It will fill each child's school hours with talking to others, thinking together, working with others—with arguing, listening, compromising, laughing. It will provide the experiences a child needs to live, happily and constructively, on a little planet packed with people.

—James L. Hymes, Jr.

In order for children to become decent, loving, and compassionate human beings, a child care center must surround each child with a nurturing environment. Nurturing, as a concept, conjures feelings identified with *affective* learning: empathy, support, warmth, positive attitudes. For nurturing to be instated as a formal program component, it must be articulated in concrete terms; not only *we nurture children,* but *how we nurture children* in this center. A center nurtures children by giving serious consideration to social/emotional factors that influence a child's development and a classroom climate. Social/emotional factors interface at early childhood levels; each area is intricately connected to the other.

A primary objective in child care centers is to socialize children through positive and meaningful interactions to prepare them for entering and functioning in a larger society. This requires early training in areas of personal care, emotional well-being, safety, health and literature, social courtesies, moral and character development, and important practical life skills.

The most important way to nurture children in social development is to create an atmosphere that recognizes and respects all people. For many young children there is an unhealthy gap between home and center environments. Language, food, clothing, religious beliefs, and childrearing patterns may vary considerably from family to family, which creates confusion and insecurity for a child caught between two worlds. A multicultural program will encourage children to affirm their heritage while assimilating the American education experience. It will create a sense of democracy within a miniature, multinational community such as a child care center.

Training Children

Training may be accomplished at early childhood levels by example and by guidance. Training requires intent, commitment, and follow-through. Teachers must first accept the fact that children cannot grow up with the skills and attitudes required to function fully and effectively in a society without strong guidance and direction during the early years.

A good way to begin is to list the characteristics that one would most like to see in a society. Virtues that come to mind are consideration, cooperation, respect, kindness, fair play, responsibility, honesty, patience, empathy, trust, good conduct, and an understanding of cultural and racial differences and similarities. Children practice what they are taught and what they experience. To become affective human beings, children must be given the opportunity to exercise autonomy, practice cooperative play, use judgment, express love, express feelings, make decisions, feel in control, exercise leadership, take pride in their identity, and develop empathy.

Example

Training by example establishes a *humanistic* framework for a nurturing curriculum. Adults model the behavior they desire from children. Children view their teachers as respectful, caring adults who are trustworthy and dependable. They do not yell or express anger inappropriately, they do not favor one child, and they know how to please children. They also view adults as real human beings with feelings and emotions who sometimes display anger or become upset.

A teacher will model the special qualities that children follow: kindness, understanding, and firmness. With skillful strategies and attentiveness to children's behavior, a teacher promotes an affective environment. When a teacher exhibits firmness and assertiveness in appropriate ways, she is gaining children's respect. A firm voice is not a yelling or unpleasant voice. A misbehaving child is taken aside, spoken to, asked to explain the behavior, asked to think about the consequences of the behavior, and given an opportunity to change the behavior. "What do you think you should do?" is a far more effective closure than "I want you to apologize," or "I'm going to tell your mother." Parents may need to be informed, but not in a way that makes a child feel threatened.

Training by example requires forethought and attention. It is not enough to say the right words. A teacher must set a nurturing tone that becomes so natural to an environment that eventually the words and their meaning become self-evident. Nurturing is built into a foundation: it begins with a philosophy that creates a context for caring relationships. Educator Judith Leipzig writes:

> As educators of very young people who are in the midst of creating their selves and their futures, it is our responsibility to think about what kinds of raw materials we are providing them. Each child should have the support, the attention, and the experiences that will help that child grow to be a competent, well-rounded, and loving person—one who has a clear picture of his or her self, one who is able to cooperate and to work on her or his own, and one who is able to both give and receive support and nurturing. As teachers of infants and toddlers, we should be doing everything in our power to support the development of individuals who will be capable of leading rich and balanced lives.[1]

Guidance

Teachers can train children by establishing classroom rules that promote respect and kindness throughout an environment. In an insightful book, *Anti-Bias Curriculum*, Louise Derman-Sparks and a task force of early childhood educators emphasize the importance of early training:

> Learning nonoppressive ways of interacting with differences requires more than introducing diversity into the classroom. It also requires gentle but active and firm guidance by adults. Unfortunately, many teachers and parents are uncertain about what to do when a preschooler exhibits biased behavior. All too often, uncertainty results in nonaction: "I was struck speechless," "I was afraid of saying or doing the wrong thing," "It made me so upset (angry), I couldn't do anything," are typical comments.
>
> Discriminatory acts are one form of aggressive behavior, as hurtful as physical aggression, and should be immediately and directly addressed. Teachers must

become aware of any attitudes or feelings that prevent them from intervening in discriminatory interactions between children, and practice appropriate techniques like role-playing.[2]

Role-Playing

Teachers can train children in manners and good conduct through role-playing techniques, of which puppetry is a favorite. Puppets can be presented in any color, shape, or form. They can be used to discourage gender identification (boys are mean, girls are kind), discrimination, unhealthy peer identification, poor manners, unhealthy eating habits, poor hygiene, and improper speech. They can speak to a child who is feeling lonely, sad, or inadequate. They can speak to a child who has a stressful home situation. Mostly, teachers should let children talk vicariously through puppets: "I wonder what is troubling Ernie today; he looks a little sad?" "Do you think it's because he lost a button on his new jacket?" "No, then what could it be . . . ?"

Themes and Projects

Teachers can develop cultural awareness and understanding by planning themes or projects that invite nurturing. A unit on families or a unit on children around the world will expose children to a widening human experience—to one that reflects diversity in living patterns, in social patterns, and in cultural patterns. A social studies unit can provide unlimited opportunities for children to learn about the people and places that make up the world.

Long-term projects are effective ways to encourage children to invest in something that they can appreciate and identify with. A carefully planned project such as making a Japanese garden incorporates forethought, research, and considerable planning. A project that is designed to beautify and enhance an environment can become a consuming preoccupation for all involved. The choice and selection of a cherry tree, a birdbath, and little stone figures may take several weeks. Designing a pathway in between shrubs and flowers will add further challenge to this wonderful project. Young children may help in planting shrubs and flowers, while older children may design a small pond with fish and lily pads. After consulting magazines, reading Japanese folktales, and sketching ideas, the project may include a gazebo. With assistance from parents and the community, a project can become a reality.

Literature

Teachers can help children understand right from wrong through literature. The wolf in *Little Red Riding Hood* or the fox in the *Gingerbread Man* are examples of favorite stories that clearly have moral implications. Stories that enable children to make observations and draw conclusions should be very carefully selected and presented. They should be stories children can identify with, enjoy, and learn from. See page 229 for examples of nurturing books.

Health, Safety, and Nutrition

Children in out-of-home environments depend on adults to teach them about ways they can nourish and protect their bodies. It is the responsibility of teachers to provide an environment that is physically and psychologically safe—one that makes a child feel secure and confident. Units on health, safety, and nutrition should be presented periodically, and reinforced daily. Children should be informed about good eating habits, good grooming habits, and good living habits. They should be cautioned about environmental risks, but encouraged to take risks that are important to their healthy development. They should be trained to care for themselves at an early age.

Writing and Reviewing Rules of Good Conduct

At early childhood levels rules of conduct should be simply stated, as shown in this example:

> In this center children are expected to:
> 1. Be courteous.
> 2. Be respectful.
> 3. Have good manners.
> 4. Be kind to one another.
> 5. Make wise choices.
> 6. Be responsible members of a group.
> 7. Be good self-managers.
>
> If there is a problem:
> 1. Teachers talk with children.
> 2. Teachers talk with parents.
> 3. Children may not be able to remain in this center, if the problem continues.
>
> Please help by being a positive member of this class.

Rules serve as reminders that help children in their interactions with peers. At four or five years old, as well as school-age levels, children should participate in writing and in reading back their own rules. If behavior becomes unruly, a teacher may take a child over to the chart to remind him or her about this agreement.

Objectives for a Caring Environment

Teachers should encourage children to:

- Respect and support others.
- Learn to take turns.
- Be cooperative and courteous.
- Develop self-control.

- Think about right and wrong, good and bad, kind and unkind practices.
- Take the perspective of others.
- Recognize and respect differences.
- Become responsible members of their classroom and of their community.

When children are expected to be responsible members of a group, they will respect freedom and not abuse its privileges. They will learn to care for property, to cooperate with their friends, to take turns, and to have good manners. They will understand what they can and cannot do to feel successful about themselves and their environment.

A teacher will create a community of caring. She will be ready to assist a child who is experiencing difficulty or frustration, but she also will encourage independent problem solving. In helping children develop socially, she will know when to step forward and when to remain in the background. In his book, *The Social Development of Young Children*, Charles A. Smith writes:

> Helping children learn social skills, such as making friends, is a troublesome effort for many adults. Ultimately, every child is alone in the social arena. We can stand by the sidelines and cheer their efforts, but they must be the ones to act. By becoming too involved in manipulating a social situation, we take the risk of alienating children from their peers. Yet, by doing absolutely nothing for them, we may contribute to their own confusion and sense of isolation. These two extremes can be avoided by becoming involved without being oppressive, and detached without being aloof.[3]

Cultivating a Nurturing Environment

The human environment that surrounds the child is the psychological core of a child care program. It is from caring and sympathetic adults that children receive affirmation and support. A relationship between a child and an adult is critical to a child's emotional well-being.

Too often children's expressions of unhappiness are ignored or trivialized by caregivers: "I don't know what's wrong with her, I couldn't find a minute to talk to her privately; I think she's just tired ... " Perhaps this is the case, or perhaps the child has a need that should be communicated to a teacher. She may have been made fun of or intentionally left out of a game. A superficial reaction to stress glosses over problems that may be far more serious than meets the eye. Teachers of young children must become sensitive to changes in behavior and record unusual patterns observed over a period of time. They must bring their observations to a parent's attention at an appropriate time.

Children's moods and feelings are usually apparent to those who choose to notice. When we *stop noticing*, children *stop responding* and they *stop trying* to please. They become programmed to do what they are expected to do. Those who no longer protest may become compliant, slowly becoming less responsive. Those who protest become caught up in power struggles that eventually break down relationships and deepen a child's sense of disharmony and alienation. Yet knowledgeable and caring adults often place unreasonable demands on children every day. Teachers can get so caught up in routines and schedules that they fail to notice the children they are trying to help.

Preventing Misbehavior

A well-designed and managed program prevents misbehavior by including the following practices: limiting the number of children in a classroom; having adequate staff; limiting the number of transitions in a day; discouraging competition; having enough for children to do; providing a balanced, integrated day; being attentive to children's needs for outdoor play, good nutrition, and good health practices; encouraging children to express feelings and be empathetic; supporting children's choices; encouraging children's interests; opening time frames to maximize independent play; and developing and discussing rules of conduct (see Table 6.1).

If teachers and staff members model appropriate behavior and consistently reinforce the standards that are operative in a given environment, children will understand and, most of the time, accept limits. Limits can be reinforced by post-

TABLE 6.1   Behavioral Guidelines

1. State problem:	Student/teacher discuss the stated problem in open, respectful, trusting manner
Purpose:	To encourage a child to verbalize a problem without anxiety or fear of reprimand
2. State feelings:	Student self-examines and expresses feelings; teacher counsels
Purpose:	To help a child come to a position of understanding and forgiveness
3. Solve problem:	Student/teacher discuss alternative ways to solve problem
Purpose:	To help a child find appropriate ways to solve a problem
4. My intentions:	Student selects a method of solving the problem and makes a written agreement with himself or herself
Purpose:	To help a child come to a position of acceptance and responsibility
5. What have I learned?	Student talks, teacher listens and reinforces child's agreement
Purpose:	To help a child bring the problem and feelings to closure
6. Follow-through:	Student and teacher agree to meet periodically to continue the self-examination process
Purpose:	To help a child sustain positive behavior and feelings toward self and others

Note: This approach may be modified for children of various ages.

ing and reviewing agreements for behavior in the classroom, on the playground, and on field trips. Children accept rules of conduct that are presented at the beginning of a child care experience. It is imperative that teachers at all levels agree on the *manner* and *methods* of discipline, so children have consistency throughout their child care experience. If bad language is not permitted at the age of three, it should not be permitted at the age of four. By agreeing on fundamental behavioral guidelines, a staff will know how to deal with problems as they occur and will undoubtedly experience fewer problems. Positive expressions of kindness, cooperation, and friendship, should be used repeatedly in a learning and play context (e.g., "Good job," "I'm proud of you"). Through direct and indirect repetition, appropriate behavior practices will be absorbed and practiced by children.

The purpose of setting disciplinary guidelines is to enable children to develop internal control mechanisms that foster growth and promote societal values. Children must be trained in basic rules of conduct before they are expected to follow general rules of conduct. As they progress in development, children will be exposed to increasingly higher levels of human interaction. In the process of developing an understanding about how social systems operate effectively, children will learn to replace physical or verbal aggressiveness with acceptable modes of interaction. They will not only learn the consequences of their actions but begin to internalize information in ways that generate feelings of empathy and compassion.

Dealing with Misbehavior

Children should never be spanked, threatened, or mistreated in any way by adults. They should not be punished by *isolation* (removing a child from a group for an extended period of time), *ridicule* (reprimanding children in front of peers), or *deprivation* (taking a snack away). Continuing patterns of misbehavior should be recorded and communicated to parents so there is agreement on how to discipline children. A parent must not only be consulted but must be *required* to share with a center's staff the responsibility for managing their child's behavior. There is no single method for dealing with children's stress and anger.

Behavior Management Strategies

There are *five strategies* that, if used consistently and carefully, will soothe and mollify upset children.

The first strategy is to develop a system of *positive reinforcement*. Children should be given positive feedback when they are expressing sympathy and cooperating with others. Teachers can reward children for good behavior in small but personalized ways. A teacher may hold a hand, slip a special smiling face on a picture, or whisper something a child wants to hear—gestures that make a little child feel important and good. Teachers can use puppets or other dramatic conveyers to emphasize or reinforce a message.

The second strategy is one of *prevention*. A teacher who knows a child recognizes what triggers and escalates anger (e.g., sharing favorite toys, interruptions, irritating peers). By redirecting a child before a crisis occurs, the teacher will help restore a child's sense of control and balance. By understanding the nature and needs of each child, a teacher will use appropriate intervention strategies. Some children need more direction than others. They can't handle long periods of free play, they can't make choices, and they, can't interact effectively with peers. These children need considerable attention before they can become self-directed and trustworthy. Some children like to test rules of behavior through argumentation or aggressive behavior. By reminding children about classroom rules that pertain to respect, the teacher will discourage a challenging child.

Finding constructive ways to manage behavior before an incident escalates into a dramatic encounter is a teacher's challenge. An important first step is to *notice,* rather than to *ignore,* behavior. If a teacher senses an argument or fight brewing, she should make her presence known and, if necessary, immediately step in to redirect or stop unkind behavior. Children should always be spoken to privately at the time of an incident. A child's misbehavior should never become the object of group attention. By ignoring unacceptable behavior, a teacher is giving a child the *wrong* message—she is basically affirming his unacceptable behavior. The child, in turn, feels confused and unsatisfied, the problem is not going away, it is worsening. He reacts by continuing the behavior. His friends are watching and implicitly labeling him "a bad boy." When a teacher deals with behavior at the moment of crisis (as difficult as this may be), she is making a statement that "I care, this is not acceptable." Eventually, the child will stop testing and begin to believe in and trust his environment.

A third strategy is to *obtain information.* Often, a child does not know what she has done wrong, or truly believes in her own innocence. Distinguishing an accuser from an aggressor may become a challenge for a teacher who did not witness the incident or is not clear what precipitated the incident. Both children feel wronged, and probably both are crying. Neither wants to accept blame. Before discussing an incident with a child, a teacher might try to obtain information from peers who witnessed the altercation. An impartial teacher will listen to both sides, make suggestions, and help children find a solution and reconcile their differences.

If a child is clearly the aggressor, a teacher should speak firmly and look for ways to resolve the problem without unnecessarily hurting a child's dignity. When a child understands that he cannot conduct himself in ways that harm or offend others, he will take responsibility for his actions, finding acceptable, less aggressive ways to solve problems. A child must, in essence, forgive himself before he can *honestly* say "I'm sorry." He must feel the need to restore a harmonious relationship with the child he has hurt. This may be done in indirect ways: by holding hands on the way to a bathroom, sharing a favorite toy, or sharing a lunch treat. These follow-up acts of kindness are extremely important to a child's emotional growth. They are far more important than a mechanical, "I'm sorry," prompted by a harried teacher.

A fourth strategy is to *remain objective.* The maturation process is never without fluctuations. A teacher who overreacts to a child's change in behavior needs to take time to self-assess and reflect. She should look at her relationship with the child, think about possible causes and ways to change or redirect negative behavior. She should not ignore the behavior, nor should she exaggerate the behavior—she simply needs to place it in perspective.

A fifth strategy is to *ask for help.* When, over a reasonable period of time, standard procedures are no longer effective, a teacher knows when it is time to ask for help. It is not unusual for children in child care environments to have problems that are not easily resolved by behavior management techniques. A dysfunctioning child may require professional intervention.

Intervention Techniques

The most beneficial way of handling a child who is having a temper tantrum or a serious fight with a peer is to remove the child from the setting for a reflective cooldown period that is not punitive but restorative. A drink of water, a walk outside, or a conversation with a teacher will help a child gain control. An extra pair of hands to handle emergencies, such as sickness, accidents, and behavioral problems, is essential in child care environments.

With some training, senior citizens can become perfect assistants. Unlike teachers who have a group to consider, senior citizens have the time to sit with children and to comfort them in their times of need. An alternative to a senior citizen is a secretary or office helper who is willing to sit with a child for a few minutes until she can gain control and reenter her group.

The time that is spent handling behavioral problems in child care environments must be an essential part of program planning. Daily activity plans must allow ample time for teacher/student interactions, and an environment must have additional staff to assist a teacher in handling behavior problems. It is far more important for children to feel secure and happy than it is for them to finish projects. Projects eventually get thrown out; a child's memories last forever.

A Discipline Policy

Most state regulations require child care centers to disseminate a discipline policy for parental review. A policy might read:

> In keeping with the Center's philosophy, children are expected to exercise self-control, respectful attitudes, concerns for others, and appropriate behavioral patterns. When problems arise, children are spoken to in a firm but supportive fashion, and are encouraged to express feelings and to acknowledge their responsibility for an incident. After a quiet, reflective interval, children will be given the opportunity to resume their play or, if necessary, asked to select a quiet place where they can reflect on their behavior. If inappropriate behavioral patterns continue, parents are notified and asked to work in partnership with the Center on their child's behalf. At this time, a behavior modification plan will be

agreed on and implemented. A child who continues to demonstrate aggressive or unhealthy behavioral patterns may need specialized help that cannot be provided at this Center.

A Shared Responsibility

What is not recognized in child care centers is that poorly trained teachers may be contributing to children's misbehavior. A center that meets developmentally appropriate criteria and hires teachers who are skilled in behavior management should not be overly burdened with behavioral problems. Skillful teachers establish a foundation of values that encourage children to respect people and property at the very beginning stages of development. They encourage good manners and kindness and discourage lying or taking things without asking permission. Teachers encourage forgiveness and discourage negative thinking. They handle behavioral problems with care and attentiveness to the feelings and needs of children, understanding that children, by nature, want to please. They will not label children or minimize their problems.

If an environment does not model cooperation and empathy, it is teachers who must assume responsibility for this neglect and its consequences. A center that is *pro-child*, affirms the importance of early training. Advice to teachers about controlling children's behavior might include:

- Talk and interact with them as often as possible.
- Be attentive to their dispositions and personalities.
- Be attentive to their vulnerabilities—to circumstances that make them feel different and inadequate.
- Record, assess, and understand their behavior.
- Support their growth and development.
- Advocate for them.
- Extend yourself for them.
- Acknowledge responsibility for the way they grow, develop, and receive and transmit information.
- Affirm and support behavior that reveals and acknowledges their movement toward social growth and notice the little gestures that often go unnoticed.
- Include parents in a center/child relationship.

A Daily Activity Schedule: Early-Childhood Level

8:00–9:00 AM	Independent play—a daily project is set up for children's enjoyment (e.g., an art activity, a science/math activity, a language activity)
9:00–9:30 AM	Opening group time—children greet, share, discuss plans for the day, and engage in a brief learning activity (e.g., a theme-related activity, a language activity, a science experiment, a creative movement, or music activity)

9:30–10:00 AM	Outdoor play—children play independently, play circle games, or share a group experience
10:00–10:15 AM	Transition—bathroom, snack
10:15–11:00 AM	Independent play in activity centers—teacher-initiated play/work projects are also set up (e.g., a cooking or art project, a creative writing or science/math project, a practical task)
11:00–11:30 AM	Transition to quiet activity (e.g., reading a story, artwork, playing a group game)
11:30–12:30 PM	Lunch and transition to rest—children may go outside before rest
12:30–3:00 PM	Rest and transition to afternoon activities (e.g., music, story, nurturing)
3:00–4:00 PM	Snack, outdoor play, or indoor large-motor independent play
4:00 PM–pick-up	Choices—a teacher-initiated play/work project is set up; a specialist may visit; children may enjoy a short film or a carefully selected television program one or two days per week; art/hands-on activities are also available

A Teacher's Role in Promoting Affective Development

A day care center must be perceived as a loving homelike environment where a child can feel secure. If teachers are too busy or too insensitive to target into a child's emotional needs, one of the most important functions of a child care center has been ignored. Teachers can promote emotional growth by using some or all of the growth-enhancing techniques described below.

Establish Feelings and Values in the Early Years

When children are nurtured in cooperative and pro-social play at an early age, they internalize attitudes and patterns of behavior. Ideally, an environment should not be bound by rules but by agreements. The more children are encouraged toward kindness, the more accepting they become. Children behave as they are conditioned to behave. They look to adults for clarification and direction. *Prejudice is bred*, it is not endemic to young children. They are not born with negative feelings toward others. In a nurturing classroom, children do not see differences. When children are open and loving they do not distinguish between black and white dolls, or between Asians and Caucasians. When an environment appropriately models equality and fairness, children become considerate and caring. They understand that people are different in some ways and alike in others. They become sensitive to their human environment by expressing empathy and compassion, by reaching out to hold hands and to hug one another.

Not all environments are nurturing, however, and not all children are untainted in the way they regard others. Louise Dermon-Sparks points out that young children's "development is harmed by the impact of sexism, racism, and handicappism."[4] Some research indicates that children begin to see differences and act differently toward others at a very young age. By age two, they are learning the appropriate use of gender labels and color names—as applied to skin colors. By three (or earlier) they begin to notice gender and racial differences to the degree that they may exhibit "pre-prejudice toward others on the basis of gender, race, or being differently abled."[5] As children mature, they often become stereotyped in their attitudes and behavior. They judge people superficially: by what they wear, how they look, how much money they carry in their pockets, by what cars their parents drive, how many vacations are taken in one year, how many activities they participate in after school. Teachers must use both indirect and direct strategies to change inappropriate attitudes or behavior so that children who may not "fit in" are not "written off" by peers.

Counsel Children

Teachers must build personal time into children's daily activities. Personal time requires personal space. An area set aside for children's personal use can be called a *den,* connoting *d*evelopment, *e*nrichment, and *n*urturing. This area can serve a dual purpose—it can be used for child-time (children play alone or with small groups of friends) or for teacher–child time (teacher and child visit together and, when appropriate, a teacher counsels a child who is unhappy or who has been misbehaving). Personal, meaningful interactions often will lead to problem solving or conflict resolution. Educator Susanne Wichert identifies the following steps that may be used in a counseling session targeted toward changing behavior:

- Calming and focusing
- Turning attention to the parties concerned
- Clarification/stating the problem
- Bargaining/resolution/reconciliation
- Affirmation[6]

This method is effective for children in child care environments because it gives them time to cool down, to discuss a problem, to think of other ways a problem might have been handled, and to resolve the problem in ways that allow a child to regain emotional composure. If a teacher is counseling a child who is distressed, she should comfort the child; encourage the child to share feelings; identify with the child ("I know how you are feeling . . . , I feel that way sometimes too"); and raise her self-esteem ("You have such a pretty smile, I wish you would smile more often").

Often a child will come to the realization that the perceived problem is really not the problem at all. A child may have been unusually distraught for other reasons: a new baby in the family, an angry parent, or a sick grandparent. When a child has someone to talk with at a time of distress, she often will release her anxieties quickly. Children's problems are not usually so complex that with a little stroking and nurturing, they cannot be resolved.

Be Available for Conversation and Consultation

Teachers should set aside time to:

- Share special moments with every child every day.
- Be available to assist a child during a crisis or upset at the time of occurrence.
- Consult frequently with parents.
- Observe and record children's behavior on a regular basis.
- Be attentive to changes in dispositions or behavior patterns.
- Report signs of dysfunction or unusual emotional stress to the director and to the parents.
- Consult a center's resource specialist in areas that suggest intervention.
- Keep an updated file on each child's progress.
- Provide opportunities for relaxation and stress reduction in a classroom.
- Maintain a consistent, supportive relationship with each child.

Help Children Develop Self-Control

Children gain self-control by understanding what is expected of them and by positively connecting with their environment. When a child feels secure about himself and his surroundings, he will conduct himself in an appropriate manner most of the time. The child who lacks self-control often finds someone else like herself to pal around with. She will exhibit less immature behavior when she is not receiving attention and when she realizes there are consequences such as being removed from a play center.

Help Children Gain Self-Esteem

If children are withdrawn and fearful, they may be lacking in self-esteem and confidence. They may not know how to make choices or to manage their time. They may experience failure in relationships and in their work. They may not know that they are cared for or loved. They are afraid to trust and unable to express feelings because they fear rejection and a greater sense of loss. A person without a sense of identity needs to build confidence slowly through relationships and experiences that engender success. *Love* is central to the process. There are many who believe that the ability to express and give love is the primary requisite for working with young children. Love should *never* be conditional. It should never be withheld from a child because a child has misbehaved. A teacher must seize every opportunity to build a child's self-esteem by praising, supporting, and identifying with a child's needs.

Help Children Develop Appropriate Behavior

Children misbehave frequently in day care centers. There is no one example; there are many examples. Children's behavior, or more precisely their misbehavior, is one of the most pervasive and troublesome aspects of working at a center. In complex and changing family patterns, there is rarely a simple explanation for negative behavior.

Children can be angry or negative even when they have been treated with affection and love. Misbehaving children want attention for whatever reason. They may not be getting quality time with parents; they may not feel very good about themselves; they may be frustrated and may have no place to ventilate their feelings. Lacking the wherewithal to find acceptable ways to express their frustrations, children find other ways to get approval. By acting out what she is feeling, the misbehaving child is getting attention (albeit the wrong kind) from peers. She is, in effect, acting the way she feels others are treating her.

There are no magical formulas and no instructional guidelines that will address the problems. There is no socioeconomic status that immunizes children from anger and aggressive behavior. When lives get off-balance, there are consequences. Much of the time, a teacher uses intuition when responding to a misbehaving child. He realizes that even under stress, he is still responsible for assisting a child in self-growth and in reaffirming values.

Be Attentive to Children's Mental and Physical Well-Being

Unfortunately there are some areas of emotional support and understanding that cannot be tapped by nurturing teachers. More and more, children are victims of child abuse and negligence. Dr. Barbara J. Meddin, a child protection specialist, and Dr. Anita L. Rosen, a private consultant, define child abuse and/or neglect as "any action or inaction that results in the harm or potential risk of harm to a child." This includes:

- Physical abuse (cuts, welts, bruises, burns)
- Sexual abuse (molestation, exploitation, intercourse)
- Physical neglect (medical or educational neglect; inadequate supervision, food, clothing, or shelter)
- Emotional abuse (actions that result in significant harm to the child's intellectual, emotional, or social development or functioning)
- Emotional neglect (inaction by the adult to meet the child's needs for nurture and support)

The signs or symptoms of child abuse are:

- Bruises or wounds in various stages of healing
- Injuries on two or more places of the body

- Injuries reported to be caused by falling but that do not include hands, knees, or forehead
- Oval, immersion, doughnut-shaped imprint burns
- Reluctance to leave school
- Inappropriate dress for the weather
- Discomfort when sitting
- Sophisticated sexual knowledge or play
- Radical behavior changes or regressive behavior
- Child withdraws or watches adults
- Child seems to expect abuse
- Revealing discussions, stories, or drawings[7]

Teachers need to watch for patterns of abuse and report observations and concerns to a director or administrator for immediate follow-up. In most states, a child welfare agency investigates each report and takes whatever action is necessary to protect the child.

Set Limits

Children tend to test limits in open, low-structure environments. They try things that would not be tolerated in highly structured environments. Examples of this may be the following: a child carries play dough around on a spoon until it crumbles into tiny pieces all over the floor; a child takes indoor blocks outdoors without permission; a child gives a portion of his lunch to a friend every day; a child wears a favorite dress-up all day because she doesn't want to risk giving it up; a child keeps little bugs in a cubbie. Teachers need to decide what is acceptable and what is not acceptable so that children understand specific boundaries in their play and play/work worlds.

Questions to Help Set Boundaries and Limitations
- Can children play superheroes indoors; can they use blocks and Tinkertoys as weapons?
- Can children carry equipment and materials from one activity center to another?
- Can they mix and use paints freely and without assistance?
- Can they add items to a water table?
- What language is acceptable and what is prohibited?
- How are children handled when they bite or hit?
- How are they handled when they have temper tantrums?
- Is there a restriction on the number of children in activity centers at one time?
- What are the rules for picking up; do children all pick up or do they pick up what they played with?
- Can children play outdoors in mud and dirt?
- Can they play with sticks and stones?
- How high can they swing; can they jump off?

- Can they go indoors for drinks without permission?
- Can they go to the bathroom or lockers without permission?
- Is there a dress code; no slippery shoes on climbing bars?
- Can children climb on fences; can they climb on a big old tree?

Make Agreements

In a play environment, teachers must always evaluate the quality of children's activities. Play is not always pure and innocent. An unhealthy or unacceptable mode of play is one that may physically or emotionally harm or hurt another child. Teachers need to make agreements and understandings with children regarding play rules. Agreements can be made regarding:

- Social relationships and attitudes
- Classroom responsibilities
- Activity center rules
- Personal behavior
- Care of equipment
- Safety and health rules
- Attitudes toward work and play
- Understandings about values

With reasonable review and a great deal of reinforcement, children will generally abide by their agreements.

Reduce Fatigue and Stress

A child-appropriate environment generates good feelings among children by reducing the elements that cause fatigue and stress. Activities and materials are matched to children's age levels, interests, and needs. There is a healthy balance between play, rest, and quiet activities. Environmental factors that affect behavior such as heat, light, and noise levels are closely monitored and adjusted when necessary. A great deal of attention also is given to health and nutritional factors that influence children's behavior. In *Keeping the Peace: Practicing Cooperation and Conflict Resolution with Preschoolers,* Susanne Wichert describes an ideal environment:

- Allow children to function with the maximum degree of independence. When children are able to do many things for themselves or with the help of another child, not only is there an enhancement of self-esteem and increased opportunity for altruistic behavior, but staff can spend less time on purely custodial tasks. Obviously, the teacher who is freed from these custodial tasks is better able to monitor for conflict and guide it to its resolution.
- Allow all persons in it to function at a low-stress level. A number of physical factors can influence stress level, among them noise level, visual clutter, use of color, and space/child ratio.

■ Be as comfortable as possible for a variety of uses. Space in a preschool classroom should aid in establishing a strong link between the parent and the center. With that aim in mind, there should be a number of places where a parent and child can be together comfortably for a while. The parent's comfort and sense of trust is passed on to the child and has a direct influence on the child's ability to feel secure and to view the values expressed at the center as consistent with the values in the child's family. The space also should have a number of "retreats" for children or adults who need time alone during the day.[8]

Praise and Reinforce Children

Children like to please. If their gifts are appreciated, they will continue to give. The basically generous and loving nature of children overflows in an affective environment. Play dough is shaped into meatballs for a teacher's lunch, "I love you" messages are tucked discreetly into pockets, a yellow dandelion and a blade of grass become a bouquet of love from a child to an adult friend. In order for children to give love, they need to feel accepted and worthy of love. Adults can instill a sense of self-worth and importance in children by acknowledging the little moments of each day when special time is needed or appreciated. Praise and reinforcement require so little effort. Teachers need only remind themselves from time to time how important it is to recognize and identify with children—to be sensitive to where they are coming from and what they need from adult friends.

Extend Love

It is unconscionable to consider caring for a child without extending love. Without love, potential fades. Young children need a great deal of physical contact and warmth. A hug or a gesture can give a child strong feelings of comfort and security throughout the day. When children experience love, they give back love. They are able to put themselves in the place of others and express sympathy. Eric Fromm drew a connection between loving others and love of ourselves: "The affirmation of one's own life, happiness, growth and freedom is rooted in one's capacity to love. . . . If an individual is able to love productively, he loves himself too."[9]

Extend Freedom

Young children need freedom in order to develop independence and self-control. Children should not have to hold hands to walk to a bathroom or use whispered voices in public places. When a child is required to behave in a way that is restrictive and unnatural, he will break free at the first opportunity. A field trip is the perfect place for a child to change the rules. Running freely, disregarding instructions, children will often behave the way they have been taught not to behave. Appropriate training for young children is not to *inhibit* behavior but to *encourage* self-control. A teacher who yells at children and threatens them with punishment does not gain respect.

Freedom is established by clear understandings and by trusting the basically good instincts and nature of children. *Freedom* is a process that begins with early training. The young child is encouraged to make choices and is entrusted with reasonable amounts of autonomy in decision making until he understands his responsibility for supporting relationships, honoring agreements, and building trust. The more cohesive a group, the more freedom children can be entrusted with. Children feel a sense of community when they are part of a team. They are unlikely to disappoint one another or their adult friends if they have participated in establishing rules of conduct and if they have learned to recognize the privileges as well as responsibilities that accompany freedom.

Give Children the Right to Make Choices

There are many ways children exert independence. Children choose playmates and activities. They choose to eat or not to eat their sandwiches; they choose to paint or not to paint a picture. The more opportunities children have to make reasonable choices, the more socially adept they will become. When children make choices, they make commitments and accept the possibility of failure. They assume responsibility for their choices. Nurturing teachers will not try to shield children from the consequences of their decisions unless the choice is clearly inappropriate or unsafe. Children, like adults, need to experience some disappointments in order to recognize and value achievement. When giving children choices, it is important to remember that it is the adult who holds the discretionary powers that guide children toward appropriate decision making. Sue Spayth Riley comments:

> I have observed that in raising children some parents think of decision making only in very lofty terms. For them, decisions are grandiose choices between earth-shaking alternatives and may be turned over to children only when they have reached the age of reason. It is quite true that earth-shaking moral decisions cannot and should not be presented to young children. The opportunity, however, to make decisions involving less significant options may be given to the very young. Practice in the process of choosing is a must, with the options being in keeping with the age and ability of each child. When children are given practice in choosing, the chances are good that they will develop decision-making ability, insight, flexibility, and the imagination to cope with the loftier choices to come later.[10]

Extend Empathy

Empathy is sharing the thoughts and feelings of another. In an affective environment, teachers naturally express empathy because they are mentally and emotionally "tuned in" to each child. They are concerned with the development of the whole child: how the child looks, feels, develops, and expresses himself. They are informed about a child's history, present environment, and overall developmental level. They know where children are coming from because they understand where children are at a given moment. An empathetic teacher recognizes the value of developing a close and caring relationship with parents and other primary adults who surround a child.

Provide a Secure and Happy Environment

An affective classroom is equipped for comfort, challenge, and investigation. There are busy corners and quiet centers, soft places for rest, and lots of things to get little hands into. Some children paint, others parade around in grown-up clothes. Two friends are listening to records; another is pestering to become a part of the group. These little tête-à-têtes bind children together. The classroom is like a big family filled with grabbing, teasing, moodiness, and hugging. At the baseline, however, there should always be forgiveness and acceptance. Little children have an infinite capacity to forgive and forget—to live and let live, to get on with their play world. Noted educator and writer Jim Greenman has emphasized the importance of providing children and adults with soft, companionable environments:

> A soft, responsive, physical environment reaches out to children. It helps children to feel more secure, enabling them to venture out and explore the world, much like homes provide the adults the haven from which they can face an often difficult and heartless world. The moments alone spaced out on a swing, rocking in a chair or a rocking horse, or kneading dough allow children to recharge.[11]

Provide Personal Space

Children identify with their classroom when they have a place to call their own. Cubbies are important symbols of independence and possession to young children. They are places children can claim and control. Though not for leftover tuna sandwiches or dying insects, cubbies perform an important self-affirmation function for every child. What the child deems important is inevitably slipped into a cubby: a piece of glass, an acorn, a stick, a present from a friend, an invitation to a birthday party—all the important collectibles that have made up a child's day.

Encourage Respect for Life

In affective settings, there is a respect for all living things. Children identify with nature and care about their environment. It is through nurturing insects, flowers, and animals that children develop a greater sense of unity with their surrounding world. A child who can relate to living things in positive ways will never be alienated or lonely. A primary way to generate compassion in young children is to give them pets. Professor Gladys F. Blue suggests that pet–person relationships are most relevant to a growing child because they provide:

- Love, attachment, and comfort
- Sensorimotor and nonverbal learning
- Responsibility, nurturance, and sense of competence
- Learning about life, death, and grief
- Therapeutic benefits to psychological and physical health
- Nurturing humaneness, ecological awareness, and ethical responsibility[12]

Children in child care centers enjoy stroking and watching baby animals or rabbits. A pet can offer children unequivocal companionship and love. Children can play imaginatively with animals. They enjoy picking them up and putting them in unusual places like cubbies, remote corners, and in handmade cages. They enjoy getting into a monologue with a pet—a conversation that is something like role-playing.

The Roles and Responsibilities of Quality Teachers

An effective educator in a child care environment must acquire a range of skills and a level of professional competency that encompasses all facets of child development. In *Early Childhood at Risk: Actions and Advocacy for Young Children,* Professor Victoria Jean Dimidjian aptly describes early childhood teachers as developmental interaction specialists. She defines their roles by these categories:

- Observer
- Environmental designer
- Facilitator
- Nurturer
- Inquiry-based explorer
- Intellectual guide and stimulator
- Information provider
- Modeler of social skills
- Disciplinarian
- Assessor/diagnostician
- Resource and referral provider
- Staff/team member[13]

These functions require not only considerable training and experience, but instinct as well. An instinctive teacher is naturally child sensitive; she knows how to manage a classroom and how to interact with children. She is objective and open minded, recognizing that behavioral changes are not unusual in child care environments. The teacher knows how to help children work through the everyday experiences that cause upsets. Using both wisdom and training, she extends herself for a child in need and, more often than not, experiences success.

In a developmental environment, a teacher and an assistant perceive their relationship as interdependent and supportive. An assistant may have insight about a child that a busy teacher has missed. She may notice changes in development and changes in behavior because she is with the child for a longer period of time during various transitions. A wise teacher will cultivate a strong relationship with her colleagues, one that creates a sense of togetherness.

Characteristics of Quality Teachers

Teachers who work with young children should be:

- Sensitive to the individual needs of children in a child care environment
- Professionals trained in child development and experienced in working with children
- Skilled in classroom management
- Kind and considerate toward children, colleagues, and parents
- Affectionate and positive role models for children to place their trust in
- Prepared and organized in their approach to teaching and training children
- Skillful in bringing out the best in young children
- Able and resourceful in developing a creative and challenging program
- Flexible in their approach to teaching and learning
- Aware of the importance of teaching children responsibility, values, and good work habits
- Aware of the importance of encouraging independence, initiative, and problem-solving skills
- Able to plan and implement field trips that complement a program and enrich children's lives
- Able to use the creative arts as a primary vehicle for self-expression, self-development, and creativity
- Able to work effectively with staff
- Aware of the importance of promoting multicultural awareness and ethnic identity throughout a program
- Creative architects in planning and equipping activity centers for children to explore and enjoy
- Creative in developing ideas and original materials for children to interact with and derive knowledge from
- Able to initiate ideas for children to develop in their own ways
- Talented in bringing out the talents in others
- Able to make each child feel important and good about himself
- Able to help children to value and love all people
- Skillful at eliminating stereotypes and biases
- Skilled in behavior management and conflict resolution
- Humorous and patient in mannerisms and style
- Loving and accepting toward children and adults

Assessing Children's Progress

The purpose of assessing children's progress is to understand and evaluate their growth patterns and development. The most careful way to assess children's progress is by observing children in their total environment on a *daily* basis. Equally important is recording children's behavioral and developmental progress on an as-needed basis. Teachers are advised to document children's progress by keeping anecdotal (brief) records on child-related concerns and areas of general development. Documentation might include *behavioral, developmental,* or *social* areas. A teacher observes a child's behavioral patterns and his physiological make-up, temperament, disposition, and personality and notes his family background and prior experiences. She observes a child's developmental characteristics: interests and talents; ability; distinguishing features; skills—physical, language, and listening skills; sensory development; thinking, recall, and discrimination skills; number concepts, reasoning, and problem-solving ability; expressive skills; and self- and task-management skills. She observes a child's social skills—ability to communicate and cooperate with peers on a fairly sustained basis.

By being aware of each child's activities and interactions throughout the day and by spending personal time with a child, a skillful teacher will not need to record everything that happens in the course of a day. Excessive preoccupation with recordkeeping may cause children to be unfairly or prematurely labeled. It also may take a teacher's time away from children and shift a classroom atmosphere away from open-learning. A teacher must use discretion in what and when she records about her children. Some items should be noted at the time of occurrence (e.g., unusual changes in behavior, confidential information, developmental milestones, a specific developmental concern, accidents, or contagious illnesses). Areas of general progress, however, such as basic skill, eye–hand coordination, or physical or behavioral development, need not be recorded daily.

Documenting and Preserving Children's Work

In a whole-child environment, teachers can access a part of a child that may not reveal itself in everyday encounters. Documentation provides an in-depth, long-term profile of a child's developmental progress. It can be accomplished in several ways, for example, by making notes and keeping informal records of children's behavior and performance, by maintaining a personal portfolio for each child, and by displaying children's works.

A *portfolio* is a uniquely personalized and insightful record of a child's progress, interests, and emerging personality. It is especially helpful at the early levels of development. A teacher may include in a child's portfolio photographs such as a child resting on a cot, riding a tricycle, or making cookies. She may include a small book of "Habits and Manners" containing messages such as: Sarah can brush her teeth, put on her coat, and almost fold her bedding. A teacher would also note first time happenings, new words, new teeth, other important milestones, and children's unique expressions. In the hands of a caring teacher, a portfolio becomes a storehouse for memories. Portfolios and journals of children's work are shared with parents during a conference, and taken home at the end of a year.

A portfolio of children's work and interests provides a vehicle for determining the following:

- How a child is responding to a program
- Aspects of a child's emerging personality
- A child's level of engagement and interest

- A child's attitude and disposition
- A child's level of commitment to a project or activity
- A child's skill and developmental level
- Specific areas of accomplishments
- Emerging interests and talents

A Developmental Checklist

A child's progress in areas germaine to his development usually is recorded on a developmental checklist. The form should not be so general as to exclude basic skills in foundation areas or so restrictive as to exclude important developmental, interactional factors. A checklist should *not* label a child, grade a child, or attempt to predict a child's educational future; it should merely be a tool for assessing progress at a given time and for *promoting* and *enhancing* a child's development over time. It is also a way of assessing one's own performance. By evaluating children, a teacher evaluates herself. Am I meeting the needs of each child? Do I need to make changes in the environment, in my program, in my performance, in my own objectives for children?

In order to assess a child with accuracy, a teacher must be informed about developmental theories and practices. He must understand the significance of self-expression and play to a child's development. A teacher needs to understand that a three-year-old who can identify colors, shapes, numbers, or words is performing in only one small area of development. If the same child can recall information, self-manage, and work independently, a teacher may assume that a child is progressing well. Progress is *never* forever. Children dip and rise in their abilities and interests much like adults do.

Checklists are valuable insofar as they identify and monitor a child's interests, emerging skills, and needs over a period of time. (See the Appendix for sample checklists.)

Conferencing with Parents

Conferences are important channels for communicating with parents about a child's adjustment and progress in a child care environment. In addition, a conference is an opportunity for a teacher to gain more information and insight about a child and an opportunity for parents to learn about a program. The challenge for a teacher is to communicate effectively and honestly. She will want to stress the positive aspects of a child's development, but she also will want to provide an objective assessment that points out areas of concern. A teacher will gradually learn how to communicate concerns to parents, some of whom may blame themselves for a child's problems. When necessary, she will provide resources and special assistance and recommend a plan for correcting deficiencies that can be followed through at home. For example, a child with poor motor skills will need materials and equipment that are specifically designed to develop eye–hand coordination. A center may lend toys for weekend use or suggest fine-motor games and toys that can be purchased at a local store.

Most important, a teacher and a parent should end a conference by agreeing to work together, to reinforce and support a child's interests. A summary of each conference should be placed in a child's file and retained for at least one year after a child's departure from the center.

Preconference Considerations

A conference should not be handled in a routine, checklist format. Parents have the right to know what a program is about so that they too can evaluate and reinforce a child's learning. By outlining areas of emphasis, a teacher will be better able to communicate a center's objectives and a child's progress. Areas to include might be:

Self-development. Degree of independence, initiative, and self-management that a child manifests toward self and environment. What particularly interests the child during self-initiated play and practical life experiences (e.g., washing tables, setting tables, sorting and classifying objects during pick-up)? What is child's attitude toward cooperating and helping with tasks? Why is this area of training important in a child care environment? How can parents help children toward self-management and responsible behavior? What responsibilities are children given in this classroom?

Social development. Degree of social maturity child expresses. How and to whom does child demonstrate sharing and friendship? How is caring and friendship nurtured in this classroom? How can parents encourage this important area of development? How is self-esteem and social awareness developed in this classroom (e.g., Person of the Week, sharing day, parent visits, celebrating birthdays, helping children to accept and understand differences, projects and activities that invoke emotions and feelings)?

Physical development. Degree of large- and small-motor abilities child is acquiring. What opportunities for both areas are available in this program? What is child particularly good at or interested in? How can parents encourage this important area of development? How are nutrition and good health practices encouraged in this classroom?

Emotional development. Degree of adjustment child is making to his or her child care experience and environment. Is child developing self-control, patience, and self-awareness? Is child able to play alone for extended periods of time? Is child able to sustain group or peer play for reasonable periods of time? How is emotional growth encouraged in this classroom? How do parents assess this important area of development?

Cognitive development. Degree of awareness, alertness, inquiry, and exploration child exhibits toward mastery and understanding of his or her physical environment. What formal and informal learning opportunities are available for children's cognitive development? What areas may or should be given extra attention by teachers and parents? Why? What basic skills are introduced to children and in what way (e.g., language, math and science concepts, spatial relationships, ordering, classification, problem solving, memory, and critical thinking skills)? How are children encouraged to think creatively and independently in this classroom?

Language development. Degree of language competency expressed by child. Does the child attend to a story? Can he or she project endings, show interest, identify with characters, recall a sequence of events (if appropriate)? Does the child participate in group circle? What whole-language program is incorporated into this program? How are phonics integrated into the language-arts program? What is important in a child-centered reading program (e.g., the process, enjoying language, reading and telling stories in unique and motivating ways, encouraging children's interest in books, stimulating thinking, and encouraging children to express themselves through language)? What specific activities may parents want to adapt for use in a home language program?

Creative development. What degree of interest and involvement does the child exhibit toward dramatic play, toward storytelling experiences, toward painting, toward music and poetry, toward original thinking, and toward discovery opportunities in the classroom and on the playground? How important is creative expression in this classroom? What areas might parents want to cultivate? What is creativity?

Suggestions for Effective Conferences

Some or all of the following may be useful when preparing for a conference with a child's parents:

- Self-evaluate the role and responsibilities of teachers.
- Review the center's objectives.
- Review the center's discipline policy.
- Prepare well in advance for parent conferences; observe and evaluate children's progress during the preceding months and especially during the pre-conference period.
- Keep a daily record of children's progress, noting milestones, interests, friends, concerns, and behavior changes.
- Review the center's curriculum guide and refer to its developmental checklist when observing children, noting areas that may be of concern.
- Spend individual time with children before a conference so that information can be updated and verified by the child's primary teacher; be certain children can perform basic skills that are age appropriate and observe their thinking patterns and language development.
- Keep an ongoing file of children's drawings, anecdotes, original writings, and so on to share with parents.
- Be able to point out the important objectives of a program.
- Emphasize the special qualities of each child by pointing out interests, attitudes, talents, and friends.

- Be relaxed and nonjudgmental with parents.
- Observe but *do not* label children.
- Make recommendations in positive and supportive ways.
- Be prepared to provide resources for learning or emotional problems, for special events or activities that might interest a child, and for parent/child field trips.
- Allow time for natural "in-time" maturation (i.e., avoid hasty decision making and recommendations).
- Begin and end a conference on a positive note.

Working with Parents

Young children prosper when centers value and nurture continuous and caring interaction among the primary adults in their lives. They gain knowledge and understanding from the role models around them throughout the day. Children perceive themselves as members of a group that resembles an extended family. In this extended family, teachers know family members and parents know classroom friends. Instinctively, children identify with and place their trust in a center/home environment that provides consistency and love.

Directors, staff, and parents must envision themselves as cooperative partners in the care, nurturing, and education of young children. They must share common goals, recognizing that each partner in the team has something important to contribute to the life of a child throughout the formative years. Such collaborative interaction and shared responsibility will give children a sense of continuity between a home and the school environment.

A child's experience in a child care center is most beneficial when there is respectful communication between a center and its parent body. Parents who are involved in their children's education are sensitive to children's developmental needs. They recognize the importance of a healthy and happy childhood and the critical role a center plays in a child's total development. (See A Parent Evaluation, in the Appendix.)

Integrating Nurturing into a Child-Centered Curriculum

Health and Nutrition

A comprehensive early childhood program will include health and nutrition as primary components in an integrated curriculum. To nurture a child's well-being is to provide basic information about physical and nutritional health and to become cognizant of the importance of mental health to child development. A healthy child is a child whose physical, nutritional, and mental needs are met and who is safe from environmental hazards.

Physical Health

The basic routines of a child care center such as dressing, hand-washing, eating, and resting are established early. Children learn self-management and body care through direct instruction and practice. They develop a greater awareness of their responsibility for self-care through vicarious classroom experiences. A nurturing curriculum, for example, may use a puppet to symbolically act out the habits and attitudes that adults are trying to reinforce in young children. One puppet may be a good rester, another a good cleaner, and another a good eater. Another puppet may have trouble following rules and be lax about self-care. The dialogue that ensues will make children think about the consequences of poor habits.

Each classroom can develop its own puppet theme to train children in health, safety, and nutrition. For example, a mother or father rabbit and seven bunnies can become active participants in a health curriculum. Each bunny can be good at some things but not good at others. The children themselves can become involved in training the bunnies. A bunny who hates to rest can become a resting friend for a child. A bunny who hates to clean up his mess can become an eating companion of another child. A bunny who never plays out-of-doors because it is too cold may get to wear a special coat and cap. A bunny who hates to wash his ears because they are too big, or who hates to wash her hands because she always plays in the dirt, will become a favorite buddy to a young child.

Professionals, such as dentists and pediatricians, should be invited to a child care center to speak about self-care and hygiene. They may extend their services by inviting children to their office for a personal visit. A visit to a doctor or a dentist usually includes a treat: a paper mask or garment, some floss, or a toothbrush. Doctors who specialize in practices for children are usually people who care about children—people who will extend themselves to a child care center.

Body awareness and sex education are integral components of a nurturing curriculum. Children start asking questions at an early age and teachers are often reluctant to provide children accurate information. Teachers can use units or themes as a way of acquainting children with their bodies. Units such as "All About Me," "Me and My Family," or "Baby Animals" provide natural settings for sex education. There are many natural opportunities to increase children's awareness—through sensory and nurturing experiences, literature, weight and height charts, and body movement records.

A wonderful way to satisfy children's curiosity about birth is to acquire classroom pets and offspring. Animals such as rabbits, mice, and guinea pigs make wonderful classroom pets. By observing and identifying with a birth experience, children learn about conception, prenatal development, and birth in natural, positive ways. Natural experiences are always preferable to instructional experiences at early childhood levels.

Mental Health

A "wellness" approach to child care education views stress reduction as a primary factor in curriculum planning. Stress in young children is one of the more serious consequences of disruptive, unbalanced living patterns. When children feel neglected, fatigued, or confused, they are limited in their coping, adjustment mechanisms. Children signal stress in many ways: irritability, sucking thumbs, deviant behavior, hostility, anger, poor concentration and short attention span, stuttering, eye blinking, preoccupation with body parts, poor eating and resting habits, withdrawal, or complaints about not feeling well.

In designing a curriculum for children in child care, each content area should be examined from a perspective of mental health/stress reduction. Activities and room arrangements should be organized to *reduce competition,* to *enhance self-confidence,* and to *promote self-expression.* Teachers should become attentive to a child's internal environment, to what is producing unhappiness and stress. By reducing stress levels, a teacher is reducing conflict and accompanying misbehavior.

A mental health program should include time for outdoor play, rest at intervals throughout the day, creative self-directed play, and recreation. On a regular basis, children should stop, rest, and breathe deeply. School-age children should be offered the opportunity to practice some form of meditation, such as yoga. When children meditate, they reduce stress levels by integrating mind and body. They feel better inside and increase their energy level. They gradually learn to respond to stress by making the adjustments that make them feel better about themselves and happier inside.

Nutrition

Nutrition is a process by which children obtain food and nutrients. Children can become familiar with the basic food groups through cooking, shopping, and experiences such as going on field trips to see how food is grown, processed, and distributed. They can help a teacher plan a nutritious meal by providing the foods that are essential to growth, energy, and health. Children can consult their classroom food chart as they plan a menu. They have learned from their chart that a nutritious lunch should include healthy amounts of the following food groups: milk and milk products, meat or meat alternatives, vegetables and fruits, breads and cereals, and limited amounts of fats and sugar. They have learned that raw vegetables are more nutritious than cooked vegetables and that water is essential to the digestive process and to general physical health. They have learned that salt and butter are not essential add-ons in nutritional planning. They also have learned about junk food! (See Nutrition Guidelines in the Appendix.)

An important part of children's nutritional training takes place when children observe and prepare food. Children need to make healthy choices of foods, and they need to learn how to handle and care for the foods they select. They need to practice personal hygiene and to perceive a cooking or food-preparation experience as an extension of themselves. Cooking, like many other aspects of development and personal expression, is an art that requires training and skill. Through selective experiences, children will learn that some foods need refrigeration, all foods need careful storage, and some need considerable preparation before they are ready to add to recipes (washing, peeling, cutting, chopping, removing seeds). As children prepare and work with foods, they observe changes in texture, volume, and consistency. Because cooking is a hands-on experience, children will quickly become knowledgeable about the process. They will learn how to prepare fresh green beans, corn, melons, and strawberries. They will learn to approximate amounts and to select foods that are in season (and therefore less costly).

Equally important is serving food. Children can become skilled and creative in the way they set a table and arrange food. Children should learn to pass food trays or plates and to show discretion in the amount they take at one time. They should learn to use their napkins and to practice good table manners (no thank you, please, would you care for . . .). Inappropriate table behavior should be dealt with quickly by a teacher. If a teacher is apathetic to table etiquette, children will not perceive eating as a pleasurable, social experience.

A nutrition curriculum should include problem solving and critical thinking as well as decision making. A teacher can help children plan by using problem-solving strategies: "I think we need a green vegetable today because yesterday we had a yellow vegetable—who can think of a green vegetable?" Children can identify all the green vegetables they can think of, the teacher can print the choices, and the children can vote on the selection. Children can think of interesting ways to prepare and serve snacks; they can make up their own recipes and keep a recipe book. School-age children can research and prepare dishes and snack foods that reflect the international ethnic backgrounds of classmates.

An important aspect of educating children in health, safety, and nutrition is that practical life training must begin during the formative years. Children learn to function as independent managers when they are informed and knowledgeable about health and hygiene. They learn to be self-sufficient, wise decision makers respecting the habits designed to promote and protect their well-being. They learn to distinguish between and choose behaviors that promote growth and those that inhibit growth

Literature

Literature can serve as a primary vehicle for nurturing children. Fictional characters can become very real to the child, particularly to one who can identify with their problems. Literature facilitates problem solving by indirect association and identification. It also serves as a catalyst for training in values and morals. When children solve their own problems, they become stronger, less vulnerable young persons. In a listening/sharing experience, children can gain insight about themselves by sharing someone else's perspective. In an article, "Learning to Share: How Literature Can Help," Susanne Krogh and Linda Lamme describe the value of books in training for nurturing:

> Literature can help children learn about sharing, employing their budding ability in role-taking. Literature takes sharing, an essentially abstract concept, and places it inside a more concrete setting. It provides children with an opportunity to take, for a while, the role of a protagonist, to step inside the shoes of someone facing a dilemma or making a decision. Specifically, it offers children an opportunity to learn why people share.[14]

Literature can serve as an entrance to the inner self—to what motivates and validates one's personage.

Some Nurturing Books for Young Children[15]

George & Martha by J. Marshall. The message: friendship. Two hippopotamuses named George and Martha have a special friendship. They always look on the bright side, and they always know how to cheer one another up. And, they also tell the truth!

We Are Best Friends by Aliki. The message: adapting and adjusting to change. Robert's best friend, Peter, is moving away. Robert tells his friend not to move because "you will miss me too much." Peter does move and, for Robert, there was no fun anymore—until he meets Will.

Tico and the Golden Wings by A. Mosel. The message: the gifts of love transcend the ordinary. Tico is a little bird born without wings and dependent on friends for survival. The day comes when Tico magically grows golden wings, to the amazement and envy of other birds. Tico uses these wings as gifts for the poor and helpless until they are all gone and replaced by plain, black wings.

Make Way for Ducklings by R. McClosky. The messages: making good choices, responsibility. Mrs. Mallard is very particular about finding a suitable place to nest and raise her offspring, and Mr. Mallard is very patient with her. They finally settle on a quiet spot on the Charles River in Boston; and just in time.

Goodnight Moon by M. Brown. The message: security. A warm, cozy, and comforting story for the very young child; "Goodnight stars . . . Goodnight air . . . Goodnight noises everywhere."

Tikki Tikki Tembo by A. Mosel. The messages: cultural awareness, respect for adults. This exquisite Chinese folktale comes to life through its adorable characters and rhythmic verse, "Oh, most honorable mother, Tikki tikki tembo-no sa rembo-chari bari ruchi-pip peri pembo has fallen into the well."

Let's Be Enemies by J. Udry. The message: friends can have disagreements and still remain friends. John went to James's house to tell him he was his enemy, but he found that friends can be enemies but still remain friends—best friends.

Daddy Makes the Best Spaghetti by A. Hines. The message: pitching in and sharing responsibilities. Corey is at a day care center and when Daddy picks him up, wonderful things happen. Corey helps with the shopping, setting the table, cooking, and then, the games begin.

William's Doll by C. Zolotov. The messages: overcoming stereotypical behavior, doing one's thing, what's wrong with being me? William wants a doll of his very own, a wish that concerns his family. Grandmother understands the nature and importance of this need and buys William a doll.

Ira Sleeps Over by B. Waber. The message: anxiety (we all need teddy bears sometimes). Ira is excited about sleeping over at his friend's house (he had never slept out before) but as the day progresses he develops anxieties about parting with Ta Ta his best bear. When his friend Reggie pulls out his bear during a ghost story, Ira rushes home to get Ta Ta.

What Mary Joe Shared by J. Udry. The messages: decision making, the need to feel special. Mary Jo needed to share with her classmates during show-and-tell but everything she thought of someone else had already shared. One day she invited her daddy to school and shared him. Mary Joe and her friends delighted in the specialness of her first sharing.

Nick Joins In by J. Lasker. The message: being different—how children with special needs feel when they are mainstreamed. Nick expresses his fears about being integrated into a new school and, at the same time, children at the school he is about to attend express their concerns, too. They quickly reconcile their differences and view Nick as a special friend.

The Little Engine That Could by W. Piper. The message: if you think you can, you probably can. As the immortal little blue engine puffs over its final hill, the enraptured listener becomes a passenger. The train says, "I think I can," and the children say "I know you can."

The Tenth Good Thing About Barney by J. Viorst. The message: regeneration; renewal. When a funeral is held for Barney, a cat, the family has difficulty thinking up a tenth good thing to say about their beloved cat. When the father covers the ground with seeds, the little boy finds one more good thing to say. Barney will help the flowers grow!

Peter's Chair by E. Keats. The message: sharing is not always easy. Peter has to give his special things to a new baby in the house. His chair is a different matter.

Timothy and Gramps by R. Brooks. The message: everyone needs someone to love. This is a tender and beautifully illustrated story about a shy and lonely little boy whose greatest pleasure is being with his grandfather. One day grandfather comes to school to share a special story with Timothy's classmates and Timothy begins to feel special too.

A Story, A Story by G. Haley. The message: we can overcome obstacles. In this beautifully illustrated African tale, a defenseless man succeeds against great odds to obtain Sky God's stories. Children will enjoy Ananse's quests, feats, and identify with his fears.

Mommies at Work by E. Merriam. The messages: identification and understanding. Children will see mommies in a variety of roles—making cookies, kissing places that hurt and places that don't hurt, working on ranches, building bridges. But best of all, mommies come home to a lot of love at the end of the day.

On Mother's Lap by A. Scott. The message: there's always room when there is love. This wonderful and tender book about a little Eskimo boy who is sensitive to a new baby on his mother's lap, tests her love for him by loading more and more on her lap before placing himself there also. Mother lets Michael know there is plenty of room on mother's lap.

The Birthday Wish by I. Chihiro. The message: we all make mistakes; being thoughtful is what counts. Allison accidentally blew out the candles on her friend's birthday cake. Allison feels very upset, but the next day, on her fifth birthday, Allison lets Judy blow out her candles.

Alexander and the Wind-Up Mouse by L. Lionni. The message: love makes it own magic. This is the story about a real mouse and a wind-up mouse and their special friendship. Alexander thought he wanted to be a wind-up mouse like Willy until the day came when Willy was put in a throwaway box with other old toys. Helped by a magical lizard and a purple pebble, Willy turns into a real mouse to live happily ever after with Alexander.

Frederick by L. Lionni. The message: we all have something special to give, even if it isn't always apparent to others. Frederick was not a worker like his mice family. Instead of gathering food for winter, he gathered sun rays, colors, and imagination. But it was Frederick who entertained his friends with poems during the long winter months when there wasn't much work to do.

Annie and the Old One by M. Miles. The message: a child experiences loss gently through the death of her grandmother. This sensitive book suggests that life and death are a part of a process. Annie is a little Navajo girl who learns that when her mother finishes weaving a rug, it will be time for her beloved grandmother to die and return to the earth. Annie resists the inevitable death of her grandmother and tries to prevent the completion of the rug. When the old one explains that it is time for her to return to the earth, Annie understands and is filled with the wonder of it all.

The Red Balloon by A. Lamorisee. The message: life can be sad and cruel but often there are happy endings. This tender story about a lonely little boy's love for a red balloon generates tremendous feeling in children (and adults). At the end of the book, when bullies taunt Pascal and throw stones at his balloon, the Sky is suddenly filled with balloons rising in freedom, carrying Pascal away from sadness and loneliness. This is a picture book that can be read with or without discussion.

For Additional ways to nurture children through literature, see *Big Multicultural Tales,* Scholastic, 1993–current.

Summary

Young children prosper when centers value and nurture continuous and caring interaction among the primary adults in their lives. They gain knowledge and understanding from the role models around them throughout the day. Children perceive themselves as members of a group that resembles an extended family. In this extended family, teachers know family members and parents know classroom friends. Instinctively, children identify with and place their trust in a center/home environment that provides consistency and love.

Directors, staff, and parents must envision themselves as cooperative partners in the care, nurturing, and training of young children. They must share common goals, recognizing that each partner in the team has something important to contribute to the life of a child throughout the formative years. Such collaborative interaction and shared responsibility will give children a sense of continuity between a home and the school environment, and they will prosper in an environment that is consistent and reinforcing.

N O T E S

1. Judith Leipzig, "Helping Whole Children Grow: Non-Sexist Childrearing for Infants and Toddlers," in *Alike and Different: Exploring Our Humanity with Children*, Bonnie Neugebauer, ed., (Washington, DC: Exchange Press, 1987), p. 43.

2. Louise Derman-Sparks and the A.B.C. Task Force, *Anti-Bias Curriculum: Tools for Empowering Young Children* (Washington, DC: NAEYC, 1989), p. 69.

3. As cited in Mary Renck Jalongo, "Promoting Peer Acceptance of the Newly Immigrated Child," *Childhood Education* 60(2) (November/December, 1983): 123.

4. Derman-Sparks, *Anti-Bias Curriculum*, p. 4.

5. Ibid., p. 2.

6. Susanne Wichert, *Keeping Peace: Practicing Cooperation and Conflict Resolution with Preschoolers* (Philadelphia, PA: New Society Publishers, 1989), p. 54.

7. Barbara J. Meddin, Anita L. Rosen, "Child Abuse and Neglect," in Janet B. McCracken, *Reducing Stress in Young Children's Lives* (Washington, DC: NAEYC, 1986), pp. 78, 80.

8. S. Wichert, *Keeping Peace*, p. 15.

9. As cited in Daniel A. Prescott, "The Role of Love in Preschool Education," in *Readings from Early Childhood Education*, ed., M. Rasmussen (Washington, DC: ACEI, 1966), p. 56.

10. Sue Spayth Riley, *How to Generate Values in Young Children* (Washington, DC: NAEYC, 1984), p. 8.

11. Jim Greenman, *Caring Spaces, Learning Places: Children's Environments That Work* (Washington, DC: Exchange Press, 1988), p. 74.

12. Gladys F. Blue, "The Value of Pets in Children's Lives," *Childhood Education* 63(2) (December 1986): 85.

13. Victoria Jean Dimidjian, *Early Childhood at Risk: Actions and Advocacy for Young Children* (Washington, DC: National Education Association, 1989), pp. 49–51.

14. Susanne L. Krogh and Linda L. Lamme, "Learning to Share: How Literature Can Help," *Childhood Education* (January/February, 1983): 189.

15. Ellen Cromwell, *Feathers in My Cap: Early Reading through Experience* (Washington, DC: Acropolis Books Ltd., 1980), pp. 197–204.

PART THREE

The Environment

An environment is a living, changing system. More than the physical space, it includes the way time is structured and the roles we are expected to play. It conditions how we feel, think, and behave; and it dramatically affects the quality of our lives. The environment either works for us or against us as we conduct our lives.

—Jim Greenman

CHAPTER

7

Indoor Environments

Families enter a child care facility from the outside. A building creates an image that is meant to attract clientele. Inside a child care center, however, there is another image that is less visible to the public. This image should reflect the real, untouched, untarnished world of childhood; a world of special moments that creates a day for children that is at once unique, special, and memorable; a day unlike any other day.

—Ellen Cromwell

Imagine a room that looks and feels and smells like little children; a room that is bristling with activities; a room that is a composite of distinct interests and dispositions; a room that, despite its individuality, is greater than its parts; a room that conveys feelings of harmony, of order, of completeness, of wholeness, of happiness; a room that welcomes all children and all adults; a room that is alive with growth and potential and possibility. Imagine a perfect environment.

In child care, an environment conveys a weblike imagery that begins with the child and expands outward creating a sense of harmony and order. Each center has its unique features as well as characteristics common to all quality environments.

Setting a Tone

Caring

Evidence of caring permeates a child-centered room from pictures on the wall to an old rocking chair that is never stationary. There is an atmosphere of pleasing, unhurried movement. Many activities are taking place, and there are many choices within each activity. A teacher is writing a story with a child while another child sits on her lap quietly observing the activity. In another part of a room, an adult is patiently helping children assemble colors for a mural. Somewhere else, children are playing in their own little play worlds, so absorbed in fantasy that they scarcely notice others in the room. One almost misses the little girl who is setting the table for a snack, carefully arranging napkins and cups near chairs that will soon be occupied by hungry little children. There is a rhythm and a naturalness to the way children are playing and working in this room. It is not by accident that the room appears remarkably complete. The room has been designed carefully and arranged by a creative and caring teacher who knows what children like.

Creativity

One is compelled to linger in this room. A huge stuffed bear named McGoo has quickly become an attention-getter and a classroom companion. Children are sitting in his lap and feeding him pretend food. He never seems to tire of the attention or affection he receives as children pass by. Nearby, one notices a mural of a snowy day, hastily painted by children. It is the first snowfall of the year. The picture, like the season, is still moist and fresh with whiteness. While some children paint, others are cutting up paper into tiny little pieces that will soon be added to the mural. Still others are listening to a scratchy, worn record; one child is avidly reading a book that contains no words, another is bargaining for a dress-up item that is on another child. Some children are chattering, smiling and some are arguing. Personalized touches are everywhere: soft pillows, a trunkful of costumes, child-sized furniture, a real telephone, mirrors, a rocker, and a wardrobe for McGoo!

Authenticity

Character permeates a room that is authentic and meaningful. Character has its unique markings: child-worn furniture; overfed pets; and scarred surfaces that have been played on, spilled on, and written on. It is unpretentious: windowboxes with bulbs announcing the arrival of spring, a large clean window surrounded by children's pictures, children's artwork with the remnants of glue still dripping down the wall, a fishbowl too small for a fish because of the rocks children keep adding to it, hairless dolls, and armless teddy bears. It is joyful—something to look forward to, something to feel good about, something that makes one feel warm and safe inside, even on snowy days. Character emanates from a room that has been truly lived in and enjoyed by children. A room with character allows children to become meaning makers, as poignantly described by V. Suransky in her book, *The Erosion of Childhood:*

> The child's mode of being in the world is such that the world becomes an invitation. It is the things in the beckoning world that invite the child, that awaken his curiosity, that invoke him . . . to make sense of that multitude of experiences lying beyond; in short to become, through his play, both an actor and a meaning maker.[1]

Like its occupants, an environment develops character and personality over time. When an environment is institutional in appearance and in feeling, it cannot grow and change with its occupants. Experiencing the same furniture grouped in the same way year after year is not developmentally appropriate: At the most critical and exciting stages of development, children are experiencing an environment that is unchanging, uninviting, and in time, unchallenging.

Environments for young children should creatively combine children's play furnishings with real-world objects and decor. Children's senses are stimulated by fabrics, textures, odors, and special touches that are identified with home. An entrance area sets the tone for a home-like environment. A brass lamp, an antique mirror and table, a colorful area rug, dried flowers, and real plants communicate that a center is a special place.

In Reggio Emilia environments, space is so intricately and sensitively designed that a visitor feels immediately at home. There is a somewhat disarming realization of having been in this environment before; of reexperiencing one's past; of reentering one's childhood. In this charmingly companionable atmosphere, time appears to be unchanging. One trusts that year after year the flowers will continue to delight children with their fragrance, the birds will return to familiar settings, and the projects begun in childhood will have blended in with the landscape.

The design and structure of physical space in Reggio Emilia schools is crucial to this program. Ceiling space is considered as visually important and functional as wall space and floor space. Ceilings are decorated with herbs, dried flowers, and transparent mobiles that catch and play with light. Soft accent lighting, natural light, shapes, patterns, and shadows interact companionably with one another creating visual impressions that change with the time of day. Every item on a wall is carefully worked into a message for children; their work, pictures, photographs, and personal space is woven into the total environment. Glass walls, dividers and windows identify parts of a room without separating children from one another. Interesting textures, plants, color-coordinated rooms, and polished floors are bathed in natural light creating an impression of harmony between a child's indoor and outdoor environment. In essence, the environment connotes an image and a feeling of a child's place—a child's home.

Playfulness

A special room has a feeling of playfulness; an environment that sustains interest and makes children want to return. There are activity centers for exploration, there are open play areas for children to move and dance in, and there are enclosed areas for imaginary play. There is quiet space to play with one's thoughts and space for small gatherings. Teresita E. Aguilar defines a playful atmosphere as one that:

- Increases the sense of freedom
- Provides an outlet for self-expression
- Encourages people to "play with" ideas rather than to "work for" solutions
- Allows for manipulation; use "people-powered" devices
- Provides risk/challenge in varying degrees
- Encourages problem-solving activities
- Incorporates the arts (music, dance, drama)
- Is flexible
- Minimizes or eliminates negative consequences for playful behaviors
- Allows for escapism, fantasy, and imagination
- Encourages and demonstrates good humor
- Allows for experimentation/exploration[2]

Working with Space

Space communicates to children. It gives them information about what they can play with and where they can play. It makes them aware of dimensions. Children perceive space as both changing and unchanging. There are certain units in a room that are designated for a particular purpose, and although the parts may change, the structure remains fairly constant throughout a year. These units are called activity or interest centers and are designed for a specific kind of play or play/ work. They are enclosed on two or three sides by frames or shelves, and they are organized in compatible patterns that reflect the purpose and use of a center.

Activity centers usually are connected by pathways that allow children to move freely from activity to activity in logical patterns. The number of centers in a room is determined by the space available and by the developmental levels of its occupants. A room for two-year-olds will have fewer centers and less equipment than one for four-year-olds. A room for eight-year-olds will have fewer play centers but more game and art centers than one for six-year-olds.

A good portion of children's play space should be left open for multipurpose use. Common space is needed for lunch, for group circles, and for cubbies. Large, open areas also may be used for a loft or to store a piece of equipment that does not fit into an activity center. A loft may become a reading area, a homework area, or a place to hang out until parents arrive. Common space is not only functional but promotes social development through natural interaction that takes place when children do not feel restricted by enclosed space.

In child care environments, space is continuously adapting to the needs and interests of its occupants, to the creative influence of teachers, and to environmental exigencies. Throughout a year, a teacher may make several changes before she feels a room is working. She examines space critically to determine if it is meeting her goals and objectives, if it is challenging, and if it is adding significantly to her environment. Sometimes only subtle changes are required: A small area rug and a soft cushion are added to a language center, a new theme is needed for a discovery center. Sometimes more dramatic changes are necessary: A heavily used block center needs a larger corner of a room, a library corner is too close to a common area. The more teachers experiment with space, the more adept they become in designing environments. Making changes is sometimes unsettling, often exhilarating, but in the long run, worthwhile. This poem from *Everychild's Everyday* aptly describes change:

> *If we change*
> *Time and space*
> *We can change*
> *Ourselves*
> *We can find new ways*
> *To communicate*
> *New words to say*
> *New topics to pursue*
> *We can find new ways*
> *To operate*
> *To invent*
> *To respond*
> *If I can change*
> *Time and space*
> *I can change habits too.*

—From *Everchild's Everyday* by Cindy Herbert and Susan Russell

Defining Space

Measuring for Children

From a child's vantage point, an environment that works is one that offers the possibility of discovery and inventiveness. For a young child, a child care room is like an oversized play room that has lots of parts, people, and hidden dimensions. Within this configuration, children begin to make mental maps. They find their way around a room by reading picture labels that describe activities and by learn-ing the patterns and the pathways that lead to favorite toys and activities. There are many choices to make and there are hidden dimensions as well. For a small res-ident, a classroom is a very big world to explore, even with a map. Each child reacts to an environment in his or her own way. Some children will plunge right into activities, others will move more cautiously, while some will stay near the door until they feel acclimated and assured that the new surroundings are safe to enter.

To a child, an environment is companionable and manageable when it is nei-ther too cluttered nor too bland. Teachers, who tend to view an environment from the eyes of adults, are often insensitive to children's impressions of space. Rooms are too often set up to please parents rather than for children's play. Teachers for-get that children may not feel comfortable in a sanitized, perfectly arranged room that looks very much like the room down the hall. If children had to choose between a comfortable, lived-in environment and a manicured room that gives a hands-off impression, they would clearly choose the former. When a room in a child care center has its own aura, children look forward to each day and each year.

Children prefer a homelike setting. They immediately notice freestanding novelty items like cardboard-box houses or imaginative handmade props. They are attracted to soothing activities like modeling with clay, playing in water, and painting—activities that do not require a great deal of interaction. As they become familiar with a room, children react to warm, soft colors, to an interesting balance of activities, and to a creative distribution of space. They absorb an atmosphere, identifying its play space, activity centers, common areas, and space that is off lim-its. Within these boundaries, they perceive a sense of order, routine, and harmony.

Measuring for Toys and Things

A child-centered environment requires a long measuring tape, one that goes around and through objects that take up play space. A preschool classroom must offer children a variety of toys and activities that generate learning and motor development. They need both *nonrealistic* (unstructured, imaginative) and *realistic* (structured, recognizable) toys. Structured toys are those that are easily recognized and identified: a bus, a drum, a doll, a long wooden train, or a riding truck. Young children primarily prefer structured, realistic toys, although novelty items (such as a feather, an animal scull, a snake skin, a wind machine, or a fossil) should always be slipped into an activity center for discovery learning.

Unstructured toys are items that may or may not be identified by name. They are less-defined objects that are labeled by the child in the context of his immediate play needs (scarves, shawls, baskets, bags, zippered containers, items with unusual shapes). Indoor materials might include interesting props such as a wagon wheel, a lantern, an old weathered chest with an intriguing lock, an unusual stuffed animal, and a surprise box; play items such as a cane, or a wand; and sensory pieces such as lace, streamers, net, fur, feathers, a fan, or a plastic horse with a long soft mane.

Outdoor materials might include gatherings from nature such as rocks, sticks, stones, bark, pinecones, nutmeats, and so on. During unstructured, outdoor play, sticks may be used as fishing poles, twigs as birthday candles, rocks as gold or silver, and little hills as miniature forts or underground tunnels for little action figures. Tactile experiences in sand, water, mud, and clay also lead to imaginative, open-ended play. These unstructured experiences are under a child's control from beginning to end. For most children, they are the best parts of a day.

A classroom also needs variety in the types of play units that are offered to children. In their excellent book, *Planning Environments for Young Children,* leading educators and writers S. Kritchevsky and Elizabeth Prescott classify play units as:

1. *Simple:* A play unit that has one use and does not have subparts (swings, jungle gym, rocking horse, tricycle).
2. *Complex:* A play unit with subparts that can be manipulated or improvised by children (art activities, a table with books to look at, an area with pets).
3. *Super:* A complex unit that has one or more additional play materials (a sand box with play materials and water, dough table with tools, movable climbing boards and boxes, and large crates).[3]

Young children (ages two to three) generally are happy (and safe) with fewer parts to interact with. They enjoy the motion of getting on and off items that are relatively fixed and uncomplicated. As children become more physically adept and imaginative in their play (ages four to five), they increasingly look for units that offer more challenge. An independent, inventive four-year-old loves to move parts around to create new structures.

Measuring for Interests

The composition of a class affects space. If boys dominate a group of children, there will be a need for an expanded large-motor construction center. If girls dominate, there will likely be a need for an expanded drama and arts center. In traditional play patterns, boys gravitate toward large-motor, active play while girls prefer less active, more focused play. Boys like rough-and-tumble direct-contact play while girls prefer less physical outlets. Although all activities should be encouraged for both sexes, if given the choice, boys and girls will probably make the same choices.

Gender-role stereotyping in play begins early and continues throughout childhood according to a study of play activities conducted by Betty S. Beeson and R. Ann Williams (1979). The study found that preschool boys still prefer wheeled vehicles, blocks, sand, tractors and climbing frames, trains and kiddie-kars, while girls prefer art activities, dolls, formal games, and house play. In crossovers, house play (or dramatic play) was the one area that was not found to be gender stereotyped—it was chosen by both boys and girls as a preferred activity. The research indicated that there may have been some changes in the gender stereotyping of play activities of young children but only in one direction. Boys' choices had expanded to include house play while girls' play choices had not expanded.[4]

Similarly, a study on toy preferences of preschool children conducted by Charles H. Wolfgang (1983) found that contemporary children attending child care do not differ from children of previous studies in their preferences for gender-specific toys; basically little had changed since earlier studies. Results of a preschool Play Materials Preference Inventory (PMPI) indicate that boys preferred categories of structured materials, letters, numbers, carpentry, number shapes, number cards, and colored pegs, while girls preferred the category of fluid constructional materials and the toy farm, doll play, housekeeping, symbolic activities as well as letter shapes and clay.[5] These natural, early preferences would suggest a disposition toward math (for boys) and language (for girls).

If early childhood is a time for making choices and expanding knowledge, children's environments should reflect their interests. If teachers take away toys that are identified with one sex, they deny children access to natural play preferences (i.e., boys tend toward blocks and girls tend toward housekeeping). The place to make changes in children's perceptions is not through contrived methods of social engineering that deny children access to the toys and experiences they enjoy, but in home environments where identity begins.

One way to discourage gender stereotyping is to expand a dramatic play or block center to include themes and activities that appeal to both sexes (e.g., a barber shop, a bank, a shoe shop, a paint store, a post office) or by adding interesting accessories in a large-motor area. Another way might be to expand an arts section to include activities such as woodworking, clay modeling, models (rockets, boats, windmills, mobiles), and innovative assemblages (creating a small farm, a castle, or pond diorama). If an arts table is not inviting to little boys, chances are they will gravitate back to a block corner where they can create in more satisfying ways.

Measuring for a Total Environment

Children and their activities fill up a room. When setting up a classroom, teachers often forget to consider children as an integral and sizeable component of space. Children physically occupy space with form, shape, and backpacks. School-age children naturally take up more space than young children, yet these rooms are often the most crowded (e.g., a 26 to 2 student/teacher ratio for children older than five years of age). Licensing personnel, who establish school-age student/teacher ratios under the current allocation of 35 square feet per child, have not given much thought to movement or personal space.

Designing a classroom to maximize the feeling of space without limiting activities is a creative challenge for a teacher. Confined space restricts activities and choices of toys. Large-motor activities, such as tumbling or push toys that require room, are usually the first items to be removed from a crowded classroom. Many teachers are not opposed to giving up large-motor toys; which are identified with noise and movement. Unfortunately, in crowded centers, large-motor development is limited to outdoor time.

Play curriculums are forcing teachers to rethink and restructure their organizational patterns and use of space. With limited space, teachers find it necessary to eliminate some activity centers or find creative ways to integrate existing centers. For example, they might combine a language center with a discovery center, or a listening/language center (it can be closed during group time) might frame a circle area. They might change the dimensions of activity centers or place compatible centers, such as dramatic play and construction, back to back using long shelves as dividers. Another alternative is to reduce the number of tables and chairs in a room by storing them until lunch or by setting up a separate lunchroom for all children in a center. By eliminating tables, teachers are eliminating a structured, school-like appearance as well as opening space.

Space includes not only cubbies and common space, but also utility objects and units such as doors, windows, sinks, heating units, built-in storage areas, and bulletin boards. It includes office space, a food preparation area, storage areas, closets, bathrooms, personal shelves for children, file cabinets and personal space for teachers, and a staff lounge/resource room. These areas must be considered when designing and measuring a room. With space at a premium, teachers can use auxiliary space for a file cabinet, personal cubbies, or to store "space-heavy" items such as a television, props for a play, or a refrigerator. As much as possible, items that are not considered part of children's play should be moved to adjacent rooms. Clearly, the layout and management of space is an important factor in child care planning, influencing both child and staff behaviors.

Other Considerations

Activity Centers

Activity centers reflect a program's philosophy, objectives, and teaching methods. They inspire and promote learning through self-initiated play. They provide a system of play that is organized and readily understood by children. Activity centers are designed for a total-child approach to teaching and learning. They are particularly important in an open, play-oriented environment because they provide balance, diversity, and organization to a child's day. Activity centers reflect a child's need for personal and social development and for physical, creative, and cognitive development. They enable children to fully express and experience themselves within a cooperative, child-centered environment. As children make choices, accept responsibility, and develop competencies, they feel a sense of security and belonging. They solve problems as they occur—if a center is too crowded, a child will voluntarily move or make a change. Children begin to take the perspective of others as they learn to share. Gradually, they discover that learning is an integral part of their play world.

Most child care centers use interest centers to organize and define space and activities. These centers have boundaries to encourage privacy and to facilitate organized play. Boundaries reduce children's natural tendency to encroach on another's space. They help to hold children's attention and to reduce noise levels.

Activity centers commonly include a block area, a dramatic play area, a science center, a listening area, an arts and crafts area, and a book nook. An easel and a sand/water table usually are placed in separate sections of a room, away from areas of great activity. Carpeted space is set aside for circle, manipulative play, and other activities requiring floor time. Because activity centers accommodate play that ranges from active to less active, they must be planned carefully. Each play center must be considered from the vantage of purpose, activity level (high or low), noise level (high or low), and its potential appeal to children (popular centers need more space to accommodate more children). Finding ways to enclose and define activity areas is always a creative challenge for a teacher with limited resources. Shelves, pegboard screens, props, and visuals are common ways to solve the problem.

School-age children also need activity centers that can be used for constructive and imaginative play, for quiet activities, and for group activities. A physical and human environment carefully tailored to ages and interests will communicate caring to children. Centers who accommodate both preschool and school-age levels of care must consider a room's full-day activities before setting up an environment.

Hide-Aways

Children seem to need little spaces tucked away from action areas to sit in, play in, and escape to. Suggestions for hide-aways are: a small playhouse, an indoor log cabin, a variplay gym that has an interior section to crawl into, a loft, large cardboard boxes, or an improvised fort set up between tables or chairs covered with sheets or blankets. Sometimes the sheet can be painted in a design that matches a play theme. An investment such as a log cabin or a play house is well worth the cost. Children feel like they are in a home within a home when they can isolate themselves in a framed play area. They can decorate and change items to suit their tastes and to accommodate their play themes.

Pathways

Activity centers (or clusters) are joined by connecting pathways. These are open-space access routes that encircle and connect activity areas and common areas. They help to ensure safety and create a sense of openness and organization. Pathways should be kept free of clutter. Children naturally find pathways as they move from activity to activity. Pathways need not be marked or coded with colored tape.

Layout

There is no quick and easy method for setting up a classroom for large numbers of children throughout the day, especially when a room must be shared by several age levels. The existing shape and design of space automatically dictates certain placements. If there are few electrical outlets in a room, a teacher would naturally begin her classroom design with a listening center and put plug-in appliances near the existing outlets. An easel for painting would logically be placed near a sink, and if a teacher does a fair amount of cooking with children, she would probably want her food preparation table area near a sink and countertop. Doors, windows, storage closets and odd-shaped corners also will influence decision making. Windows are wonderful attributes, but often hard to work with. Drafts, sunlight, and safety are always primary considerations when arranging activity centers near windows.

Durable, Safe Equipment

When purchasing equipment for activity centers, it is important to look at every piece of equipment for durability and safety. The structure and quality of toys greatly affects the way a classroom functions. Therefore, a director/teacher should give thoughtful consideration to needs before purchasing a major item: What is its intended use? Is it really needed at this time? Is it the right size for its intended use? Will it be compatible with the rest of the furnishings? How difficult will it be to assemble?

When purchasing equipment for indoor use, a director should seek input from teachers as to how a room should be equipped. In addition, she should follow guidelines for safety and durability such as these:

- Fixed equipment should be purchased from a reputable toy distributing company that stands behind its products.
- Equipment should not have sharp edges.
- Shelves should be long and wide enough to place objects for children's continuous use.
- Paint should be nontoxic.
- Large pieces (such as cubbies) ideally should be secured to a wall or placed back to back to avoid tipping over.
- Structures for climbing should be securely assembled to withstand vigorous use and not be able to be moved around by children.
- Fixtures on shelves and storage units should be secure and positioned away from children's hands.
- Materials for young children should not contain small pieces that might be swallowed, should not be flammable, and should not contain sharp objects.
- Maintenance-free surfaces such as formica tops or treated wood surfaces clean easily and retain their appearance longer than untreated or poorly painted surfaces.
- Chairs should be light enough for children to manage and sturdily constructed to prevent tipping.
- Electric or battery-operated equipment should not be purchased.
- Audiovisual equipment should be strictly monitored and off-limits to young children.
- The dimensions and potential use of lofts should be carefully considered before an investment is made.

Using Space Efficiently and Effectively

When organizing space, a director/teacher should consider the total environment. The following guidelines are important:

- Carefully consider the placement of quiet, personal space, indoor climbing equipment, and, of course, common space that requires tables and chairs.
- Place activity centers back-to-back to conserve space.
- Consider storing some seasonal equipment in order to increase space when needed.
- Locate activity centers in areas that are play-safe, physically appropriate, and harmonious to a room.
- Position heavily used centers in areas of a room that can be seen and quickly accessed by adults.
- Scale activity centers to size, and design them for durability, safety, independent play, and group play.
- Equip centers with both realistic and imaginative toys, novelty items, and a variety of sensorimotor activities.
- Provide ample space for storage, for consumables, and for large-motor items.
- Provide space for a media center for enrichment and pleasure.
- Provide personal space for teachers and for children.
- Organize and label supplies so that a room connotes a feeling of orderliness.
- Train children to respect their activity centers.
- Train children to care for their activity centers.
- Consult children before selecting new toys, games, or play equipment.
- Pay attention to *safety* factors: electrical fixtures and outlets; heating, cooling and ventilation systems; plumbing and sanitary facilities; unsafe equipment; high equipment that might not adequately protect children from falling such as lofts or nesting bridges; ground coverings and fences; entrances, exits, and corridors; fire prevention; child-safe kitchen equipment; placement and condition of doors, windows, and screens; storage and food areas; loose tiles; posting of rules, regulations, emergency numbers, and procedures; updating records on children and staff; and the placement and height of water fountains and sinks.
- Pay attention to *health* factors: disposal of wastes and diapers; bathroom and handwashing routines; toxic materials; unsafe plants; food storage; fabrics and play materials; keeping a room sanitized, free of rodents and germs; keeping medical records updated; training teachers in first-aid; training teachers to recognize the signs and symptoms of contagious diseases or other illnesses and of child neglect or abuse; training staff to prepare nutritional meals and snacks; ensuring that children get rest and good care throughout the day; having procedures and policies for emergency care, sick care, and personal care such as brushing teeth and washing hands; maintaining adequate custodial services; and enclosing an area for emergency care of a sick child.

- Pay attention to *environmental* factors: harsh lights and colors, noise levels, the look and feel of a room, and stress factors.
- Recognize a child's human and physical environment as interconnected.

When a room begins to function as an interdependent unit, each section reinforces and complements the natural flow of space. At this point, a teacher can move into a creative mode to work with her remaining space, adding touches and novelties to previously empty, unused space. Colors and unique blendings of textures will work together to form a personality—a room becomes a harmonious and integrated whole.

Summary

An indoor environment that reflects a center's philosophy and the principles of child development will create space that is both functional and meaningful to its occupants. A staff will feel positive about working in a well-designed, carefully organized environment that maximizes opportunities for creative, child-centered learning. Children will profit from a child-centered environment that is designed to challenge their imaginations and to extend their knowledge. Each room will be designed as a unique and special place for children. The total environment will truly reflect the sum of its parts.

NOTES

1. V. Suransky, *The Erosion of Childhood* (Chicago: University of Chicago Press, 1982), p. 39.
2. Teresita E. Aguilar, "Social and Environmental Barriers to Playfulness," in *When Children Play*, eds., Joe L. Frost and Sylvia Sunderlin (Wheaton, MD: ACEI, 1985), p. 76.
3. S. Kritchevsky and E. Prescott, *Planning Environments for Young Children: Physical Space* (Washington, DC: NAEYC, 1977), pp. 11, 12.
4. Betty Spillers Beeson and R. Ann Williams, "The Persistence of Sex Differences in the Play of Young Children," in *When Children Play*, p. 39.
5. Charles H. Wolfgang, "Preschool Children's Preferences for Gender-Stereotyped Play Materials," in *When Children Play*, pp. 273–78.

8 Outdoor Environments

As the playground movement grows, school designers will give greater attention to the preservation of the natural landscape immediately surrounding schools as the first, essential step in creating high-quality integrated indoor–outdoor learning environments. . . . The citizens of more and more communities in the near future will realize that playgrounds are a viable alternative for TV and boredom and a major vehicle for leaning. They will construct exciting, functional play environments and seek facilitative play leaders as they grow to understand that the cost in human effort and material resources is a wise investment in children

—Joe L. Frost

The Importance of Outdoor Play

An outdoor environment is integral to curriculum development. It is an enlarged activity center providing an educational, developmental, and recreational environment that is equal in importance to an indoor environment. It should be considered one of the primary objectives in child care planning because it:

- Sharpens senses and stimulates awareness
- Enables children to conceptualize their world as less circumscribed and bounded
- Brings children into intimate contact with nature
- Nurtures curiosity and divergent thinking
- Deepens and challenges learning
- Encourages cooperative play
- Encourages problem solving and teamwork
- Promotes children's interaction with natural and man-made resources
- Challenges and welcomes children's need for physical activity
- Gives children a strong sense of mastery and control over their environment
- Reduces stress by eliminating adult/child barriers
- Promotes and encourages physical education and gymnastic talents that may be unique to a child

For many teachers, outdoor time is considered free, unstructured time that is conditional, in part, on the weather and, in part, on indoor priorities: "We must finish our projects before we can go outdoors." On intemperate days, teachers find a reason not to take children outdoors even though the weather is acceptable for children's play. Such attitudes reveal what little emphasis teachers place on outdoor play and on its importance to growth and development.

Teachers should not minimize their role and responsibility for a child's total development, which includes ample outdoor play during various times of the day, that is, morning, afternoon, and, if appropriate, during transitions as well. Outdoor play should be given as much attention as indoor play. It should not be considered bench time for staff to converse with one another or to rest. It is a time for teachers to observe children in unstructured social interaction, to interact with children in sensitive and meaningful ways, and to share children's experiences with the natural world. It is a time to complement children for reaching new heights in physical development and to encourage children to go higher.

Outdoor time provides children a sense of renewal from the programmed activities that consume so many of their waking hours. When children play outdoors, they often free themselves from expectations and uncertainties. No classroom that can quite capture the beauty of a natural landscape. Wherever there is dirt, there is something growing: a weed, a wild flower, a little bug that will have to hurry to escape a child's curious hands. Wherever there is open space, there is something to look at, something to listen to, something to wonder about: the passing clouds, the darkness before a storm, birds, planes, and distant trains. And wherever there are children, there is some new creation somewhere in nature that is waiting to be noticed,

Children's outdoor behavior is influenced by the quality and style of their play equipment, the organization of space, the degree of freedom they have to make choices, social skills, adult/child interaction, rules and regulations, the weather, physical factors, the period of time scheduled for outside play, and the general feeling of safety and security that prevails. In a child-centered environment, children are given freedom to play with minimal supervision unless there is reason for an adult to intervene. Sometimes children enjoy an adult's companionship or prolonged peer play, but more often than not, children prefer proximal play (making contact with friends but not being dependent on them for sustained interaction). Most children prefer independence and autonomy during outdoor play, which may or may not include friends. Outdoor play may be likened to dramatic play. When children enter a pretend play world, they need little encouragement or support.

A Variety of Play Modes

Children require a variety of experiences during outdoor play time. They need to exercise their bodies, their minds, their creativity, and their social skills. Outdoor activities might include:

- Circle games (Duck, Duck, Goose; Here We Go Loopty Loo; What Can You Do Punchinello Funny Fellow?) and organized sports (Dodge Ball; Four Square; Red Rover, Red Rover)
- Independent play (swinging, climbing, rollerskating)
- Small group cluster play (playing in sandbox, playing in water, playing house, or making a fort under a tree)
- Large-motor physical play (on equipment)
- Productive play (making gardens, picking up litter)
- Sidewalk and blacktop play (riding tricycles, rollerskating, basketball, making chalk drawings)
- Rainy-day play (a canopied or protected area for marching or riding tricycles)
- Dramatic play (a log cabin or an enclosed section of a climber)
- Sand and water play (sandbox, water table, or mudpile)
- Construction play (blocks and things to haul around and build with)

Children need to *manipulate* and *investigate* when they are outdoors. They need to carry, to construct, and to take things apart. Therefore, an outdoor environment must provide things that are portable (that can be taken apart and moved around by children) as well as stationary (fixed) equipment. If children do not have enough to play with out-of-doors they will complain about having nothing to do.

Children who are unaccustomed to vigorous outdoor play may feel uncomfortable out-of-doors. They often stand near a teacher and avoid making play choices or contacts with peers. These children especially need encouragement if they are to overcome inhibitions and fears. They need to develop healthy attitudes about playing outdoors and about their ability to manage themselves in a less structured, free-choice environment.

Types of Playgrounds

Contemporary Playgrounds

As more and more children spend a majority of their outdoor time in playgrounds contiguous to schools or child care centers, there is growing interest in the quality and types of playgrounds available to children within a defined area. Gradually, traditional, ad hoc type playgrounds are being replaced by play environments that are meeting the total needs of children—a playscape concept that is developmentally appropriate. In this setting, stationary equipment is seen as only one element in a total environmental design. New designs and new concepts are blending traditional with contemporary needs. Conventional fixed playgrounds (climbing bars, a merry-go-round, a see-saw, and a set of swings) are being replaced or used in combination with more innovative contemporary playgrounds.

The premise is that children will become enthusiastic participants in a playground that is both familiar and challenging—a playground that promotes physical development as well as curiosity and creativity. By using a natural landscape to its maximum advantage, children can enjoy an infinite number of interactional possibilities for both independent and cooperative play. They can ride on a traditional whirlybird, or they can move things around and control their environment in more exciting ways. In both experiences, children become masters of their environments and feel very fulfilled when they come indoors.

A suitable, creative play space for children, therefore, will include:

- A mixture of wood and metal climbing structures with platforms, wheels, ropes, and other features
- Age-appropriate swings
- A contour slide
- Barrels, bridges, and balance beams
- Ride-on items
- Playhouses, cabins, and hideaways that invite entrance
- Assorted railroad ties, cable spools, and tires
- A fort or interesting structure to crawl in or crawl up
- Hollow blocks, logs, or large pieces of treated wood
- Wagons, wheelbarrows, trikes, doll carriages, scooters
- Plastic crates, tires, rocking boats, or items to sit in
- Large sand pits and digging equipment in all sizes, shapes, and forms

Make-Your-Own Playgrounds

Many child care centers are not in a financial position to design the perfect play-ground to meet a child's total needs. Directors have to look not at what they want to do but at what they can afford to do.

Jay Beckwith, author of *Build Your Own Playgrounds*, has designed play-grounds that produce environments in which children play longer, show less aggressive and more cooperative behavior, have improved self-concepts, develop better language skills, and engage in more novel and physically demanding motor activity than on traditional playgrounds.[1] The essential com-ponents are:

Complex. The environment should contain as many different types of experi-ences as possible.

Linked. Play events should be connected to create a natural "flow" of play activity.

Social. The total environment should foster interaction between children, and play events should be designed for group use.

Flexible. Playground flexibility can be both mechanical, (i.e., equipment mounted on springs), or functional (i.e., objects that can be used in many dif-ferent ways).

Challenging. Creative playgrounds contain events that require motor coordi-nation, balance ability, flexibility, and strength.

Development. Playgrounds should offer events that will challenge a wide range of skills and ages.

Safe. Modern playgrounds must conform to the Consumer Product Safety Commission's guidelines. The safe playground not only has fewer accidents, but also encourages more inventive and creative play because the children are able to take greater risks with less fear of injury.

Often directors have limited funds and are unable to create a satisfactory play space for children. They may need to ask parents for assistance. Parents can build forts, playhouses, and storage sheds, design and landscape an environment for children's play, make sandboxes, construct trike paths and balance beams, locate cable spools and truck tires, and provide picnic tables. If parents are less than ame-nable to helping create a playground, there are always fund-raisers—events that are, for the most part, worth the effort.

Creating Adventure Playgrounds

The adventure playground originated in Denmark in the 1930s. Over the years, these playgrounds have been implemented in England, Sweden, Japan, and more recently in the United States. The adventure playground has been seen by the Danes as an aid to socialization:

The adventure playground is one of the means by which we transfer the child from the role of observer to that of actor, the role where the child is allowed to do something and see the results of efforts. The adventure playground not only teaches the child some elementary things about the nature of culture and the "answer to challenges," but it goes beyond this. The child can also meet with challenges when busy doing something on his or her own.[2]

The premise is that children love to interact with materials, shapes, smells, and other physical phenomena in their natural environment. An outdoor play environment that maximizes space for movement and exploration will encourage children's natural curiosity. When children are not limited to defined equipment, they become inventive. They look for objects to play with: a piece of bark, twigs, berries, rocks, trenches, and small hills. Unstructured outdoor play promotes resourcefulness and inventiveness.

There is little doubt that playgrounds are becoming important dimensions of planning in child development centers. As child care centers begin to recognize the value of outdoor play to child development, play yards are becoming playscapes that are linked to the greater world. Eventually, a child in the United States or Canada will be playing in the same way as a child in Israel, Italy, France, Denmark, or England. They will be moving objects that are designed for creative play; objects that meet the objectives of child development; objects that meet the universal needs of childhood. The irrepressible, joyful engagement that a child experiences as she interacts with her natural environment connects her to the greater world to all children everywhere. When a child care center identifies itself as a part of the larger world, children become citizens of the world.

A Third Dimension: Indoor/Outdoor Space

In a whole-child environment, there is a symbiotic, complementary relationship between indoor and outdoor play experiences. The environments are physically different, but philosophically they are both in harmony with the nature and needs of the young child. Together, indoor and outdoor environments are essential facilitators of growth and development.

An intriguing perspective is that indoor and outdoor play is important enough in the life of a young child to create a transitional experience that is somewhere between an indoor and outdoor experience. The concept is one of an extended classroom. Examples of integrating indoor and outdoor environments are a beautifully designed courtyard; a screened-in porch that may be converted into a play room during cold weather seasons, and an interestingly designed deck/storage area. In each example, children will enjoy a contained outdoor area that offers specific opportunities for special activities that are not typically a part of outdoor play such as painting, housekeeping, woodworking, sand and water play, reading and game areas, picnics, or caring for accent shrubs, trees, and flowers. Most importantly, an indoor/outdoor addition to a child care center will provide an important psychological benefit by offering children still another dimension for growth and development in their expanding universe.

Planning and Safety Guidelines

The following guidelines should be considered when planning play environments in child care centers:

- Is the equipment durable and relatively safe?
- Is it properly installed and maintained?
- Is it of appropriate size for the age group?
- Does the playground provide for work/play activities such as art, gardening, and science projects?
- Are a variety of loose parts available for sand and water play, wheeled vehicle play, dramatic play, building?
- Is the playground designed to involve large groups of children simultaneously?
- Is the playground aesthetically pleasing?
- Is it economically feasible?[3]

It is important to remember that careful attention to equipment and to its use will significantly reduce accidents.

For guidelines on playground safety, write to the Consumer Product Safety Commission, S401 Westbard Ave., Bethesda, MD 20816. For guidelines on the environment in the area, write to the Environmental Protection Agency, 401 M Street, SW, Washington, DC 20460.

Summary

An outdoor environment is an extension of an indoor environment. It is a place where children can take pleasure in the arts and nature, where children can communicate feelings and ideas, where children can experience human individuality and human sociality. It is a place where children can make choices and take responsibility for their play experience and its outcome. Sometimes outdoor play is all consuming and sometimes it is less than perfect. In child care centers there are never enough balls or swings to play with. Often the toys that are left to play with are the ones nobody wants. On some days, nobody wants to be a friend, but, more often than not, children find companionship and happiness when they are engaged in outdoor play.

The full dimensions of being a child are operative in outdoor play. If play holds such potential for growth and development, why don't we give it more space and attention on calendars and in budgets?

Often, a playground holds little appeal because it is uncreative and uninviting. Safe and challenging equipment and attractive landscaping are costly items for most budget-conscious directors. A play-conscious director, however, will find a way to create and fund a landscape. She realizes that outdoor play is as fundamental and important to a little child's mental and physical health as any indoor activity. She may need to fence a play yard for security, but the director will select a fence that is high enough, but not too high to restrict a child's view beyond the immediate playscape to the larger community.

NOTES

1. Jay Beckwith, "Equipment Selection Criteria for Modern Playgrounds," in *When Children Play*, eds., Joe L. Frost and Ann R. Williams (Wheaton, MD: ACEI, 1985), pp. 209–10.
2. Jens Pedersen, "The Adventure Playgrounds in Denmark," in Joe L. Frost, "The American Playground Movement," in *When Children Play*, p. 207.
3. Frost, "The American Playground Movement," p. 168.

Conclusion

My everyday
Is my identity.
It is my now.
It is my moment
My new start
My chance to create
A new vision
For myself
For my child
What I make of this moment
Will determine
The story of us.

—From *Everychild's Everyday* by Cindy Herbert and Susan Russell

Children are strongly influenced by the quality of their human and physical environment during the formative years of development. When children are respected and valued as unique and special human beings, they will feel secure about themselves and they will begin to experience their potential. Through sustained interaction with caring and competent adults in child-appropriate environments, there is every reason to expect that every child can lead a quality life. By believing in children, by challenging children, and by providing a beacon for children to follow, adults can guide children toward tomorrow's world. In the continuum of growth and development, some things, like childhood, do not change. Eugene Ionesco put it this way:

> Childhood is the world of miracle and wonder: as if creation rose and bathed in light, out of the darkness, utterly new and fresh and astonishing. The end of childhood is when things cease to astonish us. When the world seems familiar, when we have gotten used to existence, one has become an adult.

A primary purpose of all child care environments is to establish a foundation for experiencing a quality life that *begins* with the child, *extends* to the surrounding environment, and *expands* to the larger environment. In the maturation process, a child moves toward self-affirmation. She internalizes truths and develops the skills and competencies that will enhance her life. A child gradually becomes less dependent on adults and peers and more self-reliant. She knows who she is and what she is capable of doing. She doesn't need a sticker or a gold star for completing her tasks. She is becoming aware of her strengths and to some degree, of her limitations. Someday she may become a ballerina, a teacher, a scientist, or a rock singer, but for now she is where she is—a little child experiencing her world through eyes that see beauty, friendship, and possibility.

A child care center must walk a fine line between *caring* for children and *encouraging* them to care for themselves. Adults cannot shelter children from the experience of growing up, but they can guide their progress and nurture their development to the extent that they can become self-sufficient and productive human beings.

Childhood is a time of sprouting and nurturing. It is a passageway to adulthood that is filled with the promise and potential of a spring garden. Each day and each moment is important.

APPENDIX

Resources for Teachers

A Self-Evaluation Form for Teachers

Name: _____   *Code:* Teachers may rank their responses

Session: _____   from 1 (excellent) to 3 (needs improvement).

Date: _____

Controls children in directed activities by using positive role-modeling to encourage participation and enthusiasm.

      1   2   3

Permits children an appropriate degree of freedom and choice during open activity periods.

      1   2   3

Presents materials and ideas that are interesting and innovative to children.

      1   2   3

Is prepared and organized before coming to class.

      1   2   3

Arranges and sets up table activities in an attractive, inviting manner.

      1   2   3

Has a good command of basic content areas: language, math, science, social studies.

      1   2   3

Has a basic understanding how children learn: by active, independent exploration, by playing, by cooperative experiences, by interacting with teachers, by self-initiated experiences, by solving problems and making choices.

      1   2   3

Provides many opportunities for hands-on discovery learning and creative expression.

      1   2   3

Manifests a knowledge of child development in handling emotional problems or disruptive behavior.

      1   2   3

Prepares and presents units creatively and effectively.

      1   2   3

Understands the importance of nurturing by cultivating values and developing theme-related activities.

      1   2   3

Values individuality in children's choice of activities, manner of play, expression, modes of learning, and levels of interests.

      1   2   3

Is tolerant and sensitive to children's differences and preferences.

      1   2   3

Encourages children to do their best in a noncompetitive and positive atmosphere.

    1   2   3

Provides opportunities for children to develop competencies in practical life activities such as cooking, gardening, cleaning.

    1   2   3

Reads in the field, attends workshops, and visits other schools for the purpose of obtaining new ideas about teaching, equipping, managing, and enjoying a child care environment.

    1   2   3

Praises children honestly without inhibitions, predispositions, or unrealistic expectations.

    1   2   3

Welcomes new ideas and is willing to share with others.

    1   2   3

Is effective in observing and documenting children's progress and/or problems as they occur.

    1   2   3

Is conscientious in attending to the duties and responsibilities required of staff in this center.

    1   2   3

Is tuned in to children's needs by showing caring and patience to children in stress or who are unable to cope with their environment.

    1   2   3

Understands the importance of communicating effectively with parents so that children can fully benefit from their child care experiences.

    1   2   3

Appreciates the importance of reinforcing appropriate values, morals, and positive lifestyles.

    1   2   3

Contributes to a child's lifelong learning by opening doors of understanding to the immediate community and the larger world.

    1   2   3

A Formal Evaluation for Teachers

Evaluator: _____ *Code:* Check + = excellent
Teacher: _____ Check = satisfactory
Class: _____ Check − = not satisfactory
Date: _____

Child Development—The teacher is effective in developing or promoting:

_____ Practical life readiness skills
_____ Foundational skills
_____ Self-management
_____ Language skills
_____ Reasoning and thinking skills
_____ Problem-solving skills
_____ Fine- and large-motor skills
_____ Creative expression
_____ Social skills
_____ Self-awareness and self-concept
_____ Responsibility and initiative
_____ Healthy attitudes toward self and others
_____ Self-control
_____ Independence and decision making
_____ Valuing and moral development
_____ Good work habits
_____ Cooperative learning
_____ Self-esteem and confidence
_____ An awareness of health and nutrition

The Environment—The teacher is organized so that the environment:

_____ Reflects orderliness and creativity
_____ Offers children many choices and opportunities for hands-on discovery learning
_____ Offers many opportunities for self-expression and imagination
_____ Provides interesting materials that are age appropriate
_____ Does not appear overcrowded or overstimulating
_____ Reflects children's interests and abilities
_____ Provides a healthy balance between active and quiet play
_____ Offers many opportunities for children to play independently
_____ Offers many opportunities for children to play with peers

_____ Provides personal space for children's belongings

_____ Provides storage space that is neat and uncluttered

_____ Is defined by activity centers

_____ Provides a place for communicating with parents

_____ Is language rich, offering a wide variety of activities and resources

_____ Promotes creative thinking and independent learning

_____ Is soft and cozy with special places for children to enjoy

_____ Provides many opportunities for large-motor play

_____ Provides areas for specialized instruction in movement and the creative arts

Personal Attributes—The teacher reflects:

_____ Friendliness and empathy

_____ Patience and love

_____ Organization and competency

_____ Responsibility and reliability

_____ Good teaching skills

_____ Good classroom management skills

_____ An understanding of the center's philosophy and objectives

_____ Encouragement and cooperation

_____ High professional standards

_____ Creative thinking and originality

_____ Unbiased, objective teaching qualities

_____ An ability to communicate

_____ An ability to motivate and inspire children

_____ A respect for cultural diversity

_____ Good feelings among staff and parents

_____ An interest in learning and growing in her field

_____ The potential for leadership

Parent Relationships—The teacher demonstrates an ability to work with parents in partnership:

_____ Parents are pleased with their child's program.

_____ Parents are involved in classroom activities and special events.

_____ There is an effective system of communication between the teacher and parents.

_____ Parents found their conference informative, objective, and well prepared.

_____ Parents are fully informed about field trips, special events, activities, and monthly plans.

A Developmental Checklist: Ages Two to Three

Play—Independent and group play

_____ Child is beginning to play imaginatively and creatively.

_____ Child can play independently for a reasonable period of time.

_____ Child is learning to play cooperatively with peers.

_____ Child is beginning to make choices and solve problems during peer play.

_____ Child initiates and expands play opportunities.

_____ Child is demonstrating thinking and logic during play.

_____ Child is developing small-motor skills (e.g., cutting, pasting, assembling manipulatives, organizing constructs).

_____ Child is developing large-motor skills (e.g., jumping in place, climbing on jungle gym, catching a ball, balancing on one foot, coordinating body movements during creative activities, riding a trike, performing simple gymnastic exercises).

Learning—Listening, oral language, basic skills, thinking and conceptual development, following simple directions, comprehension, recall, imitating, attending to a task, problem solving, self-management, social skills

_____ Child can manage personal needs.

_____ Child is demonstrating independence and initiative.

_____ Child can listen without much distraction.

_____ Child can focus on an idea, a story, or an activity.

_____ Child demonstrates self-control.

_____ Child is developing a good attention span during circle-time.

_____ Child can follow directions.

_____ Child demonstrates reasoning.

_____ Child is beginning to discriminate like and unlike objects.

_____ Child is beginning to understand concepts.

_____ Child can understand one-to-one correspondence.

_____ Child can recognize numbers one through five or more.

_____ Child is beginning to understand some spatial concepts (e.g., over/under, in front of/behind/between, far/near, full/empty).

_____ Child demonstrates curiosity.

_____ Child can complete a simple task.

_____ Child demonstrates perceptual/motor skills.

_____ Child demonstrates sensory awareness and discrimination.

_____ Child is developing recall.

_____ Child is beginning to count.

_____ Child can recognize basic shapes.

_____ Child can assemble simple puzzles.

_____ Child is acquiring basic language skills.

_____ Child can recognize some letters.

_____ Child can repeat rhyming words and simple verses.

_____ Child can recognize own name.

_____ Child can identify familiar words.

_____ Child is developing an awareness of sounds (phonics).

_____ Child can comprehend stories.

_____ Child can remember "What comes next?"

The Arts—Painting, arts and crafts, making wood constructs with glue and paint, music, movement, and dramatic play

_____ Child enjoys painting at an easel.

_____ Child applies himself/herself to project at hand.

_____ Child demonstrates creative thinking in artwork.

_____ Child enjoys dramatic play with peers.

_____ Child is demonstrating imagination.

_____ Child uses language to express himself/herself.

_____ Child can focus on dramatic play for a reasonable period of time.

_____ Child is learning to cooperate and to take the position of a friend in order to sustain a play experience.

_____ Child is demonstrating body coordination in creative movement activities.

_____ Child can recall simple verses and nursery rhymes.

_____ Child can coordinate movement and language in finger plays.

_____ Child is demonstrating recall.

_____ Child is developing an attention span during group activities that focus on the arts.

Nurturing—Self-development and social development

_____ Child is developing a good self-concept.

_____ Child is showing independence and initiative.

_____ Child is beginning to demonstrate self-control and patience.

_____ Child respects and cares for equipment.

_____ Child has a good attitude most of the time.

_____ Child can perform simple tasks (washing hands, putting a chair under a table, putting shoes on, getting a jacket for outdoor play or an apron for artwork).

_____ Child is learning to wait his/her turn.

_____ Child is interested in peers.

_____ Child is developing affection.

_____ Child can play cooperatively.

_____ Child is developing good manners.

_____ Child is cooperative during pick-up and transitions.

_____ Child is a good eater.

_____ Child appears to be healthy and active most of the time.

_____ Child sleeps during naptime.

_____ Child is happy.

_____ Child is beginning to self-manage.

_____ Child is beginning to express feelings in positive ways.

_____ Child is making a good adjustment to his/her environment.

Special qualities: _____

Things that child enjoys doing: _____

Things that are still difficult: _____

Ways that parents can assist in child's development: _____

_____

_____

_____

Special friends: _____

Concerns: _____

_____

_____

Recommendations: _____

_____

_____

Name of child: _____   Evaluation code:

Teacher: _____   Use check or check minus:

Date: _____   Date of parent conference: _____

A Developmental Checklist: Ages Four to Five

Play—Independent and group play

_____ Child plays imaginatively and creatively.

_____ Child displays initiative and independence.

_____ Child is able to make choices.

_____ Child is able to solve problems.

_____ Child can play cooperatively with friends.

_____ Child demonstrates self-control most of the time.

_____ Child is able to share and take turns.

_____ Child demonstrates patience toward peers and projects.

_____ Child demonstrates responsibility in the care and handling of materials.

_____ Child communicates needs.

_____ Child shows an interest in completing tasks.

_____ Child can play for reasonable periods of time without adult intervention.

_____ Child is developing social skills.

_____ Child is developing interests and competency in play tasks.

_____ Child is developing large-motor skills.

_____ Child is developing fine-motor skills.

Child is particularly interested in: _____

Child is particularly good at: _____

Learning—Language, math/science, and thinking

_____ Child is developing sensory awareness.

_____ Child can discriminate, sort, and classify materials.

_____ Child is demonstrating organization.

_____ Child can group numbers, match numbers, and work with simple sets.

_____ Child can identify numbers 1 to _____.

_____ Child can identify shapes.

_____ Child can understand a one-to-one correspondence.

_____ Child can see likenesses and differences among objects.

_____ Child enjoys table games and activities.

_____ Child can assemble puzzles with little difficulty.

_____ Child is beginning to understand qualitative terms such as equal/unequal, long/short, empty/full.

_____ Child is developing concepts.

_____ Child enjoys hands-on experiences in a discovery center.

_____ Child is developing language fluency.

_____ Child communicates needs and ideas appropriate to his or her age.

_____ Child demonstrates comprehension and recall.

_____ Child reasons and asks questions.

_____ Child demonstrates problem solving and flexible thinking.

_____ Child can recognize few, some, most, all letters.

_____ Child can identify beginning and ending consonant sounds.

_____ Child can recognize and use vowel sounds (a, e, i, o, u).

_____ Child can read familiar words.

_____ Child is developing an interest in books.

_____ Child can read simple sentences.

_____ Child enjoys language experience activities.

_____ Child enjoys writing in a personal journal.

_____ Child is beginning to write inventively.

_____ Child enjoys listening to records and storybook tapes.

_____ Child can follow directions.

_____ Child uses his/her time constructively.

_____ Child is motivated to learn.

Child is particularly interested in: _____

Child is particularly good at: _____

The Arts—Drama, Painting, Arts and Crafts, Music, Movement, Woodworking

_____ Child demonstrates originality and creativity.

_____ Child stays on task and shows pride in work.

_____ Child can cut, paste, and assemble materials.

_____ Child is interested in expressing himself/herself through many mediums of art.

_____ Child demonstrates patterning and symmetry in artwork.

_____ Child demonstrates spatial organization and perspective.

_____ Child demonstrates a good concept of self in artwork.

_____ Child demonstrates confidence and resourcefulness.

_____ Child cleans up after activities with little need for teacher intervention.

Child is particularly interested in: _____

Child is particularly good at: _____

Nuturing—Self-Development, Social Development

_____ Child is developing a good self-concept.

_____ Child is developing a sense of responsibility.

_____ Child is developing values and good social conduct.

_____ Child is patient and caring toward peers most of the time.

_____ Child demonstrates affection and love.

_____ Child expresses feelings.
_____ Child is developing emotional control.
_____ Child has a positive attitude most of the time.
_____ Child is a helper in the classroom.
_____ Child is cooperative in peer play.
_____ Child is conscientious in his/her attitude toward tasks.
_____ Child is developing a sense of community.
_____ Child is developing life skills.
_____ Child is becoming an independent thinker.
_____ Child has good manners.
_____ Child appears to be happy and well-adjusted.

Special qualities: _____
_____
_____

Areas of concern: _____
_____
_____

Recommendations: _____
_____
_____

Name of child: _____   Evaluation code:
Teacher: _____   Use check or check minus:
Date: _____   Date of parent conference: _____

A Parent Evaluation

Code: Check ____ ✓ ____

Check Minus ____ ✓ ‾ ____

Dear Parents,

The purpose of this evaluation is to determine how this Center can better serve the needs of its children and their families. Please complete this form and return to the Center by _____. Thank you for your continued cooperation and support.

_____ I am pleased with my child's adjustment and with the general quality of this Center.

_____ I have a comfortable and supportive relationship with my child's teacher(s).

_____ I understand the philosophy and objectives of this Center.

_____ I am familiar with this Center's curriculum.

_____ I have been informed about this Center's discipline policy.

_____ I understand the administrative policies and procedures of this Center.

_____ I receive written information about classroom activities.

_____ I feel that this Center is very attentive to the safety and well-being of my child.

_____ I feel welcome when I visit my child's classroom or participate in Center events.

_____ I have been invited to a conference with my child's teacher.

_____ I feel satisfied that my child's teacher will provide me ongoing information about my child's adjustment, development, and special needs.

_____ I attended and benefited from Open-Center night.

_____ I plan to register my child in this Center next year.

Suggestions:

Concerns:

Comments:

Name: _____

Date: _____

Child's Teacher: _____

Resources: Professional Organizations

Organizations that provide useful research reports, information, advice, and conferences on all aspects of child care are:

American Child Care Foundation, Inc.
1801 Robert Fulton Drive, Suite 400
Reston, VA 22091

Association for the Care of Children's
  Health
3615 Wisconsin Avenue, NW
25 E Street, NW
Washington, DC 20016

Association for Childhood Education
  International
11411 Georgia Avenue, Suite 200
Wheaton, MD 20902

California Child Care Resource and
  Referral Network
320 Judah Street, Suite 2
San Francisco, CA 94122

Child Care Information Exchange
P.O. Box 2890
Redmond, WA 98073

The Child Care Law Center
625 Market Street, Suite 815
San Francisco, CA 94105

The Children's Defense Fund
25 E Street, NW
Washington, DC 20001

The Children's Foundation
1420 New York Avenue, NW
Suite 800
Washington, DC 20005

High/Scope Educational Research
  Foundation
600 North River Street
Ypsilanti, MI 48198-2898

Innovations in Early Education:
  The International Reggio Exchange
Wayne State University: The Merrill-
  Palmer Institute
71-AE Ferry Avenue
Detroit, MI 48202

The National Association for Child Care
  Management
1800 M Street, NW
Washington, DC 20036

National Association for the Education of
  Young Children (NAEYC)
1834 Connecticut Avenue, NW
Washington, DC 20009-5786

National Child Care Association (NCCA)
1016 Rosser Street
Conyers (Atlanta), GA 30012

National Commission on Children
1111 18th Street, NW, Suite 810
Washington, DC 20036

Save the Children, Inc.
Southern States Office
1182 West Peachtree Street, NW
Suite 209
Atlanta, GA 30309

Society for Research in Child
Development
5720 South Woodlawn Avenue
Chicago, IL 60637

Southern Early Childhood Association
  (SECA)
7107 W. 12th Street
Little Rock, AR 72215-5930

Wellesley School-Age Child Care Project
  Center for Research on Women
Cheever House
Wellesley, MA 02181

World Organization for Early Childhood
  Education (OMEP)
2460 16th Street, NW
Washington, DC 20009-3575

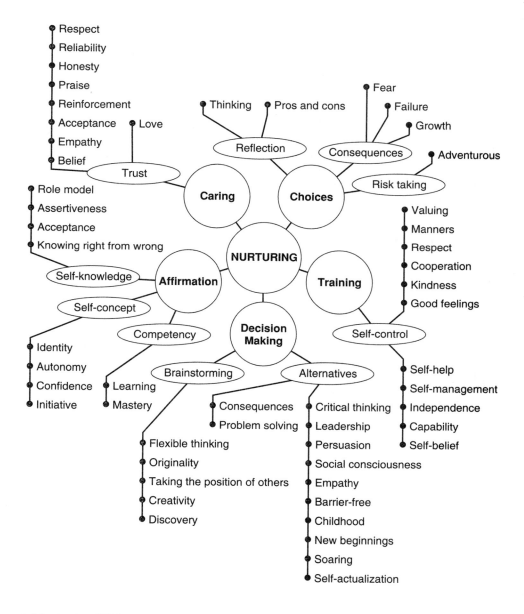

A Nurturing Web

Nutrition Guidelines

USDA Child Care Food Program Requirements

| | | Age | | |
		1–2	3–5	6–12
Breakfast	Fluid milk	½ cup	¾ cup	½ cup
	Juice or Fruit or Vegetable	¼ cup	½ cup	½ cup
	Bread or Bread Alternate	½ slice*	½ slice*	1 slice*
Snack (Supplement) select 2 out of 4 components	Fluid Milk	½ cup	½ cup	1 cup
	Juice or Fruit or Vegetable	¼ cup	½ cup	¾ cup
	Meat or Meat Alternate	½ ounce	½ ounce	1 ounce
	Bread or Bread Alternate	½ slice*	½ slice*	1 slice*
Lunch/Supper	Fluid Milk	½ cup	¾ cup	1 cup
	Meat or Poultry or Fish or	1 ounce	1½ ounces	2 ounces
	Cheese or	1 ounce	1½ ounces	2 ounces
	Egg or	1	1	1
	Cooked Dry Beans and Peas or	¼ cup	⅜ cup	½ cup
	Peanut Butter	2 tablespoons	3 tablespoons	4 tablespoons
	Vegetables and/or Fruits (2 or more)	¼ cup total	½ cup total	¾ cup total
	Bread or Bread Alternate	½ slice*	½ slice*	1 slice*

*or an equivalent serving of an acceptable bread alternate such as cornbread, biscuits, rolls, muffins, etc., made of whole-grain or enriched meal or flour, or a serving of cooked or enriched whole grain rice or macaroni or other pasta product

Source: From U.S. Department of Agriculture Food and Nutrition Service, Washington, DC: July 1989. For specific menu planning, see A Planning Guide for Food Service in Child Care Centers, revised July 1989. USDA Publication No FNS-64 (pp. 16–17). Available at most state child care agencies.

Meals

The sample menus that follow meet USDA requirements. Centers should serve milk to all children even those who bring their own lunch. This encourages parents not to send fruit drinks. Snacks should be simple, easy to prepare, nutritious, and appealing to the children. Preschoolers also can help with meal preparation. A food project such as cutting and pasting pictures of nutritious foods can be fun. Young children also can help to wash and cut vegetables and fruits (use a small, dull knife). Children can measure, pour, and mix ingredients. Keep the activity simple to suit the child's age. Work with a few at a time and make sure everyone washed their hands before handling the food.

When planning menus both USDA-required food amounts, according to age, and food groups should be considered. A beverage should be served with each snack. Milk should be served at one snack and a serving of 100% fruit juice, fruit, or vegetable should be served at least once a day. If the requirement for two food groups has been fulfilled, water may be served. Cream cheese, butter, and jam are spreads and are not to be counted as a food group. Be sure to read food labels; the grain products must be prepared with enriched flour in order to be counted.

Sample Breakfast Menus

Monday	Tuesday	Wednesday	Thursday	Friday
Orange Juice Wheatena Milk	Blueberries Wheaties Milk	Pineapple Chunks Oatmeal Milk	Orange Juice Cheerios Milk	Grapefruit Juice Scrambled Eggs Whole Wheat Toast with Butter Milk
Banana Wheaties Milk	Orange Juice Cream of Wheat with wheat germ Milk	Oatmeal Strawberries Milk	Grapefruit Juice Raisin Bran Milk	Sliced Oranges Cheerios Milk
Orange Juice Oatmeal with Milk Cinnamon Toast Milk	Pineapple Juice Raisin Bran Milk	Orange slices Cream of Wheat with Wheat Germ Milk	Peaches, sliced Wheaties Milk	Banana Peanut Butter on Whole Wheat Milk
Apple Juice Zucchini Bread Milk	Orange juice Bagels with Cream Cheese Milk	Grapefruit Whole Wheat Toast with Cinnamon Milk	Peaches Oatmeal Milk	Stewed Fruit Cold Cereal Milk

Sample Lunch Menus

Monday	Tuesday	Wednesday	Thursday	Friday

Meat Loaf
Stewed Tomatoes
Corn
Whole Wheat
  Bread with
  Butter
Pear Slices
Milk
	Spaghetti and
	  Meat Sauce
	Green Salad
	Orange
	Sesame
	  Muffin
	Watermelon
	  Chunks
	Milk
		Chicken Salad
		  with
		  Pineapple
		  Chunks
		Green Pepper
		  Sticks
		Summer Squash
		Whole Wheat
		  Bread
		Rice Pudding
		Milk
			Grilled Cheese
			  Sandwich on
			  Whole Wheat
			  Toast
			Tomato Slices
			Sliced Peaches
			Oatmeal
			Cookies
			Milk
				Tuna-Vegetable
				  Salad
				Whole Wheat
				  Bread with
				  Butter
				Banana
				Milk

Baked Chicken
Green Beans
Bulghur (cracked
  wheat)
Watermelon
  Chunks
Milk
	Hamburger-
	  Tomato-
	  Macaroni
	  Casserole
	Green Salad
	Sliced Pears
	Milk
		Grilled Cheese
		  Sandwich
		Broccoli
		Carrot Sticks
		Apricot Halves
		Oatmeal Cookie
		Milk
			Turkey Salad
			  Sandwich on
			  Whole Wheat
			4 Bean Salad
			Cherries or
			  Grapes
			Milk
				Baked Stuffed
				  Fish Fillets
				Spinach
				Broiled Tomato
				  Halves
				Whole Wheat
				  Bread
				Ice Cream
				Milk

Vegetable Soup
Egg Salad on
  Whole Wheat
Cucumbers
Peaches
Fig Newtons
Milk
	Hamburger
	  Patty on Roll
	Tomato Slices
	Cole Slaw
	Applesauce
	Milk
		Cottage Cheese
		Corn Bread
		Turnip, Celery,
		  Green Pepper
		  Sticks
		Sliced Pears
		Milk
			Roast Turkey
			String Beans
			Mashed Yellow
			  Squash
			Whole Wheat
			  Bread
			Orange Gelatin
			Milk
				Breaded Fish
				Potato Salad
				Broccoli
				Sliced Tomato
				Vanilla
				  Pudding
				Milk

Fillet of Haddock
Rice
Mixed
  Vegetables
Bread Sticks
Bananas
Milk
	Baked Chicken
	Baked Potatoes
	Carrots
	Rye Bread
	Fruit Gelatin
	Milk
		Lasagna
		Tossed Salad
		Roll
		Orange Slices
		Milk
			Chef's Salad w/
			  Egg, Ham
			  and Cheese
			Bran Muffin
			Baked Apple
			Milk
				Vegetable Soup
				Tuna Sandwich
				Celery Sticks
				Frozen Yogurt
				Milk

INDEX